Emanuel Deutsch, Reginald Bosworth Smith

Mohammed and Mohammedanism

lectures delivered at the Royal institution of Great Britain in February and March,

1874

Emanuel Deutsch, Reginald Bosworth Smith

Mohammed and Mohammedanism

lectures delivered at the Royal institution of Great Britain in February and March, 1874

ISBN/EAN: 9783337735388

Printed in Europe, USA, Canada, Australia, Japan

Cover: Foto ©Lupo / pixelio.de

More available books at **www.hansebooks.com**

MOHAMMED

AND

MOHAMMEDANISM.

MOHAMMED

AND

MOHAMMEDANISM:

LECTURES
DELIVERED AT THE
ROYAL INSTITUTION OF GREAT BRITAIN
IN FEBRUARY AND MARCH, 1874.

By R. BOSWORTH SMITH, M.A.,

ASSISTANT MASTER IN HARROW SCHOOL, LATE FELLOW OF TRINITY COLLEGE, OXFORD.

WITH AN APPENDIX

CONTAINING

EMANUEL DEUTSCH'S ARTICLE ON "ISLAM."

NEW YORK:
HARPER & BROTHERS, PUBLISHERS,
FRANKLIN SQUARE.
1875.

UXORI MEÆ,

NULLIUS NON LABORIS PARTICIPI,

HUJUSCE PRÆSERTIM OPUSCULI INSTIGATRICI ET ADMINISTRÆ,

STUDIORUM COMMUNITATIS

HAS, QUALESCUNQUE SINT, PRIMITIAS

DEDICO.

PREFACE.

The substance of these Lectures was written early in 1872: they were originally intended only for a select audience of friends at Harrow, but on the suggestion of some of those who heard them they were afterward considerably enlarged, and were delivered before the Royal Institution of Great Britain in the months of February and March, 1874.

They are an attempt, however imperfect, within a narrow compass, but, it is hoped, from a somewhat comprehensive and independent point of view, to render justice to what was great in Mohammed's character, and to what has been good in Mohammed's influence on the world. To original Oriental research they lay no claim, nor indeed to much originality at all—perhaps the subject hardly now admits of it; but, thanks to the numerous translations of the Koran into European languages, and to the great works of Oriental scholars, such as Caussin de Perceval, Sprenger, Muir, and Deutsch, the materials for forming an impartial judgment of the Prophet of Arabia are within the reach of any earnest student of the Science of Religion, and of all who care, as those who have ever studied Mohammed's character must care, for the deeper problems of the human soul.

The value of the estimate formed of the influence of Mohammedanism on the world at large must, of course, depend upon such a modicum of general historical knowledge, and such catholic sympathies, as the writer has been able, amid other pressing duties, to bring to his work. The only qualification he would venture to claim for himself in the matter is that of a sympathetic interest in his subject, and of a conscientious desire first to divest himself of all preconceived ideas, and then by a careful study of the Koran itself, and afterward of its best expounders, to arrive as nearly as may be at the truth. How vast is the interval between his wishes and his performance the author knows full well, and any one who has ever been fairly fascinated with a great subject will know also; for he will have felt that to have the will is not always to have the power, and that the framing of an ideal implies the consciousness of failure to attain to it.

A Christian who retains that paramount allegiance to Christianity which is his birthright, and yet attempts, without favor and without prejudice, to portray another religion, is inevitably exposed to misconstruction. In the study of his subject he will have been struck sometimes by the extraordinary resemblance between his own creed and another, sometimes by the sharpness of the contrast; and, in order to avoid those misrepresentations, which are, unfortunately, never so common as where they ought to be unknown—in the discussion of religious questions —he will be tempted, in filling in the portrait, to project his own personal predilections on the canvas, and to bring the differences into full relief, while he leaves the resemblances in shadow. And yet a comparison between two systems, if it is to have any fruitful results, if its object is to unite rather than divide, if, in short, it is to be of the spirit of the Founder of Christianity, must, in matters of religion above all, be based on what is common to both. There is, in the human race, in spite of their manifold diversities, a good deal of human nature; enough, at all events, to entitle us to assume that the Founders of any two religious systems which have had a great and continued hold upon a large part of mankind must have had many points of contact. Accordingly, in comparing, as he has done to some extent, the founder of Islam with the Founder of Christianity—a comparison which, if it were not expressed, would always be implied — the author of these Lectures has thought it right mainly to dwell on that aspect of the character of Christ, which, being admitted by Mussulmans as well as Christians, by foes as well as friends, may possibly serve as a basis, if not for an ultimate agreement, at all events for an agreement to differ from one another upon terms of greater sympathy and forbearance, of understanding and of respect.

That Islam will ever give way to Christianity in the East, however much we may desire it, and whatever good would result to the world, it is difficult to believe; but it is certain that Mohammedans may learn much from Christians and yet remain Mohammedans, and that Christians have something at least to learn from Mohammedans, which will make them not less but more Christian than they were before. If we would conquer Nature, we must first obey her; and the Fourth Lecture is an attempt to show, from a full recognition of the facts of Nature underlying both religions — of the points of difference as well as of resemblance — that Mohammedanism, if it can never become actually one with Christianity, may yet, by a process of mutual approximation and mutual understanding, prove its best ally. In other words, the author believes that their is a unity above and beyond that unity of Christendom which, properly understood, all earnest Christians so much desire: a unity which rests upon the belief that "the children of one Father may worship him under different names;" that they may be influenced by one spirit, even though they know it not; that they may all have one hope, even if they have not one faith.

HARROW, *April* 15, 1873.

I have to return my best thanks to my friend Mr. ARTHUR WATSON, for a careful revision of my manuscript, and for several valuable suggestions.

It may be serviceable to English readers to mention the more accessible works upon the subject, to the writers of which I desire here to express my general obligations, over and above the acknowledgment, in the text, wherever I am conscious of them, of special debts. I am the more anxious to do this fully here, as, while I am quite aware that I could not have written on this subject at all without making their labors the basis of mine, I have yet in the exercise of my own judgment often been obliged to criticise their reasonings and their conclusions. I can only hope that even where I have ventured to express a somewhat vehement dissent from my authorities, they will kindly credit me with something at least of the *verecunde dissentio* which becomes a learner, and of the zeal for truth, or for his idea of it, which becomes a writer, however diffident of himself, on a great subject.

"The Koran," translated by Sale, with an elaborate Introduction and full Notes drawn from the Arabic Commentators (1734).

"The Koran," translated by Savary (1782), also with instructive explanatory Notes.

"The Koran," translated by Rodwell (1861): the Suras arranged, as far as possible, chronologically.

Gagnier's "Vie de Mahomet" (1732); drawn chiefly from Abul Feda and the Sonna.

Gibbon's "Decline and Fall of the Roman Empire;" Chapters L., LI., LII. (1788). A most masterly and complete picture.

Weil's "Mohamed der Prophet" (1845). Able and to the point.

Caussin de Perceval's "Essai sur l'Histoire des Arabes," etc. (1847), gives particularly full information upon the obscure subject of early Arabian history, and is written from an absolutely neutral point of view.

Sprenger's "Life of Mohammad," Allahabad, 1851; and his greater work, 'Das Leben und die Lehre des Mohamad' (1851-1861), the most exhaustive, original, and learned of all, but by no means the most impartial: he is often, as I shall point out on one or two occasions in the notes, flagrantly unfair to Mohammed.

Sir William Muir's "Life of Mahomet" (1858-1861). Learned and comprehensive, able and fair; though its scientific value is somewhat impaired by theological assumptions as to the nature of inspiration, and by the introduction of a personal Ahriman, which, while it is self-contradictory in its supposed operation, seems to me only to create new difficulties, instead of solving old ones.

"The Talmud," an article in the *Quarterly Review* (October, 1867); "Islam," an article in the *Quarterly Review* (October, 1869): both full of most recondite Eastern learning. Had the lamented author lived to finish the work he shadowed forth in the last of these, he would probably have drawn a juster and more vivid picture of Islam as a whole than has ever yet been given to the world.

For less elaborate works:

Ockley's "History of the Saracens from 632–705." Picturesque; dealing largely in romance (1708–1718).

Hallam's "Middle Ages," Chapter VI. (1818); Milman's "Latin Christianity," Book IV., Chapters I. and II. (1857); both good samples of the high merits of each as an historian.

Carlyle's "Hero as Prophet" (1846). Most stimulating.

Washington Irving's "Life of Mahomet" (1849). The work of a novelist, but strangely divested of all romance.

Lecture by Dean Stanley in his "Eastern Church" (1862). Has the peculiar charm of all the author's writings. Catholic in its sympathies, and suggestive, as well from his treatment of the subject as from the place the author assigns to it on the borders of, if not within, the Eastern Church itself.

Barthélemy St. Hilaire's "Mahomet et le Koran" (1865), a comprehensive and very useful review of most of what has been written on the subject.

On the general subject of Comparative Religion:

"Religions of the World," by F. D. Maurice (1846). Perhaps of all his writings the one which best shows us the character and mind of the man.

"Études d'Histoire Religieuse," by Renan (1858). Ingenious and fascinating, but not always, nor indeed often, convincing.

"Les Religions et les Philosophies dans l'Asie Centrale," by Gobineau (1866), gives the best account extant of Bâbyism in Persia.

"Chips from a German Workshop" (1868), and "Introduction to the Science of Religion" (1873), by Max Müller. Unfortunately the author says very little about Mohammedanism, but from him I have derived some very valuable suggestions as to the general treatment of the subject. Perhaps it is well that the extraordinary learning and genius of Mr. Max Müller should be given mainly to subjects which are less within the reach of ordinary European students than is Islam, but it is impossible not to wish that he may some day give the world a "Chip" or two on the Religion of Mohammed.

For books which throw light on the specialties of Mohammedanism in different countries:

Al-Makkari's "History of the Mohammedan Dynasties in Spain" (Eng. Trans.).

Sir John Malcolm's "History of Persia" (1815).

Condé's "History of the Dominion of the Arabs in Spain" (1820-21).

Crawfurd's "Indian Archipelago" (1820).

Colonel Briggs's "Rise of the Mohammedan Power in India," translated from the Persian of Ferishta (1829).

Sir Stamford Raffles's "History of Java" (2d edition), (1830).

Burckhardt's "Travels in Arabia" (1829).

Caillé's "Travels through Central Africa to Timbuctoo" (1830).

Burckhardt's "Notes on the Bedouins and Wah-Habees" (1831).

Lane's "Modern Egyptians" (1836).

Burton's "Pilgrimage to Mecca and Medina" (1856).

Barth's "Travels in Central Africa" (1857).

Waitz's "Anthropologie der Naturvölker" (Leipsig, 1860).

Lane's "Notes to his Translation of the Thousand and One Nights" (new edition, edited by E. S. Poole, 1865).

Elphinstone's "History of India" (3d edition), (1866).

Palgrave's "Arabia" (1867).

"Our Indian Mussulmans," by W. W. Hunter (1871).

Burton's "Zanzibar" (1872).

Shaw's "High Tartary, Yarkand, and Kashgar" (1871).

Palgrave's "Essays on Eastern Subjects" (1872).

"Report of the General Missionary Conference at Allahabad" (1873).

Three articles in periodical literature, besides "Islam" mentioned above, are of very high merit, and have furnished me, in enlarging my work, with some matter for reflection or criticism:

"Mahomet," *National Review* (July, 1858).

"The Great Arabian," *National Review* (October, 1861).

"Mahomet," *British Quarterly Review* (January, 1872).

Among other works which I regret I have not been able to consult may be mentioned:

Gerock's "Versuch einer Darstellung der Christologie des Koran" (Homburg, 1839).

Freeman's "Lectures on the History and Conquests of the Saracens" (1856).

Geiger's "Was hat Mohammed aus dem Judenthume aufgenommen?"

Nöldeke's "Geschichte des Qorans."

"Essays on the Life of Mohammed and subjects subsidiary thereto," by Syed Ahmed Khan Bahador (1870).

"A Critical Examination of the Life and Teachings of Mohammed," by Syed Ameer Ali Moulla (1873).

The last two books I had not heard of when I wrote the substance of these Lectures; and in enlarging my work, I have purposely abstained from consulting them, as I have been given to understand that from a Mohammedan point of view they advocate something of the spirit and arrive at some of the results which it had been my object to urge from the Christian stand-point. I would not, of course, venture to compare my own imperfect work, derived as it is in the main from the study of books in the European languages, and from reflection upon the materials they supply, with works drawn, as I presume, directly from the fountain-head. But if the starting-points be different, and the routes entirely independent of each other, and yet there turns out to be a similarity in the results arrived at, possibly each may feel greater confidence that there is something of value in his conclusions.

CONTENTS.

LECTURE I.

INTRODUCTORY.

Comparative Religion.—Historical Religions of the World Moral in their Origin, not Theological. —Judaism; Buddhism; Christianity. —Religion in Greece; Question of Originality of Mohammedanism.—Two Views of Religion.—Obscurity of all Origins, above all of Religion.—Dim Knowledge of Founders of Other Religions; Full Knowledge of Mohammed.—Bible and Koran Contrasted.—Difficult in Other Creeds to Distinguish the Foundation from the Superstructure; Possible in Islam.—Problems Connected with Mohammed's Character.—Survey of the Saracen Conquests, and of what Mohammedanism Overthrew.—Its Position now—is it Losing or Gaining Ground?—China; East Indian Archipelago; Africa—Extraordinary Success of its Missionaries there now.—Its Progress in the African Continent Traced Historically.—What it has Done for Africa, and what Christians have Done. —Its Probable Future in Africa.—Armenia and Koordistan—Revival there.—India; Few, if any, Converts to Christianity.—Causes ordinarily Suggested for its Success Reviewed.—National and Religious Prejudices Stand in Way of a Fair Judgment.—Principles which must Guide Investigation.—Do Religions Differ in Kind?—Sacred Books and their Influence.—Missionary Work; its Limits and Legitimate Objects.—Can the World be Christianized?...........Page 25

LECTURE II.

MOHAMMED.

History of Opinions about Mohammed: The Troubadours; the Middle Ages; the Reformers; Biblical Commentators; Gagnier; Sale; Gibbon;

Carlyle; Other Modern Writers.—Arabia before Mohammed; its Religion; its Social Condition; War; Poetry; Plunder; Chivalry.—Could Mohammedanism have been Predicted?—Was it the Voice of the Spirit of the Time, or of Individual Religious Genius?—Moral and National Upheaval.—Pre-Mohammedans.—Youth of Mohammed; his Call to be Prophet, and its Phenomena; his Long Struggles.—The Hegira.—Sincerity of Mohammed Examined.—His Personal Characteristics.—The Prophetic Office.—Mohammed's Life at Medina.—His Faults.—His Supposed Moral Declension Examined.—Was he Consistent?—Did he Use the Koran for his Private Purposes?—Illustrations. —The Exact Nature and Limits of his Mission; Illustrations.—His Death...Page 80

LECTURE III.

MOHAMMEDANISM.

Essence of Mohammedanism; Claims to be Universal; How far Borrowed from Jews.—Judaism and Christianity as Known to Arabs.—Mission of Mohammed.—Other Articles of Faith: Practical Duties Enjoined; Pilgrimage, its Use and Abuse; How far Alien to Mohammedanism and to Christianity.—The Kaaba; the Hadj.—Dictum of Dr. Deutsch.—The Talmud and its Influence.—Mohammed's Concessions to the Jews, and his Efforts to Gain them over.—Why he Failed.—The Koran: its Characteristics; its History; Influence; Variety; Poetry.—Relation of Mohammed to Miracles, Compared with that of Christ.—The Miraculous Generally.—Fatalism.—What the Koran Says.—Opposite Effects of the Same Doctrine.—Mohammed's Views of Prayer, Predestination, and Free-will.—Wars of Islam—an Essential Part of the System or not?—How Accounted for. —Connection of the Spiritual and Temporal Power—in Eastern Christendom, in Western Christendom, and in Islam.—Character of Early Mohammedan Wars.—Religious Enthusiasm.—The Crusades.—Results of Mohammedan Conquests.—Literature, Science, and Civilization.—Attitude of Christianity and Christians toward Religious Wars. —Morality of War.—What Wars are Christian?............Page 130

LECTURE IV.

MOHAMMEDANISM AND CHRISTIANITY.

The Future Life of Mohammedanism; of Other Religions.—Use Mohammed made of Heaven and Hell; Their Legitimate Use.—Does Mohammedanism Encourage Self-indulgence?—Morality of Mohammedanism.—Mohammed's Attitude toward Existing Institutions Compared with that of Other Founders: Solon; Moses; Christ.—How he Dealt with Polygamy, Slavery, the Poor, and the Orphan; with the Lower Animals; with Moral Offenses.—How ought Christianity to Regard Mohammedanism?—How does it?—Three Monotheistic Creeds; Heroes Common to All.—Spirituality of Each.—Mohammed and Moses Compared.—Iconoclasm.—Reverence for Christ.—Three Reasons Suggested for Mohammed's Rejection of Christianity.—Mohammed's Views of Christ; of the Virgin Mary; of the Trinity; of the Crucifixion; of God.—Lessons to be Learned from them.—Has Mohammedanism Kept Back the East by Hindering the Spread of Christianity?—Is it a Curse or a Blessing to the World at Large?—Limits of Mohammedanism and of Christianity.—Aspects of Mohammedanism in Different Countries: Africa; Persia; India; Turkey; Spain.—Contrast between Christianity and Mohammedanism and their Founders.—Is the East Progressive or not?—Corruptions of Mohammedanism Illustrated by other Religions.—Necessity of Revival in all Religions.—Wahhabees in Arabia and in India.—Revival in Eastern Anatolia.—Limits to the Influence of the West on the East.—Despotism; Polygamy; Slavery; the Slave-trade.—Is Mohammedanism Reconcilable with the Highest Civilization?—With Christianity?—Modifications Possible or Necessary.—Mohammed's Place in History.....Page 188

APPENDIX TO LECTURE I.............................267

APPENDIX TO LECTURE III...........................276

ISLAM. BY EMANUEL DEUTSCH.........................281

LECTURES

DELIVERED AT THE

ROYAL INSTITUTION OF GREAT BRITAIN

IN FEBRUARY AND MARCH, 1874.

LECTURE I.

Delivered at the Royal Institution, London,
February 14, 1874.

INTRODUCTORY.

Sua cuique genti religio est, nostra nobis.—Cicero.

Ἀλλ' ἐν παντὶ ἔθνει ὁ φοβούμενος αὐτὸν, καὶ ἐργαζόμενος δικαιοσύνην, δεκτὸς αὐτῷ ἐστι.—St. Peter.

The Science of Comparative Religion is still in its infancy; and if there is one danger more than another against which it should be on its guard, it is that of hasty and ill-considered generalization. Hasty generalization is the besetting temptation of all young Sciences; may I not say of Science in general? They are in too great a hurry to justify their existence by arriving at results which may be generally intelligible, instead of waiting patiently till the result shapes itself from the premises; as if, in the pursuit of truth, the chase was not always worth more than the game, and the process itself more than the result. Theory has, it is true, its advantages, even in a young Science, in the way of suggesting a definite line which inquiry may take. A brilliant hypothesis formed, not by random guess-work, but by the trained imagination of the man of Science, or by the true divination of genius, enlarges the horizon of the student whom the limits of the human faculties themselves drive to be a specialist, but who is apt to become too much so. It throws a flood of light upon a field of knowledge which was before, perhaps, half in shadow, bringing out each object in its relative place and in its true proportions; finally, it gathers scattered facts into one focus, and, explaining them provisionally by a single law, it makes an appeal to the fancy, which must react on the other mental powers, and be a most powerful stimulus to further research. In truth, much that is now demonstrated fact was once hypothesis, and would never have been demonstrated unless it had been first assumed. But since there are few Keplers in the world — men ready to sacrifice, without hesitation, an hypothesis that had seemed to explain the universe, and become, as it were, a part of themselves, the moment that the facts seem to require it—great circumspection will always be needed lest the facts may be made to bend to the theory, instead of its being modified to meet them.

Bearing this caution in mind, we may, perhaps, think that the Science of Comparative Religion, young as it is, has yet been in existence long enough to enable us to lay it down, at all events provisionally, as a general law, that all the great religions of the world, the commencement of which has not been immemorial—coeval, that is, with the human mind itself—have been in the first instance moral rather than theological; they have been called into existence to meet social and national needs; they have raised man gradually toward God, rather than brought down God at once to man.

Judaism, for instance, sprang into existence at the moment when the Israelites passed, and because they passed, from the Patriarchal to the Political life; when from slavery they emerged into freedom; when they ceased to be a family, and became a nation. "I am the Lord thy God, which brought thee out of the land of Egypt, and out of the house of bondage." The Moral Law which followed—the Theocracy itself—was the outcome of this fundamental fact. The nation that God has chosen—nay, that he has called into existence—is to keep his laws and to be his people. Consequently, all law to the ancient Hebrew was alike divine, whether written, as he believed, by the finger of God on two tables, or whether applied by the civil magistrate to the special cases brought before him. Moral and political offenses are thus offenses against God, and the ideas of crime and sin are identical alike in fact and in thought.

Again, take a glance at the religion of Buddha. We speak of Buddhism, and are apt to think of it chiefly as a body of doctrine, drawn up over two thousand years ago, and at this day professed by four hundred and fifty millions of human beings; and we wonder, as well we may, how a *summum bonum* of mere painlessness in this world, and practically, and to the ordinary mind, of total extinction when this world is over, can have satisfied the spiritual cravings of Buddha's contemporaries, and in its various forms can now be the life-guidance of a third of the human race. But we forget that, in its origin at least, Buddhism was more of a social than of a religious reformation. It was an attack upon that web of priestcraft which Brahmanism had woven around the whole frame-work of Indian society.* It was the leveling of caste distinctions, the sight of a "man born to be a king" throwing off his royal dignity, sweeping away the sacerdotal mummeries which he had himself tested and found unfruitful, preferring poverty to riches, and Sûdras to Brahmans. It was Buddha's overpowering sense of the miseries of sin, his dim yearnings after a better life, his moral system—of which the sum is Love

---

* See Max Müller's "Chips from a German Workshop," vol. i., p. 210 –226, especially p. 220; and Spence Hardy's "Legends and Theories of the Buddhists," Introduction, p. 13-20. Cf. also Beal's "Buddhist Pilgrims," Introduction, p. 49, seq.

—which wrought upon the hearts of his hearers. "He founded, it is true, a new religion, but he began by attacking an old." He reconstructed society first, and it was his social reform that led to his religion, rather than his religion which involved his social reconstruction. The half we may, perhaps, think would have been more than the whole—

"Quæsivit cœlo lucem ingemuitque repertâ."

Nor is it much otherwise with Christianity itself. Christ was before all things the Founder of a new Society; not, it is true, of a political Society: had it been so, more of his countrymen would have seen in his person the Messiah that was to come, and in his kingdom the golden age of their own poets and prophets. The political frame-work, indeed, of the world Christ came neither to destroy nor to reconstruct, except indirectly and remotely. He recognized the logic of facts; above all, the tremendous logic of the Roman Empire. Tribute was to be paid to Cæsar, even though that Cæsar was a Tiberius. The new Society was potentially a world-wide one, a vast democracy in which Jew and Roman, slave and freeman, rich and poor were on a footing of absolute equality. Enthusiastic love to Christ himself, evidenced by purity of heart, by forgetfulness of self, and by enthusiastic love to all mankind, was the one condition and the one test of membership.

It is true that to this new Creation of his Christ gives a name, which we are accustomed to look upon as conveying mainly theological ideas; he calls it "the Kingdom of Heaven," but how does he explain the term himself? His great precursor, John the Baptist, had predicted its immediate advent. Christ says, It is here already—it is *within* you. At the very opening of his work, he speaks of it as already existing; the outline was there, even if the details were not filled in. Now if the Kingdom of Heaven existed before it had dawned, even upon the most favored of his followers, that he was more than "that Prophet," it would seem to follow that the essence of his kingdom was, not the doctrine which they did not and could not as yet accept, but the higher life they saw Christ leading—the life of the soul; and which, seeing, they reverenced, and reverencing, as far as might be, wished to imitate. The Sermon on the Mount, so far as that which is indescribable can be described at all, and that which is the fountain-head of goodness in infinitely varied types can be judged by one or two of the rills which issue from it, is little else than Christ's own life translated into words; and those who, least imperfectly, retranslated his words back into their own lives, were the very "salt of the earth." They were members of the Kingdom of Heaven, even though they did not believe, as some did not even to the end, that he who "spake as never man spake" was something more than man.

If we go back to the *ipsissima verba*, so far as we can now get at them, of Christ himself, how much of the doctrine that we are apt to attribute to Christ we shall find to be Pauline—how much more Patristic, Scholastic, Puritan! How little dogma, and how much morality, there is in the Founder of our religion; how few words, and how many works; how little about consequences, how much about motives; in a word, how little theology, and how much religion! I do not of course mean to deny that Moses, Buddha, Christ himself were founders of a theology as well as of a life; I only say that the life came first, since it was that which was most called for by the time, and it was their new views of life which prepared their followers to receive and develop their new views of God. "If any man will *do* his will, he shall know of the doctrine whether it be of God." "He that loveth not his brother whom he hath seen, how can he love God whom he hath not seen?" "Blessed are the pure in *heart*, for they shall see God."

I am aware that distinguished German philosophers, Max Müller among them,* have laid it down that men can not form themselves into a people till they have

---

* "Introduction to the Science of Religion," Lecture III., p. 144-153.

come to an agreement about their religion, and that community of faith is a bond of union more fundamental than any other bond at all. But I do not think that if the distinction which I have drawn between the primeval and the historical religions of the world be kept in sight, there is much necessary antagonism between their view and mine; that a new religion is, in order of time, the outcome and not the cause of a general movement toward a higher life, whether moral or national. Religion is, no doubt, practically all that they say it is—a tie so strong that it can give an ideal unity, as it did in Greece, to tribes differing from one another in degrees of civilization, in interests, and in dialect; but it does not follow that it was historically ever the original moving power in the aggregation of scattered tribes, or that a new religion was at first a revelation of God rather than a revelation of morality. There must have been a previous community of race and language for the religion to work upon; there must also have been a strong, though very possibly an ill-directed and a desultory upheaval of society. The fragments still existing of the primeval creed are no doubt a factor in that upheaval, and feel its force; but the new religion is the result and not the cause of the general movement. It is not till later that it pays the debt it owes to what gave it birth, by lending a higher sanction to each institution of the new society, and so does in truth become, what philosophers say it is, the most important bond in a national life. First the aspirations, then that which satisfies them! First a new conception of the relation of men to one another, then that conception sanctioned, vivified, lit up by the newly perceived relation of all alike to God!

I would also remark that Greece itself, though Max Müller appeals to it in favor of his own conclusions, seems to supply an argument in favor of my view. For even in the Persian wars the common danger and the common hatred of the "Barbarian" failed to bring about more than a very transitory coalition between two or three of the leading states. The ideal unity of the Greek races was only an ideal, and Panhellenism never went so far as to unite the different states into a homogeneous people. If there had been a real and spontaneous movement among the autonomous cities of Greece toward centralization, a great reformer might have taken advantage of it, and working upon the "dim recollection of the common allegiance they owed from time immemorial to the great Father of Gods and men, the old Zeus of Dodona, the Panhellenic Zeus,"* have welded the fragments into a nation. The One would not mere-

---

* "Science of Religion," p. 148.

ly have been dimly discerned behind the Many by the highest minds, but the perception would have been converted into a practical reality. The intellectual mission of Socrates might have taken something of the shape and realized something of the results of the mission of Mohammed. But there was no such national movement in Greece, and therefore no opportunity either for the birth of a new religion or a revival of the old one. In Greek Polytheism we see historically nothing but decay, Mythology having completely overgrown the Religion. The gross stories of Homer and of Hesiod, which so scandalized Socrates and Plato, had, even at that early time, concealed from all but the highest minds the vague primitive belief, common probably to the whole Indo-Germanic race, in one Father who is in Heaven.

To what extent the principle I have laid down as to the origin of the three great historical religions is also true of that of Mohammed will develop itself gradually in the sequel.

It has been remarked, indeed, by writer after writer, that Islam is less interesting than other religions, inasmuch as it is less original. And this is one of the favorite charges brought against it by Christian apologists. In the first place, I am inclined to think that the charge of want of originality, though it can not be denied, has been overdone by recent writers; most conspicuously so by M. Renan, who, ingenious and beautiful as his Essay is, seems disposed to explain the whole fabric of Islamism by the ideas that existed before Mohammed, and the political direction given to it by his successors, most notably by Omar; in fact, it seems to me that the only element left out, or not accounted for, in his analysis of Mohammedanism, is Mohammed himself. His Mohammedanism resembles a Hamlet with not only the Prince of Denmark, but with Shakespeare himself cut out. The disjointed members and some few elements of the fabric remain—about as much as we should have of the Hamlet of Shakespeare in the Amlettus of Saxo-Grammaticus; but the informing, animating, inspiring soul is wanting.

It is undeniable that a vague and hearsay acquaintance with the Old Testament, the Talmud, and the New Testament, and the undefined religious cravings of a few of his immediate predecessors or contemporaries, influenced Mohammed much, and traces of them at second hand may be found in every other page of the Koran; but then, in the second place, it may be asked whether want of originality is any reproach to a religion: for what is religion?

It is that something which, whether it is a collection of shadows projected by the mind itself upon the mirror of the external world, explaining the Macrocosm by the

Microcosm, and invested with a reality which belongs only to the mind that casts them, if indeed even to that, or whether it is indeed an insight of the soul into realities which exist independently of it, and which underlie alike the world of sense and the world of reason; it is something, at all events, which satisfies the spiritual wants of man. Man's spiritual wants, whatever their origin, are his truest wants; and the something which satisfies those wants is the most real of all realities to him.

The founder, therefore, of a religion which is to last must read the spiritual needs of a nation correctly, or at all events must be capable of seeing the direction in which they lead, and the development they will one day take. If he read them correctly, he need not care about any originality beyond that which such insight implies; he will rather do well to avoid it. The religious world was startled a few years ago by the revelations of an Oriental scholar that much supposed to be exclusively the doctrine of the New Testament is to be found in the Talmud, as though some reflection was thereby cast upon the Founder of our religion! Positivists, again, have laid great stress on the fact that some of the moral precepts supposed to be exclusively Christian are to be found in the sacred writings of Confucius and the Buddhists. But what then? Is a religion less true because it recognizes itself in other garbs, because it incorporates in itself all that is best in the system which it expands or supplants? What if we found the whole Sermon on the Mount dispersed about the writings of the Jewish Rabbis, as we unquestionably find some part of it? Christ himself was always the first to assert that he came, not to destroy, but to fulfill. But it is strange that the avowed relation of Christianity to Judaism has not protected Islam from the assaults of Christian apologists, grounded on its avowed relation to the two together!

But what of interest, I am free to admit, the religion of Mohammed loses on the score of originality, it gains in the greater fullness of our knowledge of its origin. It is the latest and most historical of the great religions of the world.

Renan has remarked that the origin of nearly all the leading phenomena of life and history is obscure. What, for instance, can Max Müller tell us of the origin of language? What well-authenticated facts can political philosophers like Hobbes or Locke, or even scientific antiquaries like Sir Charles Lyell or Sir John Lubbock, tell us of the origin of society? What can Darwin tell us of the origin of life? Trace the genealogy of all existing languages into the three great groups of Aryan, Semitic, and Turanian; find, if you can, the parent language from which even these three families have originally diverged; are we any nearer an explanation of what language really is? Our hopes, indeed, are aroused by hints dropped throughout Max Müller's fascinating book that he has a secret to divulge to those who have gone through an adequate process of initiation. But to our disappointment we find that the explanation of "Phonetic Types" is only a roundabout way of saying— what, no doubt, is true—that language is instinctive, and that we know nothing whatever of its origin. That sound expresses thought we knew before; but how does it express it? That is the question. Trace elaborately through Geological Periods, if you can, the steps by which the Monad has been developed into Man, and show that there is no link wanting, and that Nature, so far as we can trace, never makes a leap. Perhaps not; but there is a leap somewhere, and who can say how vast the leap before the Protoplasm can have received the something that is not Protoplasm but Life, and which has all the dignity of life, even though it be a Monad's?

So, too, if the Science of Religion last long enough, we may one day be able to trace a continuity of growth from the very dawn of man's belief till, as in history so in religion,

> "We doubt not through the ages one increasing purpose runs,
> And the thoughts of men are widened with the process of the suns."

We shall find, however, that, even in the dimmest dawn of history, the essence of religion was already there, not forming, but already formed; a feeling of mystery which, as it is the beginning of philosophy, so, perhaps, it is the very first beginning of religion; the distinction between right and wrong; the idea of a Power which is neither Man's nor external Nature's, though it is evidenced by them both; the sense that there is something in this world amiss; and the fear, or, possibly, the hope, that it may be unriddled by and by.* Where did those ideas come from? And do we know any thing more of the origin of religion itself by having traced it to some of its elements?

And what is true of religion generally is also true, unfortunately, of those three religions which I have called, for want of a better name, historical — and of their founders. We know all too little of the first and earliest laborers; too much, perhaps, of those who have entered into their labors. We know less of Zoroaster and Confucius than we do of Solon and Socrates; less

---

* I do not mean to touch here upon the disputed question whether there are races without any definite religious ideas at all. Sir John Lubbock ("Origin of Civilization," cap. iv.) has brought together the testimony of many missionaries and travelers as to a great variety of tribes which seem to be, at all events, without any thing beyond the elements I have named; but I much doubt whether these elements, or some of them, do not exist in all tribes, even in the lowest. It is certain that a longer acquaintance and minuter observation among savage tribes, especially the African, have often led to the reversal of an opinion naturally but hastily formed in the first instance. See Waitz, "Anthropologie der Naturvölker," vol. ii., p. 4.

of Moses and of Buddha than we do of Ambrose and Augustine. We know indeed some fragments of a fragment of Christ's life; but who can lift the veil of the thirty years that prepared the way for the three? What we do know indeed has renovated a third of the world, and may yet renovate much more; an ideal of life at once remote and near; possible and impossible; but how much we do not know! What do we know of his mother, of his home life, of his early friends, and his relation to them, of the gradual dawning, or, it may be, the sudden revelation, of his divine mission? How many questions about him occur to each of us that must always remain questions!

But in Mohammedanism every thing is different; here, instead of the shadowy and the mysterious, we have history.* We know as much of Mohammed as we do even of Luther and Milton. The mythical, the legendary, the supernatural is almost wanting in the original Arab authorities, or at all events can easily be distinguished from what is historical.† Nobody here is the dupe of

---

* Cf. Renan, "Études d'Histoire Religieuse," p. 220 and 230.

† The belief in Jinn, beings created of smokeless fire 2000 years before Adam, as a part of the original Arab mythology, was not discarded by Mohammed (Koran, Sura i., 7–8; xlvi., 28, 29; lvii., 17–18; lxxii., 1, etc.); but, in other respects, the miraculous and mythological element in Mohammedanism comes almost exclusively from Persian sources. Persia has revenged the destruction of her national faith by corrupting in many particulars the simplicity of the creed of her conquerors. For an exhaust-

himself or of others; there is the full light of day upon all that that light can ever reach at all. "The abysmal depths of personality" indeed are, and must always remain, beyond the reach of any line and plummet of ours. But we know every thing of the external history of Mohammed—his youth, his appearance, his relations, his habits; the first idea and the gradual growth, intermittent though it was, of his great revelation; while for his internal history, after his mission had been proclaimed, we have a book absolutely unique in its origin, in its preservation, and in the chaos of its contents, but on the authenticity of which no one has ever been able to cast a serious doubt. There, if in any book, we have a mirror of one of the master-spirits of the world; often inartistic, incoherent, self-contradictory, dull, but impregnated with a few grand ideas which stand out from the whole; a mind seething with the inspiration pent within it, "intoxicated with God," but full of human weaknesses, from which he never pretended—and it is his lasting glory that he never pretended—to be free.*

---

ive account of Arab ideas on the Jinn, their creation, their influence on human affairs, and their abode, see Note 21 to the Introduction of Lane's edition of "The Thousand and One Nights." The legends illustrating the power of Solomon over the Genii are well known. The notes to Lane's edition of the "Arabian Nights" form a storehouse of accurate information upon Arab manners and customs.

* It was a proverbial saying in very early times among Mussulmans that "Mohammed's character was the Koran."

Upon the striking resemblances between the Koran and the Bible—the book with which it is most naturally compared—and the still more striking differences, I need not now dwell at length, especially as the latter have been admirably drawn out by Dean Stanley.*

To compress, as best I may, into a few sentences what he has said so well, making only a few amendments where, from my point of view, they seem to be called for: The Koran lays claim to a verbal, literal, and mechanical inspiration in every part alike, and is regarded as such by almost all Mohammedans. The Bible makes no such claim, except in one or two controverted passages; and there are few Christians who do not now admit at least a human element in every part of it. The text of the Koran is stereotyped; in the Bible there is an immense variety of readings. The Koran has hitherto proved to be incapable of harmonious translation into other languages; the Bible loses little or nothing in the process. The Bible is the work of a large number of poets, prophets, statesmen, and lawgivers, extending over a vast period of time, and incorporates with itself other and earlier, and often conflicting documents; the Koran comes straight from the brain, sometimes from the ravings, of an unlettered enthusiast, who yet in this proved

---

* "Lectures on the Eastern Church," Lecture VIII., p. 266-273.

himself to be poet and prophet, statesman and lawgiver in one. Finally, the strength of the Koran lies in its uniformity, in its intolerance, in its narrowness; the strength of the Bible in its variety, its toleration, its universality. In all these points, as in the more important one of the morality of its highest revelations, the supremacy of our sacred books over the one sacred book of the Mohammedans is indisputable.

Dean Stanley asks somewhat triumphantly, but on the whole rightly enough, whether there is a single passage in the Koran that can be named, as a proof of inspiration, with St. Paul's description of Charity. But it is worth remarking that a traditional sermon of Mohammed's has been preserved, quoted by Washington Irving,* which, though it is in no way equal to this, the sublimest passage of the greatest of the Apostles, yet shows a real insight into the nature and comprehensiveness of this Christian grace; and may at all events serve as a comment on 1 Corinthians xiii. It is in the form of an Apologue: " When God made the earth, it shook to and fro till he put mountains on it to keep it firm." Then the angels asked, " O God, is there any thing in thy creation stronger than these mountains?" And God replied, " Iron is stronger than the mountains, for it

---

* "Life of Mahomet," p. 87. He is quoting from Abu Hurairah.

breaks them."—"And is there any thing in thy creation stronger than iron?" "Yes, fire is stronger than iron, for it melts it."—"Is there any thing stronger than fire?" "Yes, water, for it quenches fire."—"Is there any thing stronger than water?" "Yes, wind, for it puts water in motion."—"O our Sustainer! is there any thing in thy creation stronger than wind?" "Yes, a good man giving alms; if he give it with his right hand and conceal it from his left, he overcomes all things." But Mohammed did not end here, or restrict his notion of charity to the somewhat narrow sense which, in common language, it bears now, that of liberal and unostentatious almsgiving: he went on to give almost as wide a definition of charity as St. Paul himself. "Every good act is charity; your smiling in your brother's face; your putting a wanderer in the right road; your giving water to the thirsty, is charity; exhortations to another to do right are charity. A man's true wealth hereafter is the good he has done in this world to his fellow-man. When he dies, people will ask, What property has he left behind him? But the angels will ask, What good deeds has he sent before him?"

But from one point of view the Koran has to the comparative mythologist, and therefore to the student of human nature, an interest quite unique, and not the less absorbing that it springs out of the very defects that

I have pointed out. By studying the Koran, together with the history of Mohammedanism, we see with our own eyes, what we can only infer or imagine in other cases, the precise steps by which a religion naturally and necessarily develops into a mythology.

In the Koran we have, beyond all doubt, the exact words of Mohammed without subtraction and without addition. We see with our own eyes the birth and adolescence of a religion. In the history of Mohammedanism we descry the parasitical growth that fastens on it, even in its founder's lifetime. We see the way in which a man who denied that he could work miracles is believed to work them even by his contemporaries, and how in the next generation the extravagant vision of the nocturnal flight to the seventh heaven, with all its gorgeous imagery, and the revolutions of the moon around the Kaaba, is taken for sober fact, and is propagated with all the elaboration of details which, if they came from any body, could have come only from Mohammed himself; and yet all of it with the most perfect good faith. We see how a man, who, though he had once in an outburst of anger uttered a prophecy which turned out true, always denied that he could predict the future, and was yet, in spite of himself, credited with all the supernatural insight of a seer. Lastly, we mark how the formalities and the sacrifices and the idolatries which he spent his life in overthrowing, revived in another shape out of the frequency of prayers and fasts that he enjoined, and of the pilgrimages he permitted. The holy places themselves became more holy, as having been the scene of his preaching and of his death, and so in time received more than human honors. We know from history what the outgrowth and superstructure have been, and we read in the Koran how narrow the foundation was.

But from the Bible, by its very nature, and owing to those peculiarities which constitute its special strength, we fail to know, in the same sense, the exact limits of the foundation of the Christendom that has overspread the world. In the outward shape in which it has come down to us, and in the questions connected with the authorship of its different parts and the variety of its contents, the Bible resembles not so much the Koran as the Sonna, which is, of course, rejected by the Sheeah half of the Mohammedan races. Even in the Gospels as we have them, comment and inference, and the individuality of the writer, are mixed with verbal accuracy and exact observation. We can detect conflicting currents of feeling and of thought which it taxes the ingenuity and honesty even of harmonists to harmonize. The New Testament is not less, but more valuable because of these discrepancies. Its undesigned discrepancies have been as valuable in widening the base of our Christianity as its undesigned coincidences are in assuring it. Whether we may legitimately apply the inferences to be drawn from our full knowledge of the growth of Mohammedanism to our imperfect knowledge of the growth of other religions is, of course, open to argument, but the interest and importance of the inquiry can hardly be overestimated.

But over and above the interest attaching to the one religion of the world which is strictly historical in its origin, and which therefore may, rightly or wrongly, be used to explain the origin of those of which we know less, there is the fascination that must always attach to those mixed characters of whom we know so much, and yet so little; who have made the world what it is, and yet whom the world can not read.

"Hero, impostor, fanatic, priest, or sage:"

which element predominates in the man as a whole we may perhaps discover, and most certainly we can say now it was not the impostor; but taking him at different times and under different circumstances, the more one reads the more one distrusts one's own conclusions, and, as Dean Milman remarks, answers with the Arab, "Allah only knows."*

---

* "Latin Christianity," vol. i., p. 555.

Nor does Mohammedanism lack other claims on our attention. Its ultimate enthusiastic acceptance by the Arabs, the new direction given to it by the later revelations to Mohammed, its rapid conquests, the literature and civilization it brought in its train, the way in which it crumpled up the Roman Empire on one side and the Persian on the other; how it drove Christianity before it on the west and north, and Fire-Worship on the east and south; how it crushed the false prophets that always follow in the wake of a true one, as the jackals do the trail of a lion; how it spread over two continents, and how it settled in a third, and at one time all but overwhelmed the whole, till Charles the Hammer, on the field of Tours, turned it back upon itself; how the indivisible empire, the representative on earth of the Theocracy in heaven, became many empires, with rival Kaliphs at Damascus and Bagdad, at Cairo, Cairoan, and Cordova; how horde after horde of barbarians of the great Turkish or Tartar stock were precipitated on the dominions of the faithful, only to be conquered by the faith of those whose arms they overthrew; how, when the news came that the very birthplace of the Christian faith had fallen into their hands, "a nerve was touched," as Gibbon says, "of exquisite feeling, and the sensation vibrated to the heart of Europe;" how Christendom itself thus became for two hundred years half Mohammedanized, and tried to meet fanaticism by counter-fanaticism—the sword, the Bible, and the Cross against the scimiter, the Koran, and the Crescent; how, lastly, when the tide of aggression had been checked, it once more burst its barriers, and, seating itself on the throne of the Cæsars of the East, threatened more than once the very centre of Christendom—all this is matter of history, at which I can only glance.

And what is its position now?

It numbers at this day more than one hundred millions, probably one hundred and fifty millions, of believers as sincere, as devout, as true to their creed as are the believers in any creed whatever. It still has its grip on three continents, extending from Morocco to the Malay peninsula, from Zanzibar to the Kirghis horde. It embraces within its ample circumference two extensive empires, one Sonnee, the other Sheeah; the first of which, though it has often been pronounced sick unto death or even dead, is not dead yet, and is even showing signs of reviving vitality. It still grasps the cradles of the Jewish and of the Christian faith, and the spots most dear to both—Mount Sinai and the Cave of Machpelah, the Church of the Nativity and the Church of the Holy Sepulchre. Africa, which had yielded so early to Christianity—nay, which had given birth to Latin Christianity itself; the Africa of Cyprian and Tertullian, of Antony and of Augustine—yielded still more readily to Mohammed; and from the Strait of Gibraltar to the Isthmus of Suez may still be heard the cry which with them is no vain repetition of "Allahu-Akbar"—God is great; there is no god but God, and Mohammed is his prophet.

And if it be said, as it often is, that Mohammedanism has gained nothing since the first flame of religious enthusiasm, fanned, as it then often was, by the lust of conquest, has died out, I answer that this is far from the truth.

In the extreme East, Mohammedanism has since then won and maintained for centuries a moral supremacy in the important Chinese province of Yun-Nan, and has thus actually succeeded in thrusting a wedge between the two great Buddhist empires of Burmah and of China. Within our own memory, indeed, after a fifteen years' war, and under the leadership of Ta Wên Siu— one of those half-military, half-religious geniuses which Islam seems always capable of producing—it succeeded in wresting from the Celestial Empire a territorial supremacy in the western half of this province. Two years ago an embassy of intelligent and, it is worth adding, of progressive and tolerant Mussulmans from Yun-Nan, headed by Prince Hassan, son of the chieftain who has now become the Sultan Soliman, appeared in England, and the future of the Panthays,* as they are called, began at length to attract attention, not so much, I fear, from the extraordinary interest attaching to their religious history—that interests few Englishmen—as to the possible opening to our Eastern trade, the only Gospel which most Englishmen care now to preach, and one which we did consistently for many years propagate by our commercial wars in China and Japan, at the expense of every principle of religion and humanity. Unfortunately the interests of our trade were not sufficiently bound up with the existence of the Panthays to call for any representations on our part, and Prince Hassan was compelled to return to Asia without any prospect of moral support from us or from the Sultan of Turkey. On arriving at Rangoon he was met by the news that the Mussulmans had at length been overpowered by the fearful odds arrayed against them; that Tali-Fu, the capital, had fallen, and men, women, and children to the number of some thirty thousand had been massacred by the victors. The fate of Momien, the other stronghold, was of course only a question of time; but though the short-lived Mohammedan sovereignty has been destroyed, and what was won by the sword

---

* A name given to them by their Burmese neighbors, from whom the word has passed into the Western World. It is said to be a corruption of the Burmese "Putthee," *i. e.*, Mohammedan.

has since perished by the sword, Mohammedanism itself has not been extinguished in the Celestial Empire. Within the last eight years that vast tract of country called Western Chinese Tartary, or Eastern Turkestan, has thrown off the yoke of China, and has added another to the list of Mussulman kingdoms. Khotan and Yarkand and Kashgar are united under the vigorous rule of the Atalik Ghazee,* Yakoob Beg. Whatever may be his private character, the abolition of the slave-trade throughout his dominions, his rigid administration of justice, his readiness to establish commercial relations with India, and the respect shown for Christianity even by the Meccan pilgrims among his subjects, are some indication of what Mohammedanism may yet have in store for it in Central Asia under the influence of a master mind, and with the modifications that are possible or necessary to it. Throughout the Chinese Empire, at Karachar, for instance, there are scattered Mussulman communities who have higher hopes than Buddhism or Confucianism, and a purer morality than Taoism can supply. The Pan-

---

* The title was given him by the Ameer of Bokhara. It means "Guardian of the Champions of Religion." For the abolition of the slave-trade, see the best authority on the subject—Shaw's "High Tartary," p. 347; and for the view of Christians taken by some pilgrims to Mecca from Central Asia, p. 65. The letters received from Mr. Forsyth's Mission (see London *Times*, of March 17, 1874) seem quite to bear out the view I had formed of Yakoob Beg's position.

thays themselves, it is believed, still number a million and a half; and the unity of God and the mission of God's prophet are attested day by day by a continuous line of worshipers from the Atlantic to the Pacific Ocean.

Nay, even beyond, in the East Indian Archipelago, beyond the Strait of Malacca, if I may venture just now so to call it, in Java and Sumatra, in Borneo and Celebes, Islam has raised many of the natives above their former selves, and has long been the dominant faith. It established itself in the Malay Peninsula and Sumatra in the fourteenth, and in Java and Celebes in the fifteenth century; and it is interesting to note, as is remarked by Crawfurd, that about the time it was being gradually expelled from Western Europe, it made up for its expulsion by extending itself to the East of Asia. The Arab missionaries were just in time, for they anticipated by only a few years the first advent of grasping Portuguese and ambitious Spaniards. It can not, of course, be supposed that among races so low in the scale of humanity as are most of the Indian islanders, Mohammedanism would be able to do what it did originally for the Arabs or for the Turkish hordes; but it has done something even for them. It expelled Hindooism from some islands, and a very corrupt Buddhism from others. It was propagated by missionaries who cared very much for the souls they could win, and nothing for the plunder they could carry off. They conciliated the natives, learned their languages, and intermarried with them; and in the larger islands their success was rapid, and, so far as nature would allow, complete.* The Philippines and the Moluccas, which were conquered by Spain and Portugal respectively, did not become Mohammedan, for they had to surrender at once their liberty and their religion. It is no wonder that the religion known to the natives chiefly through the unblushing rapacity of the Portuguese, and the terrible cruelties of the Dutch, has not extended itself beyond the reach of their swords. Here, as elsewhere in the East, the most fatal hinderance to the spread of Christianity has been the lives of Christians.† I will only add further that the Mussulmans of the East India Islands are very lax in their obedience to many of the precepts of their law, that they are tolerant of other religions, and that the women enjoy a liberty, a position, and an influence which contrasts favorably with that allowed to them in any other Asiatic country.‡

---

* Crawfurd's "Indian Archipelago," vol. ii., p. 275 and 315.

† For the cruelties of the Portuguese, see Crawfurd, vol. ii., p. 403, and for the Dutch, see especially vol. ii., p. 425, seq., and 441. For some startling facts as to the comparative morality of some native and Christian communities in India, see a paper by the Rev. J. N. Thoburn, in the Report of the Allahabad Missionary Conference, held in 1872-73, p. 467-470.

‡ Crawfurd, vol. ii., p. 260 and 269-271; and Sir Stamford Raffles's "Java," vol. i., p. 261; and vol. ii., p. 2-5.

In Africa, again, Mohammedanism is spreading itself by giant strides almost year by year. Every one knows that within half a century from the Prophet's death the richest states of Africa, and those most accessible to Christianity and to European civilization, were torn away from both by the armies of the faithful, with hardly a struggle or a regret; but few except those who have studied the subject are aware that, ever since then, Mohammedanism has been gradually spreading over the northern half of the continent.

Starting from the northwest corner, it first marched southward from Morocco, and by the time of the Norman Conquest had reached the neighborhood of Timbuctoo, and had got firm hold of the Mandingoes; thence it spread southward again to the Foulahs; and then eastward by the thirteenth century to Lake Tchad, where finally the Arab missionaries from the West joined hands with those from the East in the very heart of Africa.* Of course enormous tracts of heathenism were left, and are still left, in various parts of this vast area, and it is mainly among these that at this day Mohammedan missionaries are meeting every where with a marked success which is denied to our own. We hear of whole tribes laying aside their devil-worship, or immemorial Fetich,

---

* "Anthropologie der Naturvölker," by Dr. Theodor Waitz, p. 248-251.

and springing at a bound, as it were, from the very lowest to one of the highest forms of religious belief. Christian travelers, with every wish to think otherwise, have remarked that the negro who accepts Mohammedanism acquires at once a sense of the dignity of human nature not commonly found even among those who have been brought to accept Christianity.

It is also pertinent to observe here that such progress as any large part of the negro race has hitherto made is in exact proportion to the time that has elapsed, or to the degree of fervor with which they originally embraced or have since clung to Islam. The Mandingoes and the Foulahs are salient instances of this; their unquestionable superiority to other negro tribes is as unquestionably owing to the early hold that Islam got upon them, and to the civilization and culture that it has always encouraged.

Nor can it be said that it is only among those negroes who have never heard any thing of a purer faith that Mohammedanism is making such rapid progress. The Government Blue Books on our West African settlements, and the reports of missionary societies themselves, are quite at one on this head. The Governor of our West African colonies, Mr. Pope Hennessy, remarks that the liberated Africans are always handed over to Christian missionaries for instruction, and that their children are baptized and brought up at the public expense in Christian schools, and are therefore, in a sense, ready-made converts. Yet the total number of professing Christians, 35,000 out of a population of 513,000—very few even of these, as the Governor says, and as we can unfortunately well believe from our experience in countries that are not African, being practical Christians—falls far short of the original number of liberated Africans and their descendants.* On the other hand, the Rev. James Johnson, a native clergyman, and a man of remarkable energy and intelligence as well as of very Catholic spirit, deplores the fact that, of the total number of Mohammedans to be found in Sierra Leone and its neighborhood, three fourths were not born Mohammedans, but have become so by conversion, whether from a nominal Christianity or from Paganism.†

---

* Papers relating to Her Majesty's Colonial Possessions. Part II., 1873, 2d division, p. 14.

† Ibid., p. 15. As Mr. Pope Hennessy's Report has been much criticised, chiefly on the ground that he is a Roman Catholic (see a letter to the London *Times*, of Oct. 21, 1873, signed "Audi alteram partem"), and as I have based some statements upon it, it may be worth mentioning that I have had a conversation with Mr. Johnson, who is a strong Protestant himself, and that he bore testimony to the *bona fides* of the Report, and to its accuracy even on some points which have been most questioned. He told me that Mohammedanism was introduced into Sierra Leone, not many years ago, by three zealous missionaries who came from a great distance. It seems now to be rapidly gaining the ascendency, in spite of all the European influences at work. It may perhaps be questioned, since he does not dwell much upon it, whether Mr. Pope Hennessy, in his re-

And, what is still more to our purpose to remark here, Mohammedanism, as it spreads now, is not attended by some of the drawbacks which accompanied its first introduction into the country. It is spread, not by the sword, but by earnest and simple-minded Arab missionaries. It has also lost, except in certain well-defined districts, much of its intolerant and exclusive character. The two leading doctrines of Mohammedanism, and the general moral precepts of the Koran, are, of course, inculcated every where. But, in other respects, the Mussulman missionaries exhibit a forbearance, a sympathy, and a respect for native customs and prejudices, and even for their more harmless beliefs, which is no doubt one reason of their success, and which our own missionaries and schoolmasters would do well to imitate.

We are assured, on all hands, that the Mussulman population has an almost passionate desire for education; and those in the neighborhood of our colonies would throng our schools, first, if the practical education given were more worth having, and, secondly, if the teachers would refrain from needlessly attacking their cherished and often harmless customs. Wherever Mohammedans are numerous, they establish schools them-

---

marks on the diminished number of Christians in Sierra Leone, made allowance for the return of a certain number of true Christians, such as Bishop Crowther, to their own countries.

selves; and there are not a few who travel extraordinary distances to secure the best possible education. Mr. Pope Hennessy mentions the case of one young Mohammedan negro who is in the habit of purchasing costly books from Trübner in London, and who went to Futah, two hundred and fifty miles away, to obtain an education better than he could find in Sierra Leone itself.* Nor is it an uncommon thing for newly converted Mussulmans to make their way right across the Desert from Bornu, or from Lake Tchad, or down the Nile from Darfour or Wadai, a journey of over one thousand miles, that they may carry on their studies in El-Azhar, the great collegiate Mosque at Cairo, and may thence bring back the results of their training to their native country, and form so many centres of Mohammedan teaching and example.†

Nor as to the effects of Islam when first embraced by a negro tribe can there be any reasonable doubt. Polytheism disappears almost instantaneously; sorcery, with its attendant evils, gradually dies away; human sacrifice becomes a thing of the past. The general moral elevation is most marked; the natives begin for the first

---

* Ibid., p. 10.

† Waitz, p. 251. He calculates the number of students returning each year to be about fifty. To his book, and to the authorities to whom he refers, I owe many of the facts mentioned in the text illustrative of the influence of Islam on the native mind and character.

time in their history to dress, and that neatly. Squalid filth is replaced by a scrupulous cleanliness; hospitality becomes a religious duty; drunkenness, instead of the rule, becomes a comparatively rare exception. Though polygamy is allowed by the Koran, it is not common in practice, and, beyond the limits laid down by the Prophet, incontinence is rare; chastity is looked upon as one of the highest, and becomes, in fact, one of the commoner virtues. It is idleness henceforward that degrades, and industry that elevates, instead of the reverse. Offenses are henceforward measured by a written code instead of the arbitrary caprice of a chieftain—a step, as every one will admit, of vast importance in the progress of a tribe. The mosque gives an idea of architecture at all events higher than any the negro has yet had. A thirst for literature is created, and that for works of science and philosophy as well as for commentaries on the Koran.* There are whole tribes, such as the Jolofs on the River Gambia, and the Haussas, whose manly qualities we have had occasion to test in Ashan-

---

* Waitz, p. 252-254. Aristotle and Plato are known to not a few Mohammedans in the interior. Barth, in his "Travels in Central Africa," vol. v., p. 63, mentions that Sidi Mohammed, of Timbuctoo, maintained that they were both Mussulmans—that is to say, worshipers of the true God. Cf. vol. iii., p. 373, for the case of a Pullo at Massera, who had read Plato and Aristotle in Arabic, was well acquainted with the history of Spain, and sympathized with the Wahhabees.

tee, which have become to a man Mohammedans, and have raised themselves infinitely in the process; and the very name of Salt-water Mohammedans given to those tribes along the coast who, from admixture with European settlers, have relaxed the severity of the Prophet's laws, is a striking proof of the extent to which the stricter form of the faith prevails in the far interior.

It is melancholy to contrast with these wide-spread beneficial influences of Mohammedanism the little that has been done for Africa till very lately by the Christian nations that have settled in it, and the still narrower limits within which it has been confined. Till a few years ago the good effects produced beyond the immediate territories occupied by them were absolutely nothing. The achievement of Vasco de Gama, for which Te Deums were sung in Europe, proved for centuries to be nothing but the direst curse to Africa. If the oceanic slave-trade has been, to the eternal credit of England in particular, at last abolished by Christian nations, it can not be forgotten that Africa owes also to them its origin, and on the West Coast, at all events, its long continuance. The message that European traders have carried for centuries to Africa has been one of rapacity, of cruelty, and of bad faith. It is a remark of Dr. Livingstone's* that the only art that the natives of

---

* Livingstone's "Expedition to the Zambesi," p. 240.

Africa have acquired from their five hundred years' acquaintance with the Portuguese has been the art of distilling spirits from a gun-barrel; and that the only permanent belief they owe to them is the belief that man may sell his brother man; for this, he says emphatically, is not a native belief, but is only to be found in the track of the Portuguese. The stopping of the oceanic slave-trade by England is an enormous benefit to Africa; but, if we except the small number of converts made within the limits of their settlements, it has been the only benefit conferred by Europeans. The extension of African commerce is of more than doubtful benefit at present. The chief articles that we export from thence are the produce of slave-labor, and, what is worse, of a vastly extended slave-trade, in the inaccessible interior.*

Nor is it wholly without reason that, in spite of Krapf and Moffat, of Baker, of Frere, and of Livingstone, and of a score of other single-hearted and energetic philanthropists, the white man is still an object of terror, and his professed creed an object of suspicion and repug-

---

* For the introduction, or rather the invention, of the slave-trade by the Portuguese in the year 1444, see Helps's "Spanish Conquest in America," vol. i., p. 35, seq., and the quotation there given from the Chronicle of Azurara, relating the capture of two hundred Africans by a Portuguese company at Lagos, and their shipment to Portugal. A disastrous precedent from that time down to the end of the last century, only too fatally followed by all the Christian nations of Europe which had the chance.

nance, to the negro race. Truly, if the question must be put, whether it is Mohammedan or Christian nations that have as yet done most for Africa, the answer must be that it is not the Christian. And if it be asked, again, not what religion is the purest in itself and ideally the best—for to this there could be but one answer—but which, under the peculiar circumstances—historical, geographical, and ethnological—is the religion most likely to get hold on a vast scale of the native mind, and so in some measure to elevate the savage character, the same answer must be returned. The question is, indeed, already half answered by a glance at the map of Africa. Mohammedanism has already leavened almost the whole of Africa to within five degrees of the equator; and, to the south of it, Uganda, the most civilized state in that part of Central Africa, has just become Mohammedan.* Last year, a mosque

---

* See some interesting remarks by Mr. Francis Galton at a meeting of the British Association at Leeds, on Sept. 22, 1873. I have also to thank him for giving me, in conversation, his experience of Mohammedanism in Africa, and for directing me to the best authorities on the subject. Along the coast-line Mohammedanism of a degraded kind has of course extended much farther south, beyond Zanzibar to Mozambique and the Portuguese colonies. There are Mohammedans to be found even among the Kaffirs and in Madagascar. The original Portuguese settlers found the Arabs established along the coasts of Mozambique and in the interior. They exterminated the former; but as they failed to dispossess the latter, it is possible that some of the *terra incognita* in the interior may be still Mohammedan.

was built on the shores of the Victoria Nyanza itself, and the Nile, from its source to its mouth, is now, with very few exceptions, a Mohammedan river.

That Mohammedanism may, when mutual misunderstandings are removed, as I hope to show in a future Lecture, be elevated, chastened, purified by Christian influences and a Christian spirit, and that evils such as the slave-trade, which are really foreign to its nature, can be put down by the heroic efforts of Christian philanthropists, I do not doubt; and I can, therefore, look forward, if with something of anxiety, with still more of hope, to what seems the destiny of Africa, that Paganism and Devil-worship will die out, and that the main part of the continent, if it can not become Christian, will become, what is next best to it, Mohammedan.

Anyhow, it is certain that the gains of Mohammedanism, in Africa alone, counterbalance its apparent losses from Russian conquests, and from proselytism every where else; nor can I believe, notwithstanding predictions inspired by the wish, that its work is yet done, or nearly done, in any of the countries that have ever owned its sway.

I speak of the apparent losses from Russian conquest, for the onward march of the Russian Colossus through Central Asia, so far from carrying any form of Christianity with it, seems to intensify the religious convictions of the half-conquered or threatened races. What was dead in the religion before, it revives; to what was only half alive, it gives fresh vigor. Islam has now become with them a patriotism as well as a creed; and Mr. Gifford Palgrave, an able and accurate observer, has lately described how the distinctive precepts of the Mohammedan religion—those enjoining the observance of the month of Ramadhan, the reading of the Koran, the pilgrimage of the Hadj, the abstinence from gaming, from tobacco, and from intoxicating drinks—are now much more rigidly observed in the debatable territories; and, more than this, the Abkhasians with their immemorial antiquity, and the heroic Circassians driven from their homes after a desperate struggle by Muscovite oppression and bad faith, dropping such traces of Christianity as they had, but carrying with them a legacy of immortal hate to the creed and country of their tyrants, have crossed the frontier of the more liberal Turkish Empire, and, coalescing with Koords, Turkomans, and Arabs, have settled down in the uplands of Armenia, and are there forming the nucleus of a new and vigorous and united Mohammedan nation.*

In India, where the two religions are brought face to face, and where, if any where, we may expect the great

---

* Palgrave's "Essays on Eastern Questions," iv. and v.

drama to play itself out, Mohammedanism gives no sign of yielding. Unlike Brahmanism, which the thousand influences of Western civilization are sapping in every direction, Mohammedanism, on the contrary, seems to concentrate the strength it already has, and, owing to the efforts of its zealous missionaries, is giving symptoms at once of a Revival and of a Reform that may, at any time, change the religious destinies of the country. The Faithful are as courageous, as sincere, as ardently monotheistic as they ever were; witness it in the Indian Mutiny, the Wahhabee Revival, and the last terrible argument of assassination. The heroism and self-devotion of our missionaries seems to be wasted on them in vain, and except in individual cases I see no sign that it will ever be otherwise. Buddhism and Brahmanism may be driven out of India, but Mohammedanism never, except by the Mohammedan method of the sword.*

Such are the leading facts of Mohammedanism viewed from the outside; and now how are we to account for them?

One thing is certain, that the explanations so readily offered by historians and Christian apologists till within a very recent period will not suffice now. People who think they have nothing to do with a system except to

---

* See Appendix to Lecture I.

attack it, are not those who can best explain the causes of its vitality or its success. One historian tells us that Mohammedanism triumphed by the mere force of arms; another, by the use Mohammed made of the tendency so deeply planted in man to fall victims in masses to any well-conceived imposture; a third traces his success to his skillful plagiarisms from faiths purer than his own; and a fourth to the elevated morality, or to the lax morality, inculcated in the Koran—for both of these are strangely enough urged almost in the same breath by the same people; while, lastly, others dwell on the inherent strength of the founder's character, and the enthusiasm that must accompany a crusade against idolatry.* We feel that most of these have some truth in them, some of them have much; and one or two of them are not only not true, but they are the very reverse of the truth. But we also feel that none of them singly, nor all of them together, adequately account for the phenomena they profess to explain.

In treating of Mohammedanism, as remarked by M. Barthélemy St. Hilaire,† we have to try *in limine* to discard alike our national and our religious prejudices. It was not till Mohammedanism had existed for eight

---

* See some of these explanations admirably dealt with by F. D. Maurice, "Religions of the World," Lecture I.

† "Mahomet et le Koran," Preface, p. 6.

hundred years that it was possible to discard the one, and not till very lately that it was even attempted to discard the other. Since the conquest of Constantinople, or rather since the brilliant naval victory of Don John of Austria at Lepanto, and its final repulse by John Sobieski from the walls of Vienna two hundred and thirty years later, Mohammedanism has ceased, in Europe at least, to be an aggressive and conquering power; and since then it has been possible for the states of Christendom to breathe more freely, and to forget the infidel in the ally or the subject.

Religious prejudice is more difficult to overcome. Men who are ardently attached to their own religion find it difficult to judge another dispassionately, and from a neutral point of view. The philosopher who, according to Gibbon's famous aphorism, looked upon all religions of the Roman Empire as equally false, and the magistrate who looked upon all as equally useful, would be alike incapacitated for viewing the Mussulman creed from the Mussulman stand-point. Perhaps the populace, who looked upon all religions as equally true, would have been the best judge of the three; but I doubt whether in this, as in most epigrammatic sentences, something of truth has not been sacrificed to the antithesis. Nature does not arrange herself in antithetical groups for our convenience; and I doubt whether the mass of any people, at any time, have looked upon all religions as equally true.

But the comparative study of religion is beginning to teach, at all events, the more thoughtful of mankind, not indeed that all religions are equally true or equally elevating, but that all contain some truth; that no religion is exclusively good, none exclusively bad; that any religion which has a real and continued hold on a large body of mankind must satisfy a real spiritual need, and is so far good. God is in all his works, and not the least so in the thoughts and aspirations of his creatures toward himself; and what we have to do is to feel after him in each and all, assured that he is there, even if haply in our ignorance we can find no trace of him.

Truly, when we are dealing with religion at all, even though it be Polytheism or Fetichism, we are "treading upon holy ground;" and in order that we may treat that creed, sublime in its simplicity, which is our special subject, with that union of candor and of reverence which alone befits it, it is necessary before concluding this introductory Lecture that I should lay down clearly one principle which must guide us in our investigation.

It is this, that for the purposes of scientific investigation, religions must be regarded as differing from one another in degree rather than in kind. This is the one postulate, itself the result of a careful induction, upon which alone the existence of any true science of religion must depend. Without a clear perception of this truth, you enter upon the study of the religions of the world with a preconceived idea, which will color all your conclusions, and will invalidate them the more gravely the more favorable those conclusions are to your own creed. The ordinary distinctions of kind, therefore, drawn between true and false, natural and supernatural, revealed and unrevealed religions are, for our present purpose, unreal and misleading. The fact is that from one point of view all religions are more or less natural, from another all are more or less supernatural; and all alike are to be treated from the same stand-point, and investigated by the same methods. In the Science of Religion, to quote an expression of Max Müller's used in this place, Christianity "owns no prescriptive rights, and claims no immunities." It challenges the freest inquiry; and as it claims to come from God himself, so it fears not the honest use of any faculties that God has given to man. Christianity is indeed a revelation, and what it really reveals is true; and, so far, if the alternative must needs be put in this shape, no Christian would have any doubt in which category to place his own creed.

But does Christianity claim any such monopoly of what is good and true as is implied in this crude classification, or will any one say that there is no real revelation of God in the noble lives of Confucius or Buddha, and no fragments of divine truth in the pure morality of the systems which they founded? Truth, happily for man, is myriad-sided, and happy he who can catch a far-off glance of the one side of it presented to him! Claim, if you like, for the Bible what the Koran does claim for itself and the Bible does not—a rigid or a verbal inspiration. Grant that the truth revealed passed mechanically through the mind of the sacred writer without contamination and without alloy, yet who can say that, since the Verities with which religion deals are all beyond the world of sense, the precise meaning attached by him to any one word in his creed is the same as that attached to it by any other?—*quot homines tot sententiæ.* The recipient subject colors every object of sensation or of thought as it passes into it, and is conscious of that object, not as it entered, but as it has been instantaneously and unconsciously transformed in the alembic of the mind. In religion, as in external nature, the human mind is, as Bacon says, an unequal mirror to the rays of things, mixing its own nature indissolubly with theirs. And this relative element once admitted into religion at all, it follows that to divide religions by an impassable barrier into true and false, natural and revealed, is like dividing music into sacred and secular, and history into sacred and profane. It is a division convenient enough for those—the majority of the human race—who are content with an artificial classification, and who care for no religion but their own; but, for scientific purposes, it is a cross division, it begs the question at issue, and is as unphilosophical as it is misleading.*

Nor do Sacred Books, whatever be the theory of inspiration on which they rest, lend to the religion to which they belong any distinction of kind; they fix the phraseology of a religion, and we are apt to believe that they also fix the thought. They do not do so, however. The "poetic and literary terms thrown out,"† to use Mr. Matthew Arnold's happy expression, by the highest minds at the highest objects of thought, as faint approximations only to the truth respecting them, become enshrined in the Sacred Canon. They are misunderstood, or half understood, even by those who hear them from the Psalmist's or the Prophet's own lips, and in a few years the misunderstanding grows till it becomes fixed and rigid.‡ Poetic imagery is mistaken for scientific

---

* For a full discussion of the ordinary methods of classifying religion, see Max Müller's "Science of Religion," p. 123–143.

† "Literature and Dogma," passim; but see especially p. 38–41 and 58.

‡ For admirable illustrations of this, see "Literature and Dogma," cap. ii. and v., p. 123. This part of Mr. Arnold's work, it may be pretty confidently asserted, is done once for all; and its influence will be felt, avowedly or not, throughout the domain of Biblical criticism.

exactness, and dim outlines for exhaustive definitions. A virtue is attached to the words themselves, and the thought, which is the jewel, is hidden by the letter, which is only the casket. If it be true that man never knows how anthropomorphic he himself is, still less do sacred writers know the anthropomorphism and the materialism which will eventually be drawn even from their highest and most spiritual utterances. How little did the author of the prayer at the dedication of the Temple of Solomon—the grandest assertion, perhaps, in the Old Testament of the infinite power and the infinite goodness of God, his nearness to us and his distance from us—imagine that the time would ever come when it would be held that in that Temple alone, and by Jews alone, men could worship the Father!

Christians may and must rise from an impartial study of the religions of the world with their belief vastly deepened that their Sacred Books stand as a whole on a far higher level than other Sacred Books, and that the ideal life of Christianity, while it is capable of including the highest ideals of other creeds, can not itself be attained by any one of them. But the value of this belief will be exactly proportioned to the extent to which they have been able, for the purposes of scientific duty, to divest themselves of any arbitrary assumption in the matter; and they must also acknowledge that it is possible and natural for sincere Mohammedans or Buddhists to arrive at the same conclusions concerning their own faiths. It is not easy to be thoroughly convinced of this, or to act upon it; for intolerance is the "natural weed of the human bosom," and there is no religion which does not seem superstitious to those who do not believe in it.*

But this belief is far from necessitating in practical life a religious indifference; nor, however it may seem so at first sight, is it averse to all missionary efforts. Missionaries will not cease to exist, nor will they lose their energy, their enthusiasm, and their self-sacrifice. But they will go to work in a different way, will view other religions in a different light, and will test their success by a different standard. They will no doubt be forced to acquiesce in what seems the will of Providence, that a national religion is as much a part of man's nature as is the genius of his language or the color of his skin; they will admit that the precise form of a creed is a matter of prejudice and of circumstance with most of us, and that, in spite of the rise of historical religions which have shattered other faiths and

---

* See Grote, vol. vi., p. 156, seq., on the death of Socrates. The boast of Cicero, "Majores nostri superstitionem a religione separaverunt" (De Nat. Deorum, ii., 28), is the natural belief of every one, even of the Fetich-worshiper, concerning his own, and none but his own, creed.

risen upon their ruins, nine tenths of the whole human race have died, and will in all probability continue to die, in the profession of that faith into which they were born; but this will no longer seem to them, as it must seem now, a mysterious and overwhelming victory of evil over good, which appalls the moral sense, and, if a man be not better than the letter of his creed, must tend to shake at once his belief in the universal Fatherhood of God and the true brotherhood of humanity; they will rather, in proportion to the strength of their belief in the goodness of God, believe that his creatures can not grope after him, even in the dark, without getting that light which is sufficient for them; they will not seek to eradicate wholly any existing national faith, if only it be a living one; nor, as the phrase is, will they aim at "bringing its adherents over to Christianity;" they will seek rather to bring Christianity to them, to infuse a Christian spirit into what is, at worst, not an anti-Christian, but merely a non-Christian, or, it may be, a half-Christian faith.

The Apostles did not cease to be Jews because they became Christians, or to look up to Moses less because they reverenced Christ more. And yet the difference between Judaism and Christianity, between the forms and the ceremonies and the exclusiveness of the one, and the spirituality and the freedom and the universality of the other, is at least as great, as I hope to show, as the difference between a sincere believer in the teachings of the Prophet of Arabia and a humble follower of the character of Christ.

St. Paul, the one model given us in the New Testament of what a missionary should be, in dealing with the faith of a cultivated people much dissimilar to his own—a faith, most people would say now, differing in kind as well as in degree from Christianity—never thought himself of drawing so broad a distinction between the two. He might well have been disposed to do so, for the Polytheism of Athens had long ceased to be an adequate expression of the highest religious life of the people. It was in its decadence even when it had inspired the profoundest utterances of Æschylus or Sophocles; it could not have inspired them then, even had there existed genius like theirs to be inspired. Its oracles were dumb; and yet St. Paul dropped not a word of scorn for the echoes that still lingered and the flames that were still flickering on its shattered altars. He did not talk of false gods or of devil-worship, of imposture or of superstition. Those whom our translation calls "superstitious" he calls "God-fearing." He quotes their great authors with sympathy and with respect. He professes only to give articulate utterance to their own thoughts, and to declare more fully to them that God whom, unknowingly, they already worshiped.

And so, again, in writing to the converts to be found even in the metropolis of the world, and, it must be added, the head-quarters of its vices, while he lashes its moral iniquities and its religious corruptions with an unsparing hand, yet, with a toleration wholly alien to the Jewish race, and without forfeiting his supreme allegiance to his Master, he strikes at the root of the impassable distinction between revealed and unrevealed religion, by pointing out that those who, not having the law, yet did by nature the things contained in the law, were in truth a law unto themselves. He showed that the Eternal could reveal himself as well by his unwritten as by his written law, and that the voice of conscience is, in very truth, to every one who follows it, the voice of the living God.

The missionaries of the future, therefore, will try to penetrate to the common elements which, they will have learned, underlie all religions alike, and make the most of those. They will be able, with a sympathy which is real because it is drawn from a knowledge of the history of their own faith, to point out the abuses which have crept, and always will creep, into an originally spiritual creed. They will inculcate in their teaching and exhibit in their lives, as they do now, something of that highest morality which they have learned from their Master, and which they will then have learned is the very essence of their faith, and which, in its broad outlines at least, in the "secret" as well as in the "method" of Jesus,* may adapt itself to the wants of every nation and every creed.

They will never, therefore, think it necessary to present Christianity to those of an alien creed as a collection of defined yet mysterious doctrines, which must be accepted whole or not at all; but will rather be content to show them Christ himself as he appeared to his earliest disciples — before the mists of metaphysics had gathered around his head, and the watchwords of theology had half hidden him from the view—glorious in his moral beauty, sublime in his self-surrender, divine in his humanity and by reason of it. And they may then leave it to the moral sense of some, at least, in every section of the race, whose greatest glory and Ideal

---

* "Literature and Dogma," p. 343. "Of the all-importance of righteousness there is a knowledge in Mohammedanism, but of the method and secret of Jesus, by which alone is righteousness possible, hardly any sense at all." There is substantial truth in this; but few can read Mr. Arnold's own account of what he conceives the secret and method of Jesus to have been, without feeling that all the higher religions of the world—any religion, in fact, which, controlling the lower part of man's nature and stimulating the higher, makes him to be at peace with himself, which gives hope in adversity, and calmness in the prospect of death —must contain much both of the one and of the other.

Representative he is, to judge of him aright, and to recognize in his person the supreme and the final Revelation of God. Here, in the ambition to set before the eyes of all a higher Ideal, and a more perfect example than any they have yet known; in the proclamation of the truth, which Christ came to proclaim, of the universal Fatherhood, and the perfect love of God—here is ample work for the enthusiasm of humanity; in this sense Christ may live again upon the earth, and in this sense, and only in this, is it likely that Christianity will overspread the world. I have premised this much, even at the risk of anticipating some of the conclusions to which we shall, I believe, ultimately come, because I think it necessary to prevent any misunderstanding as to my point of view.

Ἐξ οἵων οἷος; how far the way was prepared for Mohammed by circumstances, and what part he himself bore in the great revolution that goes by his name; what we are to say on the nature of his mission, on the much-disputed question of his sincerity, of the inconsistencies in his career and the blots upon it, this will form the subject of my next Lecture.

LECTURE II.

February 21, 1874.

MOHAMMED.

Μεγάλων ἑαυτὸν ἀξιοῖ ἄξιος ὤν.—Aristotle.
There goeth the son of Abdallah, who hath his conversation in the heavens.—The Koreishites.

A COMPLETE history of the opinions that have been held by Christians about Mohammed and Mohammedanism would not be an uninstructive chapter, however melancholy, in the history of the human mind. To glance for a moment at a few of them.

During the first few centuries of Mohammedanism, Christendom could not afford to criticise or explain; it could only tremble and obey. But when the Saracens had received their first check in the heart of France, the nations which had been flying before them faced around, as a herd of cows will sometimes do when the single dog that has put them to flight is called off; and though they did not yet venture to fight, they could at least calumniate their retreating foe. Drances-like, they could manufacture calumnies and victories at pleasure:

> "Quæ tuto tibi magna volant; dum distinet hostem
> Agger murorum, nec inundant sanguine fossæ."

The disastrous retreat of Charles the Great through Roncesvalles is turned by romance-mongers and troubadours into a signal victory; Charles, who never went beyond Pannonia, is credited, in the following century, with a successful crusade to the Holy Sepulchre, and even with the sack of Babylon! The age of Christian chivalry had not yet come, and was not to come for two hundred years.

In the romance of "Turpin," quoted by Renan, Mohammed, the fanatical destroyer of all idolatry, is turned himself into an idol of gold, and, under the name of Mawmet, is reported to be the object of worship at Cadiz; and this not even Charles the Great, Charles the Iconoclast, the destroyer of the Irmansul in his own native Germany, would venture to attack from fear of the legion of demons which guarded it. In the song of Roland, the national epic of France, referring to the same events, Mohammed appears with the chief of the Pagan Gods on the one side of him, and the chief of the Devils on the other; a curious anticipation, perhaps, of the view of Satanic inspiration taken by Sir William Muir. Marsilles, Kaliph of Cordova, is supposed to worship him as a god, and his favorite form of adjuration is made to be "By Jupiter, by Mohammed, and by Apollyon"—strange metamorphosis and strange collocation! Human sacrifices are offered to him, if nowhere else indeed, in the imagination and assertions of Christian writers of the tenth and eleventh centuries, under the various names of Bafum, or Maphomet, or Mawmet; and in the same spirit Malaterra, in his "History of Sicily," describes that island as being, when under Saracenic rule, "a land wholly given to idolatry,"* and the expedition of the Norman Roger Guiscard is characterized as being a crusade against idolatry. Which people were the greater idolaters, any candid reader of the Italian annalists of this time, collected by Muratori, can say. It is not a little curious that both the English and French languages still bear witness to the popular misapprehension: the French by the word "Mahomerie;" the English by the word "mummery," still used for absurd or superstitious rites.† Nor has a Mohammedan nothing to complain of in the etymology and history, little known or forgotten, of the words "Mammetry"‡ and "Paynim," "termagant"

---

* Bk. ii., p. 1. "Terram idolis deditam."

† Renan, "Études d'Histoire Religieuse," p. 223, note.

‡ Mammetry, a contraction of Mahometry, used in early English for any false religion, especially for a worship of idols, insomuch that Mam-

and "miscreant;" but to these I can only refer in passing.

In the twelfth century "the god Mawmet passes into the heresiarch Mahomet,"* and, as such, of course he occupies a conspicuous place in the "Inferno." Dante places him in his ninth circle among the sowers of religious discord; his companions being Fra Dolcino, a communist of the fourteenth century, and Bertrand de Born, a fighting troubadour: his flesh is torn piecemeal from his limbs by demons, who repeat their round in time to re-open the half-healed wounds. The romances of Baphomet, so common in the fourteenth and fifteenth centuries, attribute any and every crime to him, just as the Athanasians did to Arius. "He is a debauchee, a camel stealer, a cardinal, who, having failed to obtain the object of every cardinal's ambition, invents a new religion to revenge himself on his brethren!"†

---

met or Mawmet came to mean an idol. In Shakespeare the name is extended to mean a doll : Juliet, for instance, is called by her father "a whining mammet." See Trench "On Words," p. 112. Paynim = Pagan or Heathen. Termagant, a term applied now only to a brawling woman, was originally one of the names given to the supposed idol of the Mohammedans. Miscreant, originally "a man who believes otherwise," acquired its moral significance from the hatred of the Saracens which accompanied the Crusades. The story of Blue Beard, the associations connected with the name "Mahound," and the dislike of European chivalry in mediæval times for the mare—the favorite animal of the Arabs—are other indications of the same thing.

* Renan, loc. cit. † Renan, p. 224.

With the leaders of the Reformation, Mohammed, the greatest of all Reformers, meets with little sympathy, and their hatred of him, as perhaps was natural, seems to vary inversely as their knowledge. Luther doubts whether he is not worse than Leo; Melanchthon believes him to be either Gog or Magog, and probably both.* The Reformers did not see that the Papal party, fastening on the hatred of priestcraft and formalism, which was common doubtless to Islam and to Protestantism, would impute to both a common hatred of Christianity, even as the Popes had accused the iconoclastic Emperors of Constantinople eight centuries before.

Now, too, arose the invention—the maliciousness of which was only equaled by its stupidity, but believed by all who wished to believe it—of the dove trained to gather peas placed in the ear of Mohammed,† that people might believe that he was inspired by the Holy Ghost — inspired, it would seem, by the very Being whose separate existence it was the first article of his creed to deny! In the imagination of Biblical commentators later on, and down to this very day, he divides with the Pope the credit or discredit of being

---

* See "Quarterly Review," Art. Islam, by Deutsch, No. 254, p. 296.

† A similar story is told of the great Schamyl; only in this case it is Mohammed himself who takes the form of a dove, and imparts his commands to the hero.

the subject of special prophecy in the books of Daniel and the Revelation, that magnificent series of tableaux, a part of which, on the principle that "a prophecy may mean whatever comes after it," has been tortured into agreement with each successive act of the drama of history; while, from another part, lovers of the mysterious have attempted to cast, and, in spite of disappointment, will always continue to cast, the horoscope of the future. He is Antichrist, the Man of Sin, the Little Horn, and I know not what besides; nor do I think that a single writer, with the one strange exception of the Jew Maimonides, till toward the middle of the eighteenth century, treats of him as otherwise than a rank impostor and a false prophet.

France and England may, perhaps, divide the credit of having been the first to take a different view, and to have begun that critical study of Arabian history or literature which, in the hands of Gibbon and of Muir, of Caussin de Perceval and of St. Hilaire, of Weil and of Sprenger, has put the materials for a fair and unbiased judgment within the reach of every one. Most other writers of the eighteenth century, such as Dean Prideaux and the Abbé Maracci, Boulainvilliers and Voltaire, and some subsequent Bampton lecturers and Arabic professors, have approached the subject only to prove a thesis. Mohammed was to be either a hero or an impostor; they have held a brief either for the prosecution or the defense; and from them, therefore, we learn much that has been said about Mohammed, but comparatively little of Mohammed himself.

The founder of the reaction was Gagnier, a Frenchman by birth, but an Englishman by adoption. Educated in Navarre, where he had early shown a mastery of more than one Semitic language, he became Canon of St. Geneviève at Paris; on a sudden he turned Protestant, came to England, and attacked Catholicism with all the zeal of a recent convert. Having been appointed to the Chair of Arabic at Oxford, he proceeded to write a history of Mohammed, founded on the work of Abul Feda, the earliest and most authentic of Arabic historians then known.

The translations of the Koran into two different European languages by Sale and Savary soon followed; and from these works, combined with the vast number of facts contained in Sale's Introductory Discourse, Gibbon, who was not an Arabic scholar himself, drew the materials for his splendid chapter, the most masterly of his "three masterpieces of biography"—Athanasius, Julian, and Mohammed. "He has descended on the subject in the fullness of his strength," has been inspired by it, and has produced a sketch which, in spite of occasional uncalled-for sarcasms and characteristic inuendoes, must be the delight and despair even of those who have access, as we now have, thanks especially to Sprenger and Muir, to vast stores of information denied to him. But Gibbon's unfair and unphilosophic treatment of Christianity has, perhaps, prevented the world from doing justice to his generally fair and philosophic treatment of Mohammedanism; and, as a consequence of this, most Englishmen, who do not condemn the Arabian prophet unheard, derive what favorable notions of him they have, not from Gibbon, but from Carlyle. Make as large deductions as we will on the score of Carlyle's peculiar views on "Heroes and Hero-worship," how many of us can recall the shock of surprise, the epoch in our intellectual and religious life, when we found that he chose for his "Hero as prophet," not Moses, or Elijah, or Isaiah, but the so-called impostor Mohammed!

I admitted above that the religion of Mohammed was in its essence not original. Mohammed never said it was: he called it a revival of the old one, a return to the primitive creed of Abraham; and there is reason to believe that both the great religions of the Eastern world existing in his time, Sabæanism, that is, and Magianism, had been, in their origin at least, vaguely monotheistic. They had passed through the inevitable stages of spirituality, misunderstanding, decline, and, lastly, intentional corruption, till the God whom Abraham, according to the well-known Mussulman legend, had been the first to worship, because, while he had made the stars and sun to rise and set, he never rose nor set himself, had withdrawn behind them altogether; the heavenly bodies, from being symbols, had become the thing symbolized; temples were erected in their honor, and idols filled the temples.

And as with Sabæanism, so with Magianism; Ormuzd and Ahriman were no longer the principles brought into existence, or existing, by the permission of the one true God, who, as Zoroaster had taught, would tolerate neither temples nor altars nor symbols; worshiped only on the hill-tops with the eye of faith, quickened though it might be by the glory of the rising or setting sun presented to the bodily eye. Fire had itself become the Divinity; and what offering could be more acceptable to such a God than the human victim, overwhelmed by the mysterious flame, whose divine power he denied?

And combined with these two religions, which had been spiritual in their origin, and, probably, more prominent and popular than either, was the grossest Fetichism—the worship of actual stocks and stones, or of the "grim array" of three hundred and sixty idols in the Kaaba; among which the aerolite — once believed to have been of dazzling whiteness, but long since blackened by the kisses of sinful men—was at once the most ancient and the most sacred.

Nor were Judaism and Christianity themselves unknown in Arabia. The destruction of Jerusalem by Titus had caused a very general migration of Jews from Palestine, southward and eastward, beyond the limits of the Roman Empire, and from that time onward the northern part of Arabia was dotted over by Jewish colonies. In the third century a whole Arabian tribe, even in the south of the Peninsula, had adopted the Jewish faith; and the history of Mohammed proves that the neighborhood of Yathrib* contained many Jewish tribes, which, though they maintained in the land of their exile that proud religious isolation which was their national birthright, were not without their influence on Arab politics.

As to Christianity, it is possible that the very first converts made by St. Paul to the faith which once he had destroyed were of Arab blood.† In the fourth century we hear of Christian churches at Tzafar and at Aden, under the protection of the half-Christianized Himyarite king; and the Abyssinian conquest made a form of Christianity to be the dominant religion, at all

---

* Not called Medina, *i. e.*, Medinat-an-Nabi, "the City of the Prophet," till after the Hegira.

† Epistle to Galatians, i. 17.

events in appearance, in Yemen. But neither of these religions ever struck deep root in the Arabian soil: either the people were not suited to them, or they were not suited to the people. They lived on, on sufferance only, till a faith, which to the Arabs should be the more living one, should sweep them away.

Such were the religious conditions under which Mohammed had to work; and what were the social conditions? Arabia from time immemorial had been split up into a vast number of independent tribes, always at war with one another. The scanty sustenance which an arid soil yielded they were fain to eke out by trading themselves, or by plundering others who conducted caravans along the sea-coast of the Hedjaz, to exchange the spices and precious stones of India or of Hadramaut or of Yemen with the manufactures of Bozra and Damascus. Their hand was against every man, and every man's hand was against them; and a prophecy is hardly needed to explain the fact that an impenetrable country was never penetrated by foreign conquerors. Nor were they as uncivilized as has often been supposed. They were as passionately fond of poetry as they were of war and plunder. What the Olympic Games did for Greece in keeping up the national feeling, as distinct from tribal independence, in giving a brief cessation from hostilities, and acting as a literary centre, that the annual fairs at Okatz and Mujanna were to Arabia. Here tribes made up their dissensions, exchanged prisoners of war, and, most important of all, competed with one another in extempore poetic contests. Even in the "times of ignorance," each tribe produced its own poet-laureate; and the most ready and the best saw his poem transcribed in letters of gold,* or suspended on the wall of the entrance of the Kaaba, where it would be seen by every pilgrim who might visit the most sacred place in the country. There was a wild chivalry, too, about them, a contempt of danger and a sensibility of honor, which lends a charm to all we hear of their loves and their wars, their greed and their hospitality, their rapine and their revenge. The Bedouin has been the same in these respects in all ages. "Be good enough to take off that garment of yours," says the Bedouin robber politely to his victim; "it is wanted by my wife;" and the victim submits, with as good a grace as he can muster, to the somewhat unreasonable demands of a hypothetical lady. El Mutanabi, a poet, prophet, and warrior, three hundred years after the Hegira, but who no doubt had

---

* Called Moállacât. Sprenger and Deutsch agree that this word means, not "suspended," but "strung loosely together," and question the truth of the story of the suspension in the "Kaaba." Some of these poems, as, for instance, that of the poet Labyd, still survive, and are a standing proof of the untaught poetic genius of the Arabs.

his prototypes before it, was journeying with his son through a country infested by robbers, and proposed to seek a place of refuge for the night: "Art thou then that Mutanabi," exclaimed his slave, "who wrote these lines—

"'I am known to the night, and the wild and the steed,
To the guest and the sword, to the paper and the reed?'"

The poet-warrior felt the stain like a wound, and throwing himself down to sleep where he then was, met his death at the hands of the robbers.* The passion indeed for indiscriminate plunder had, before the time of Mohammed, so far given way to the growing love of commerce that a kind of Treuga Dei, or Truce of God, was observed—in theory at least—during four months of the year. But what the law forbade then, *ex hypothesi* it allowed at other times, and it is likely that the enforced abstention gave at once the zest of novelty and a clear conscience to the purveyors of the trade when the four months were over.

Such, very briefly, was the condition of the Arabs when, to use an expression of Voltaire, quoted by Barthélemy St. Hilaire, "The turn of Arabia" came;† when

---

* Burton's "Pilgrimage to Mecca," vol. iii., p. 60, where he tells this story and translates the Arabic lines. See the whole of chap. xxiv. for a graphic account drawn from personal observation of Bedouin knight-errantry and poetry and generosity.

† P. 211. See cap. ii., generally, for a description of Pre-Mohammedan Arabia.

the hour had already struck for the most complete, the most sudden, and the most extraordinary revolution that has ever come over any nation upon earth.

One of the most philosophical of historians has remarked that of all the revolutions which have had a permanent influence upon the civil history of mankind, none could so little be anticipated by human prudence as that effected by the religion of Arabia. And at first sight it must be confessed that the Science of History, if indeed there be such a science, is at a loss to find that sequence of cause and effect which it is the object and the test of all history, which is worthy of the name, to trace out.

The Emperor Justinian, not the least shrewd of the Byzantine emperors, who, some forty years before, had thought it necessary to protect his empire from every possible and from many impossible dangers, had neglected to erect a line of fortresses on the side of his empire which, in defiance of nature, really was the most vulnerable.* "By a precaution which inspired the cowardice it foresaw," he had erected a fortress even at Thermopylæ, where the *religio loci* would rather have called for a Spartan rampart of three hundred men, if only they had been forthcoming. He had kept the

---

* Cf. Gibbon, vol. v., p. 102–111.

Sclavonians out of Constantinople by one long wall, and the Russians out of the Crimea by another; he had fortified Amida and Edessa against the fire-worshipers; had built St. Catharine's, half monastery and half fortress, in the wilderness of Mount Sinai; and had even taken precautions against the savages of Æthiopia: but he had trusted to the six hundred miles of desert which nature had interposed between him and a set of robber tribes, intent only on molesting one another. What hostile force could pass such an obstacle?

But we can see now, and Mohammed himself perhaps saw, that the ground was in many respects prepared for a great social and religious revolution. "It detracts nothing from the fame of a great man to show, so far as we can, how his success was possible."* It is only another proof, if proof were wanting, that genius is little else than insight joined to sustained effort; the eye sees what it brings with it the power of seeing; and the great man differs from his contemporaries chiefly in this, that he can read the dark riddle of his time with an eye a few degrees less obscured than those around him. He is the greatest product of his age, but he is still its product, and he is only the father of the age that is to succeed in so far as he owns his parent-

---

* M. Barthélemy St. Hilaire, "Mahomet et le Koran," p. 51.

age. He marches indeed in front of his age; but his influence will be permanent or fleeting precisely so far as he discerns the direction in which it would advance at a slower pace without him.* When he tries to go beyond this, and to force the world out of its groove to adopt hobbies of his own, then begins the region of the remote, the selfish, the personal; in this the great man fails, and hence the commonplaces on the failure of greatness, and the greatness of failure, with which we are all familiar. "Perish my name," said Danton, "but let the cause triumph;"† and personal failure of this kind is to the great man no failure at all—it is only another word for success. The truth is that greatness, so far as it is the truest greatness, rarely fails altogether of its object; and that failure is great only when the end proposed is good, and the human means, though inadequate to its attainment, are yet a real advance toward it.

It must be remembered therefore as regards what seems the sudden birth of the Arabian nation, fully armed, like Athena from the head of Zeus, that the annual resort to Mecca for purposes of trade, poetry,

---

* Cf. Guizot's "Lectures on History," vol. iii., lect. xx.; and Mill's Review of them in "Dissertations and Discussions," vol. ii., p. 249, 250.

† A similar saying is attributed to Cavour: "Perish my name and memory, so that Italy be made a nation!"

and religion, had pointed to the Holy City as to a possible metropolis; and to the Koreishites, the hereditary guardians of the Kaaba, as the potential rulers of a future people; while, as regards the new religion, there was the groundwork of Monotheism underlying all the abuses and corruption of Magianism and Sabæanism. There was also a class of people, called Hanyfs, who prided themselves on preserving the original creed of Abraham, and even his sacred books; while Ibn-Ishac,* the earliest-known historian of Islam, records a meeting of four or five among the Koreishites at which it was

---

* He died A.H. 151. His work has been preserved for us in the Sirat-er-racoul of Ibn-Hisham, who died in the year of the Hegira 213. The fullest and most trustworthy historian, in the judgment of Muir and Sprenger, whose writings have come down to us, is the Katib al Wakidy, or secretary of the historian Wakidy: died A.H. 207. The MS. was discovered by Sprenger at Cawnpore. Among other discoveries of Sprenger may be mentioned a portion of the biography of Mohammed by Tabari, who died A.H. 310, and a complete biographical dictionary, termed Içaba, of the companions of Mohammed, compiled by Ibn-Hidjr, in the fifth century, from writers, whose names he gives, of earlier and incontestable authority. It contains the biographies of some 8000 people. And it may be hoped that the government of India, which numbers among its subjects more than thirty million Mussulmans, may recognize, if they have not already done so, the imperial importance of publishing the three remaining folios of the work. Sprenger brought out one volume, but an order of the Court of Directors suspended the publication of the rest. See Sprenger, Preface, p. 12, where it may be observed how modestly he passes over his own great discoveries, and does not even allude to the slight shown the work by the Directors. Learned and critical Mohammedans, it would seem, do not think so highly of Wakidy and his secretary as Muir and Sprenger do; they prefer Ibn-Hisham. See Muir, vol. i., p. 77–105.

resolved to open a crusade against idolatry, and to seek for the original and only true faith; and they straightway abandoned their homes and spread over the world in the quest of this Holy Grail.*

Mohammedanism therefore is no real exception to the principle I have laid down above as to the origin of the Historical Religions of the world, though, at first sight, it may appear to be so. To Mohammed's own mind it is quite true that the theological element was the predominant and inspiring one, but Mohammed's mind itself was the outcome, at least as much as it was the cause, of the great revolution which goes by his name. There was a general social and religious upheaving at the head of which the Prophet placed himself, and which partly carried him on with it, partly he himself carried it on; the train was already laid, and the spark from heaven was all that was needed to set the Arab world ablaze. In this sense it is perhaps true, as Renan has remarked and the Koran itself declares, that Mohammedanism was preached before the time of Mohammed; but there were Mohammedans before Mohammed only in the sense in which there were Zoroastrians before Zoroaster, Lutherans before Luther, and Christians before Christ. Renan has himself re-

---

* Sprenger, p. 81. These four "inquirers" were Waraka, Othman, Abayd, and Zayd.

marked elsewhere, though he seems to have forgotten it in dealing with Mohammedanism, that the glory of a religion belongs to its founder, and not to his predecessors or to his successors.* It is easy, he says himself, to try to awake faith, and it is easy to be possessed by it when once it has been awakened; but it is not easy to inspire it. It is the grandest gift, a very gift of God.

But though, as I have said, the hour had come, the youth of Mohammed gave few signs that he was the man. The portents which ushered in his birth, and that attended his early youth, are the offspring of an-

* It seems to me, though I would speak with the utmost diffidence in venturing to dissent from the greatest European authority on the subject, that Sprenger errs in the same direction as Renan when he says in his volume, published at Allahabad (p. 171), that Abu Bakr did more for the success of Islam than the Prophet himself; and again (p. 174), after enumerating all those who, merely from their vague Monotheism, he calls the predecessors of Mohammed, he says that even after Mohammed was acknowledged as the messenger of God, Omar had more influence on the development of the Islam than Mohammed himself. "The Islam is not the work of Mohammed; it is not the doctrine of the impostor . . . it is the offspring of the spirit of the time, and the voice of the Arabic nation. . . . There is, however, no doubt that the impostor has defiled it by his immorality and perverseness of mind." It is fair to say that this tone seems somewhat moderated, or even altered in the author's subsequent and greater work. Cf., however, vol. ii., p. 83-88. One is inclined to ask, if Islam was merely the spirit of the time, who proved himself best able to read that spirit? Was it Abu Bakr and Omar, or was it Mohammed that produced the Koran? And is it their personality, or his, which has stamped itself with ineffaceable clearness for all time upon the Eastern world?

other country and of a later age. The celestial light that beamed in the sky and from his newly opened eyes; the Tigris overflowing its banks; the palace of Chosroes toppling over to the ground; the sacred fire of Zoroaster, which had burned for one thousand years, suddenly extinguished; the mules that talked and the sheep that bowed to him, were unknown to the contemporaries of Mohammed, and Mohammed himself says nothing of them! He was a man of few words, and he had few friends: notable chiefly for his truthfulness and good faith, they called him "Al Amyn," the Trusty. His tending his employer's flocks; his journeys to Syria; possibly his short-lived friendship there with Sergius or Bahira, a Nestorian monk; his famous vow to succor the oppressed; his employment by Kadijah in a trade venture, and his subsequent happy marriage with her, are about the only noteworthy external incidents in his early life.

Up to the age of forty there is nothing to show that any serious scruple had occurred to him individually as to the worship of idols, and in particular of the Black Stone, of which his family were the hereditary guardians. The sacred month of Ramadhan, like other religious Arabs, he observed with punctilious devotion; and he would often retire to the caverns of Mount Hira for purposes of solitude, meditation, and prayer. He was melancholic in temperament, to begin with; he was also subject to epileptic fits, upon which Sprenger has laid great stress, and described most minutely,* and which, whether under the name of the "sacred disease" among the Greeks, or "possession by the devil" among the Jews, has in most ages and countries been looked upon as something specially mysterious or supernatural. It is possible that his interviews with Nestorian monks, with Zeid, or with his wife's cousin Waraka, may have turned his thoughts into the precise direction they took. Dejection alternated with excitement; these gave place to ecstasy or dreams; and in a dream, or trance, or fit, he saw an angel in human form, but flooded with celestial light, and displaying a silver roll. "Read!" said the angel. "I can not read," said Mohammed. The injunction and the answer were twice repeated.† "Read," at last said the angel, "in the

---

* Sprenger, vol. i., cap. iii., p. 207. He thinks Mohammed suffered from hysteria, followed by catalepsy, rather than epilepsy; for the Prophet does not seem to have lost all consciousness. It is worth remarking that Sprenger's medical knowledge is not very favorable in its result to Mohammed. He starts by saying, p. 210, that all hysterical people have a tendency to lying and deceit. This is his major premise. His minor is that Mohammed was hysterical, and the inference is obvious. Accordingly, we are not surprised to find him (vol. i., cap. iv., p. 306, note) speaking of the "*vision*" of the flight to Jerusalem as one "lie," and that to the seventh heaven as another lie.

† Cf. Sura xcvi. Deutsch (Islam, p. 306) renders the word usually translated "Read" by "Cry," comparing Isaiah xi. 6.

name of the Lord, who created man out of a clot of blood; read, in the name of the Most High, who taught man the use of the pen, who sheds on his soul the ray of knowledge, and teaches him what before he knew not." Upon this Mohammed felt the heavenly inspiration, and read the decrees of God, which he afterward promulgated in the Koran. Then came the announcement, "O Mohammed, of a truth thou art the Prophet of God, and I am his angel Gabriel."*

This was the crisis of Mohammed's life. It was his call to renounce idolatry, and to take the office of Prophet. Like Isaiah, he could not at first believe that so unworthy an instrument could be chosen for

---

* Strangely enough, Sir William Muir, vol. ii., p. 89–96, selects this period, above all others in Mohammed's life, as the one in which to suggest his peculiar view that the Prophet's belief in his inspiration was Satanic in its origin; and he supports his view by a somewhat elaborate parallel with the temptations which presented themselves to Christ at the beginning of his work. Whether such a *Deus ex machinâ* is required to untie the knot is hardly within my province to inquire, since the whole matter is alike incapable of proof and disproof; but it seems pertinent to remark, first, that the developed and quasi-scientific conception of such a being as Sir William Muir pictures is Persian rather than Jewish in its origin, and is found in Palestine only after the Captivity; and, secondly, that if the spirit of evil did suggest the idea to Mohammed, he never so completely outwitted himself, since friend and foe must alike admit that it was Mohammed's firm belief in supernatural guidance that lay at the root of all he achieved. Without this we should never have heard of him except as one of a thousand short-lived Arabian sectaries; with it he created a nation, and revivified a third of the then known world.

such a purpose. "Woe is me, for I am undone, because I am a man of unclean lips, and I dwell in the midst of a people of unclean lips;" but the live coal was not immediately taken from the altar and laid upon his, as upon Isaiah's lips. Trembling and agitated, Mohammed tottered to Kadijah and told her his vision and his agony of mind. He had always hated and despised soothsayers, and now, in the irony of destiny, it would appear that he was to become a soothsayer himself. "Fear not, for joyful tidings dost thou bring," exclaimed Kadijah. "I will henceforth regard thee as the prophet of our nation." "Rejoice," she added, seeing him still cast down; "Allah will not suffer thee to fall to shame. Hast thou not been loving to thy kinsfolk, kind to thy neighbors, charitable to the poor, faithful to thy word, and ever a defender of the truth?" First the life, and then the theology, in the individual as in the tribe and the nation.

But the assurances of the good Kadijah, and the conversions of Zeid and Waraka, did not bring the live coal from the altar. A long period of hesitation, doubt, preparation followed. At one time Mohammed even contemplated suicide, and he was only restrained by an unseen hand, as he might well call the bright vision of the future, pictured in one of the earliest Suras of the

Koran,* when the help of God should come and victory, when he "should see the people crowding into the one true Faith, and he, the Prophet, should celebrate the praise of his Lord, and ask pardon of him, for he is forgiving." Three years, the period of the Fatrah, saw only fourteen proselytes attach themselves to him. His teaching seemed to make no way beyond the very limited circle of his earliest followers. His rising hopes were crushed. People pointed the finger of scorn at him as he passed by: "There goeth the son of Abdallah, who hath his converse with the heavens!" They called him a driveler, a star-gazer, a maniac-poet. His uncles sneered, and the main body of the citizens treated him with that contemptuous indifference which must have been harder to him to bear than active persecution. Well might he, to take an illustration suggested by Sir W. Muir himself,† like Elijah of old, go a day's journey into the wilderness, and request for himself that he might die, and say, "It is enough, O Lord; now take away my life, for I am not better than my fathers;" or, again, "I have been very jealous for the Lord God of hosts, because the people have forsaken thy covenant, thrown down thine altars, and slain thy prophets with the sword; and I, even I,

---

* Sura cx. † Muir, vol. ii., p. 228.

only am left, and they seek my life to take it away." At times his distress was insupportable:

> "And had not his poor heart
> Spoken with That, which, being every where,
> Lets none who speaks with Him seem all alone,
> Surely the man had died of solitude."

But out of weakness came forth strength at last; out of doubt, certainty; out of humiliation, victory. Another vision, in which he was commanded to preach publicly, followed; and now he called the Koreishites of the line of Hachim together, those who had most to lose and least to gain by his reform, and boldly announced his mission. They tried persuasion, entreaties, bribes, and threats. "Should they array against me the sun on my right hand, and the moon on my left," said Mohammed, "yet while God should command me, I would not renounce my purpose." These are not the words, nor this the course, of an impostor.

Ten more years passed away; his doctrine fought its way amid the greatest discouragements and dangers by purely moral means, by its own inherent strength. Kadijah was dead; Abu Taleb, his uncle and protector, died also. Most of Mohammed's disciples had taken refuge in Abyssinia, and at last Mohammed himself was driven to fly for his life with one companion, his early convert, Abu Bakr. For three days he lay concealed in a cavern, a league from Mecca. The Koreishite pursuers scoured the country, thirsting for his blood. They approached the cavern. "We are only two," said his trembling companion. "There is a third," said Mohammed; "it is God himself." The Koreishites reached the cave; a spider, we are told, had woven its web across the mouth, and a pigeon was sitting on its nest in seemingly undisturbed repose. The Koreishites retreated, for it was evident the solitude of the place was unviolated; and, by a sound instinct, one of the sublimest stories in all history has been made the era of Mohammedan Chronology.

It is unnecessary to follow connectedly and in detail any other incidents in Mohammed's life. The above may be found, with some variety in the details, in any History of Mohammed,* but I have thought it essential to dwell upon them, however familiar they may be to some of us, as they seem to me, apart from their own intrinsic beauty, to supply the key to almost every thing else in Mohammed's career.

The question of the sincerity of Mohammed has been much debated; but to me, I must confess, that to question his sincerity at starting, and to admit the above indisputable facts, is very like a contradiction in terms. Nor could any one have done what Mohammed did without

---

* See especially Washington Irving, p. 32, 33; and Muir, vol. ii.

the most profound faith in the reality and goodness of his cause. Fairly considered, there is no single trait in his character up to the time of the Hegira which calumny itself could couple with imposture: on the contrary, there is every thing to prove the real enthusiast arriving slowly and painfully at what he believed to be the truth.

It has been remarked by Gibbon that no incipient prophet ever passed through so severe an ordeal as Mohammed, since he first presented himself as a prophet to those who were most conversant with his infirmities as a man. Those who knew him best—his wife, his eccentric slave, his cousin, his earliest friend, he who, as Mohammed said, alone of his converts, "turned not back, neither was perplexed"—were the first to recognize his mission. The ordinary lot of a prophet was in his case reversed; he was not without honor save among those who did not know him well. Strange that Voltaire, who himself wrote on Mohammed, and even made him the subject of a drama, should, with Mohammed's example before him, have ventured on his immoral paradox that " No man is a hero to his valet." Explained in one sense, that a small mind can not fully understand or appreciate a great one, it is a feeble truism; explained in another, which was the sense Voltaire meant, that the hero is only a hero to those who see him at a distance, and that there is no such thing as true greatness, it is an audacious falsehood. It is almost equally strange that Gibbon, who has done such full justice to Mohammed in the general result, should say at starting, " Mohammed's religion consists of an eternal truth and a necessary fiction—There is one God, and Mohammed is his Prophet." It was, as I have endeavored to show, no fiction to Mohammed himself or to his followers; had it been so, Mohammedanism could never have risen as it did, nor be what it is now.

But before we go on to consider those points in Mohammed's career which are really open to question, it may be well to recall a few prominent characteristics of the man who has stamped his impress so deeply on the Oriental world. Minute accounts of his appearance and of his daily life have been preserved to us; they may be found in most of the biographies, and Sir William Muir in particular has given us copious extracts from the writings of the secretary of Wakidy.*

Mohammed was of middle height and of a strongly built frame; his head was large, and across his ample forehead, and above finely arching eyebrows, ran a strongly marked vein, which, when he was angry, would turn black and throb visibly. His eyes were coal-black, and piercing in their brightness; his hair curled slightly;

---

* Muir, vol. iv., Supplement to Chap. XXXVII.; cf. also Deutsch's "Islam," p. 302–304.

and a long beard, which, like other Orientals, he would stroke when in deep thought, added to the general impressiveness of his appearance. His step was quick and firm, "like that of one descending a hill." Between his shoulders was the famous mark, the size of a pigeon's egg, which his disciples persisted in believing to be the sign of his prophetic office; while the light which kindled in his eye, like that which flashed from the precious stones in the breastplate of the High-Priest, they called the light of prophecy.

In his intercourse with others, he would sit silent among his companions for a long time together; but truly his silence was more eloquent than other men's speech, for the moment speech was called for, it was forthcoming in the shape of some weighty apothegm or proverb, such as the Arabs love to hear. When he laughed, he laughed heartily, shaking his sides and showing his teeth, which "looked as if they were hailstones." He was easy of approach to all who wished to see him, even as "the river-bank to him that draweth water therefrom." He was fond of animals, and they, as is often the case, were fond of him. He seldom passed a group of children playing together without a few kind words to them; and he was never the first to withdraw his hand from the grasp of one who offered him his. If the warmth of his attachment may be measured, as in fact it may, by the depth of his friends' devotion to him, no truer friend than Mohammed ever lived. Around him, in quite early days, gathered what was best and noblest in Mecca; and in no single instance, through all the vicissitudes of his checkered life, was the friendship then formed ever broken. He wept like a child over the death of his faithful servant Zeid. He visited his mother's tomb some fifty years after her death, and he wept there because he believed that God had forbidden him to pray for her. He was naturally shy and retiring: " as bashful," said Ayesha, " as a veiled virgin." He was kind and forgiving to all. " I served him from the time I was eight years old," said his servant Anas, " and he never scolded me for any thing, though I spoiled much." The most noteworthy of his external characteristics was a sweet gravity and a quiet dignity, which drew involuntary respect, and which was the best, and often the only protection he enjoyed from insult.

His ordinary dress was plain, even to coarseness; yet he was fastidious in arranging it to the best advantage. He was fond of ablutions, and fonder still of perfumes; and he prided himself on the neatness of his hair and the pearly whiteness of his teeth. His life was simple in all its details. He lived with his wives in a row of humble cottages, separated from one another by palm branches, cemented together with mud. He would kindle the fire, sweep the floor, and milk the goats himself. Ayesha tells us that he slept upon a leathern mat, and that he mended his clothes, and even clouted his shoes, with his own hand. For months together, Ayesha is also our authority for saying that he did not get a sufficient meal. The little food that he had was always shared with those who dropped in to partake of it. Indeed, outside the Prophet's house was a bench or gallery, on which were always to be found a number of the poor who lived entirely on the Prophet's generosity, and were hence called the "people of the bench." His ordinary food was dates and water, or barley bread; milk and honey were luxuries of which he was fond, but which he rarely allowed himself. The fare of the desert seemed most congenial to him, even when he was sovereign of Arabia. One day some people passed by him with a basket of berries from one of the desert shrubs. "Pick me out," he said to his companion, "the blackest of those berries, for they are sweet—even such as I was wont to gather when I fed the flocks of Mecca at Adgad."

Such were some of the characteristics of the man whom the Arabs were now called upon to recognize as the prophet of their country, and as a messenger direct from God.

Monotheism, pure and simple, if it is to be a life as well as a creed, almost postulates the prophetic office.

The Creator is at too great a distance from his creatures to allow of a sufficiently direct communication with them. The power, the knowledge, the infinity of God overshadow his providence, his sympathy, and his love. Renan has remarked that in only two ways can such a gap be bridged over: first, if, as in the Indian Avatar, from time to time, or, as in Christianity, once for all, there is an actual manifestation of the Godhead upon earth; or, secondly, if, as in Judaism or in Buddhism, the Deity chooses a favored mortal, who may give to his brother men a fuller knowledge of the divine mind and will.* The latter would seem the form most congenial to the Semitic mind, if one may be allowed to use that convenient but, since the bold generalizations in which Renan has indulged respecting them, somewhat misleading word. The Arabs themselves looked up to Adam, Noah, Abraham, and Moses as prophets; Mohammed did the same, and added Christ to their number. He held that each successive revelation had been higher than the preceding one, though each was complete in itself, as being adequate to the circumstances of the time. Was there, Mohammed might ask, any reason to suppose that Christ had been the last of the prophets, and that his revelation was absolutely as well as relatively final; and

---

* Renan, p. 278.

were there not evils enough in Arabia and in the world to call for a further communication from heaven? To say that Arabia needed renovation was to say in other words that the time for a new prophet had come, and why might not that prophet be Mohammed himself? Sprenger, the most recent and exhaustive writer on the subject, has shown that for some hundred years before Mohammed the advent of another prophet had been expected and even predicted. So strong was the general conviction on the subject that the Arab tribes were guided by it even in their politics.*

But, if we admit the sincerity of Mohammed and the naturalness of his belief up to the time of the Hegira, what are we to say of him during his first years of exile at Medina, and again of his subsequent successes?

It is unquestionably true that a change does seem to come over him. The revelations of the Koran are more and more suited to the particular circumstances and caprices of the moment. They are often of the nature of political bulletins or of personal apologies, rather than of messages direct from God. Now appears for the first time the convenient but dangerous doctrine of ab-

---

* Sprenger, vol. i., p. 245, quotes a saying of the Arabs that the children of Shem are prophets, of Japhet kings, of Ham slaves. We are told that the Arab women were at this time in the habit of praying for male children, in the hope that of them the long-expected prophet might be born.

rogation, by which a subsequent revelation might supersede a previous one.*

The limitation to the unbounded license of Oriental polygamy which he had himself imposed, he relaxes in his own behalf: † the greatest stain, and an indelible one, on his memory, though it is possible that he may have justified himself to his own mind by the Ethiopian marriage not condemned in the case of Moses.‡ The public opinion even of the harem was scandalized by his marriage with Mary, an Egyptian, a Christian, and a slave. His marriage with Zeinab, the wife of Zeid, his freedman and adopted son, divorced as she was by Zeid for the express purpose that Mohammed might marry her, was still worse. It was felt as an outrage even upon the lax morality of an Oriental nation, till all reclamations were hushed into silence by a Sura of the Koran which rebuked Mohammed, not for his laxity, but for his undue abstinence!§

---

* Sura xvi., 103; ii., 100.
† Sura xxxiii., 49; lxvi., 1.
‡ See Lecture IV., p. 210.
§ Sura xxxiii., 37. See a good passage on the subject in the *British Quarterly Review* for January, 1872, p. 131.

It should be remembered, however, that most of Mohammed's marriages are to be explained at least as much by his pity for the forlorn condition of the persons concerned as by other motives. They were almost all of them with widows who were not remarkable either for their beauty or their wealth, but quite the reverse. May not this fact, and

The doctrine of toleration gradually becomes one of extermination; persecuted no longer, he becomes a persecutor himself; with the Koran in one hand, the scimiter in the other, he goes forth to offer to the nations the threefold alternative of conversion, tribute, death. He is once or twice untrue to the kind and forgiving disposition of his best nature; and is once or twice unrelenting in the punishment of his personal enemies, especially of the Jews, who had disappointed his expectation that they would join him, and of such as had stung him by their lampoons or libels. He is even guilty more than once of conniving at the assassination of inveterate opponents; and the massacre of the Bani Koreitza, though they had deserted him almost on the field of battle, and their lives were forfeit by all the laws of war, moved the misgivings of others than the disaffected. He might, no doubt, believing, as he did, in his own inspiration, have found an ample precedent for the act in the slaughter of the Canaanites by Joshua two thousand years before, or even in the wars of Saul and David with neighboring tribes; but, judged by any but an Oriental standard of morality, and by his own con-

---

his undoubted faithfulness to Kadijah till her dying day, and till he himself was fifty years of age, give us some ground to hope that calumny has been at work in the story of Zeinab? There are some indications on the face of it that this is the case.

spicuous magnanimity on other occasions, his act, in all its accessories, was one of cold-blooded and inhuman atrocity.

Can we explain away or extenuate these blots on his memory, or, if we can not, are they inconsistent with substantial sincerity and single-mindedness? Here is a problem of surpassing interest to the psychologist, and I have only time to touch lightly upon it.

In the first place, the change in his character and aims is not to be separated from the general conditions of his life. At first he was a religious and moral reformer only, and could not, even if he would, have met the evils of his time by any other than by moral means. If he was without the advantages, he was also free from the dangers, of success. A religion militant is, as all ecclesiastical history shows, very different from a religion triumphant. The Prophet in spite of himself became, by the force of circumstances, more than a prophet. Not, indeed, that with him height ever begot high thoughts. He preserved to the end of his career that modesty and simplicity of life which is the crowning beauty of his character; but he became a temporal ruler, and, where the Koran did not make its way unaided, the civil magistrate naturally used temporal means. Under such circumstances, and when his followers pressed upon him their belief in the nature of his mission, who can draw the line where enthusiasm ends and self-deception or even imposture begins? No one who knows human nature will deny that the two are often perfectly consistent with each other. Once persuaded fully of his divine mission as a whole, a man unconsciously begins to invest his personal fancies and desires with a like sanction: it is not that he tampers with his conscience; he rather subjects conscience and reason, appetite and affection, to the one dominating influence; and so, as time goes on, with perfect good faith gets to confound what comes from below with what comes from above. What is the meaning of the term " pious frauds," except that such acts are frauds in the eyes of others, acts of piety in the eyes of the doer? The more fully convinced a man is of the goodness of his cause, the more likely is he to forget the means in the end; he need not consciously assert that the end justifies the means, but his eyes are so fixed upon the end that they overlook the interval between the idea and its realization. He has to maintain a hold over the motley mass of followers that his mission has gathered around him. Must he not become all things to all to meet their several wants? Perhaps he does become so, and, in the process, what he gains in the bulk of his influence he loses in its quality. Its intensity is in inverse proportion to its extension. No man—I quote here, with only such slight alteration as adapts them to my subject, the noble words of George Eliot: "No man, whether prophet, statesman, or popular preacher, ever yet kept a prolonged hold over a mixed multitude without being in some measure degraded thereby. His teaching or his life must be accommodated to the average wants of his hearers, and not to his own finest insight. But, after all, we should regard the life of every great man as a drama, in which there must be important inward modifications accompanying the outward changes."* Rigid consistency in itself is no great merit —rather the reverse: what one has a right to demand in a great man is that the intensity of the central truth he has to deliver should become, not less, but more intense; that that flame shall burn so clear as to throw into the shade other objects which shine with a less brilliant light; that the essence shall be pure even if some of the surroundings be alloyed; and this, I think, if not more than this, with all his faults, we may affirm of Mohammed.

On the whole the wonder is to me not how much, but how little, under different circumstances, Mohammed differed from himself. In the shepherd of the desert, in the Syrian trader, in the solitary of Mount Hira, in

---

* "Romola," ch. xxv., p. 214—American edition.

the reformer in the minority of one, in the exile of Medina, in the acknowledged conqueror, in the equal of the Persian Chosroes and the Greek Heraclius, we can still trace a substantial unity. I doubt whether any other man, whose external conditions changed so much, ever himself changed less to meet them: the accidents are changed, the essence seems to me to be the same in all.

Power, as the saying is, no doubt put the man to the test. It brought new temptations and therefore new failures, from which the shepherd of the desert might have remained free. But happy is the man who, living

> "In the fierce light that beats upon a throne,
> And blackens every blot,"

can stand the test as well as did Mohammed. A Christian poet has well asked—

> "What keeps a spirit wholly true
> To that ideal which he bears?
> What record? not the sinless years
> That breathed beneath the Syrian blue."

But it is a current misconception, and, subject to the above explanation, a very great one, that a gradual but continuous and accelerating moral declension is to be traced from the time when the fugitive unexpectedly entered Medina in triumph. "Truth is come—let falsehood disappear," he said, when, after his long exile, and after the temptations of Medina had done their worst for him, he re-entered the Kaaba, and its three hundred and sixty idols, the famous Hobal among them, vanished before him; and in his treatment of the unbelieving city he was marvelously true to his programme. There was now nothing left in Mecca that could thwart his pleasure. If ever he had worn a mask at all, he would now at all events have thrown it off; if lower aims had gradually sapped the higher, or his moderation had been directed, as Gibbon supposes, by his selfish interests, we should now have seen the effect; now would have been the moment to gratify his ambition, to satiate his lust, to glut his revenge. Is there any thing of the kind? Read the account of the entry of Mohammed into Mecca, side by side with that of Marius or Sulla into Rome. Compare all the attendant circumstances, the outrages that preceded, and the use made by each of his recovered power, and we shall then be in a position better to appreciate the magnanimity and moderation of the Prophet of Arabia. There were no proscription lists, no plunder, no wanton revenge.

The chief blots in his fame are not after his undisputed victory, but during his years of checkered warfare at Medina, and, such as they are, are distributed very evenly over the whole of that time. In other words, he did very occasionally give way to a strong temptation; but there was no gradual sapping of moral principles and no deadening of conscience—a very important distinction. One or two acts of summary and uncompromising punishment; possibly one or two acts of cunning, and, after Kadijah was dead, the violation of one law which he had from veneration for her imposed on others, and had always hitherto kept himself, form no very long bill of indictment against one who always admitted he was a man of like passions with ourselves, who was ignorant of the Christian moral law, and who attained to power after difficulties and dangers and misconceptions which might have turned the best of men into a suspicious and sanguinary tyrant.*

It is no doubt true that some of the revelations of the Koran, particularly the later ones, bear the appearance of having been given consciously for personal and temporary purposes, and these have led, with some show of reason, even such impartial writers as Sir William Muir to accuse Mohammed of "the high blasphemy of forging the name of God." But it would be strange indeed

---

* Yet Sprenger (vol. i., p. 359), on no more grounds than those here mentioned, can say of Mohammed that when he attained to power in Medina, "er wurde zum wollüstigen Theokraten und blutdürstig Tyrannen, Pabst und König." What Christian Pope or King—to say nothing of Oriental rulers, with whom alone is it fair to compare him—had as great temptations and succumbed to them as little as did Mohammed?

if, viewed in the light of what I have said above as to Mohammed's unfaltering belief in his own inspiration, he had not occasionally, or even often, revealed in the Koran the mental processes by which he justified to himself acts about which he may have himself, at first, felt scruples, or which his contemporaries may have called in question. And it seems pertinent to ask, by way of rebutting the charge, whether he was not at least equally ready, when occasion required, to blame himself for what he had said or done, and to call the whole Mussulman world to be witnesses of his self-condemnation? And, again, if he was ever, in the matter of the Koran, a conscious impostor, why was he not so much oftener? If he had once knowingly tripped, and gained thereby, the path must have been too slippery and the descent must have seemed too easy and inviting for him to recall his footsteps. But what are the facts? Take two samples.

On one occasion, in a moment of despondency, he made a partial concession to idolatry. He thought to win over the recalcitrant Koreishites to his views by allowing that their gods might make intercession with the supreme God.

"What think ye of Al-Lat, and Al-Uzza, and Manah, the third besides? They are the exalted Females, and their intercession with God may be hoped for."

The Koreishites, overjoyed, signified their adhesion to

Mohammed, and it seemed that they would bring over all Mecca with them. His friends would have passed the matter over as quietly as possible. So great was the scandal among the Faithful that some of his earliest historians omit it altogether. But the Prophet's conscience was too tender for that. In an hour of weakness Mohammed had mistaken expediency for duty, and having discovered his mistake, he would recall the concession, at all hazards, as publicly as he had made it, even at the risk of the imputation of weakness and of imposture. The amended version of the Sura ran thus:

"What think ye of Al-Lat, and Al-Uzza, and Manah, the third besides? They are naught but empty names which ye and your fathers have invented."*

I will give one more instance. It is a memorable one. Mohammed was engaged in earnest conversation with Wallid, a powerful Koreishite, whose conversion he much desired. A blind man in very humble circumstances, Abdallah by name, happened to come up, and, not knowing that Mohammed was otherwise engaged, exclaimed, "Oh, Apostle of God, teach me some part of what God has taught thee." Mohammed, vexed at the interruption, frowned and turned away from him. But

---

* Sura liii.; cf. also xvii., 75, and xxii., 51; see Muir, vol. ii., p. 149–158, and Sprenger, vol. ii., p. 17, where there is a curious dissertation on the word Gharânyk, used for Females—"swans which mount higher and higher toward God."

his conscience soon smote him for having postponed the poor and humble to the rich and powerful, and the next day's Sura showed that this "forger of God's name" was at least as ready to forge it for his own condemnation as in his defense. The Sura is known by the significant title "He frowned," and runs thus:

"The Prophet frowned, and turned aside,
   Because the blind man came unto him.
And how knowest thou whether he might not have been cleansed from
   his sins,
Or whether he might have been admonished, and profited thereby?
   As for the man that is rich,
   Him thou receivest graciously;
And thou carest not that he is not cleansed.
But as for him that cometh unto thee earnestly seeking his salvation,
And trembling anxiously, him dost thou neglect.
   By no means shouldst thou act thus."

And ever after this we are told that, when the Prophet saw the poor blind man, he went out of his way to do him honor, saying, "The man is thrice welcome on whose account my Lord hath reprimanded me," and he made him twice Governor of Medina.*

Mohammed never wavered in his belief in his own

---

* Sura lxxx., with Sale's note ad loc.; and Muir, vol. ii., p. 128. Sir Wm. Muir tells the story much as I have related it, but seems quite unable to see its grandeur, for he only remarks upon it: "This incident illustrates at once the anxiety of Mohammed to gain over the principal men of the Koreish, and, when he was rejected, the readiness with which he turned to the poor and uninfluential." Was ever moral sublimity so marred, or heroism so vulgarized? How Mohammed towers above even his best historians!

mission, nor, what is more extraordinary, in his belief as to its precise nature and well-defined limits. He was a prophet charged with a mission from God; nothing less, but nothing more. He might make mistakes, lose battles, do wrong acts, but none the less did he believe that the words he spoke were the very words of God. To every Sura of the Koran he prefixed the words, "In the name of God, the Compassionate, the Merciful," even as the Hebrew prophet would open his message with his "Thus saith the Lord;" and before every sentence and every word of the Sacred Book is to be read, between the lines, the word "say," indicating that Mohammed believed, what Moses and Isaiah only believed on special occasions, that in his utterances he was the mere mouthpiece, and therefore the unerring mouthpiece, of the Infinite and the Eternal. He might win his way against superhuman difficulties, preserve a charmed life, do deeds which seemed miracles to others, gain the homage of all Arabia, and present in his own person an ideal of morality never before pictured by an Arab; and yet he never forgot himself, or claimed to be more than a weak and fallible mortal.

As his view of his own mission is an all-important point in estimating his character, let us deal, in concluding this Lecture, with facts alone, and watch his conduct at a few critical epochs which I have purposely selected, as throwing light upon the matter, in its different aspects, away from their chronological order and from very different periods of his life.

When the Persian monarch Chosroes was contemplating with pride, like Nebuchadnezzar of old, the great Artemita that he had built and all its fabulous treasures, he received a letter from an obscure citizen of Mecca, bidding him acknowledge Mohammed as the Prophet of God. Chosroes tore the letter into pieces. "It is thus," exclaimed the Arabian Prophet when he heard of it, "that God will tear his kingdom and reject his supplications." No prediction could have seemed at the time less likely to be accomplished, since Persia was at its height, and Constantinople at its lowest. But Mohammed lived to see its fulfillment, and yet never claimed in consequence, as others might have done, the power of prophecy.

While he had as yet only half established his position, a powerful Christian tribe tendered their submission, if only he would leave their chief some remnant of his power. "Not one unripe date," replied Mohammed.* We remember how the French rhetorician the other day, knowing that his nation, if they are slaves to nothing else, are always slaves to an epigram, prolonged re-

---

* Muir, vol. iv., p. 59.

sistance to the bitter end by his famous declaration that not "an inch of their territory nor a stone of their fortresses" would the French surrender. And we may imagine the effect produced upon the handful of Mohammed's Meccan followers who were still in exile at Medina by such an answer, coming from one who was certainly no vapid rhetorician, who preferred silence to speech, and who never said a thing he did not really mean.

Moseilama, the most formidable of the rival prophets whom Mohammed's success stirred up, thinking that Mohammed's game was a merely selfish one, and that two might play at it, sent to Mohammed to offer to go shares with him in the good things of the world, which united they might easily divide. The letter was of Spartan brevity: "Moseilama the apostle of God to Mohammed the apostle of God.—Now let the earth be half mine and half thine." Mohammed's reply was hardly less laconic: "Mohammed the apostle of God to Moseilama the liar.—The earth is God's; he giveth it to such of his servants as he pleaseth, and they who fear him shall prosper."

Again mark his conduct under failure or rebuff. He had lost, within three days of each other, Abu Taleb, his one protector, and his venerable wife Kadijah—that toothless old woman, as Ayesha long afterward, in the bloom of her beauty, called her; the wife who, as Mohammed indignantly replied, " when he was poor, had enriched him; when he was called a liar, had alone believed in him; when he was opposed by all the world, had alone remained true to him."* What was he to do? Silence and the desert seemed the one chance of safety, but what did he do? Followed only by Zeid, his faithful freedman, he went to Tayif, the town after Mecca most wholly given to idolatry; and, like Elijah in Samaria, he boldly challenged the protection and obedience of the inhabitants. They stoned him out of the city. He returned to Mecca defeated, but not disheartened; cast down, but not destroyed; quietly saying to himself, " If thou, O Lord, art not angry, I am safe; I seek refuge in the light of thy countenance alone." †

After the tide had turned in his favor, and the battle of Bedr had, as it seemed, put the seal to his military success, he was signally defeated and wounded almost

---

* Sprenger characteristically remarks (vol. i., p. 151) that Mohammed's faithfulness to Kadijah to her dying day was due probably not to his inclination, but to his dependence on her. Why, then, the interval before Mohammed married again? And why, long afterward, his noble burst of gratitude to her memory when Ayesha contrasted her own youth and beauty with Kadijah's age and infirmities, and asked, "Am not I much better than she?" "No, by Allah," replied Mohammed—"No, by Allah; when I was poor she enriched me," etc. Was Mohammed dependent upon the dead? For cynical remarks of a similar kind, see, among many other instances, Sprenger, vol. ii., p. 19, 23, 86.

† See the story in full in Muir, vol. ii., p. 198-203.

to the death at Mount Ohud. People began to desert him; but a Sura, Mohammed's "order of the day," appeared: "Mohammed is no more than a prophet. What if he had been killed, needs ye go back? He that turneth back injureth not God in the least, but himself."* The spell of his untaught eloquence recalled them to themselves, and we are assured that his defeat at Ohud advanced his cause as much as did his victory at Bedr.

Ayesha, his favorite wife, one day asked of him, "Oh, Prophet of God, do none enter Paradise but through God's mercy?" "None, none, none," replied he. "But will not even you enter by your own merits?" Mohammed put his hand upon his head and thrice replied, "Neither shall I enter Paradise unless God cover me with his mercy." There was no "false certitude of the divine intentions," the besetting temptation of spiritual ambition; no facile dogmatizing upon what he had only to hint to be believed—his own pre-eminent position in the unseen world. It would have been safe to do so: ἐς ἀφανὲς τὸν μῦθον ἀνενείκας οὐκ ἔχει ἔλεγχον;† and how few could have resisted a like temptation!

And at the last grand scene of all, when the Prophet had met his death, as he had always told his doubting followers he must, and Omar, the Simon Peter of Islam,

---

* Sura iii., 138.
† Hdt., ii., 23.

in the agony of his grief, drew his scimiter and, wildly rushing in among the weeping Mussulmans, swore that he would strike off the head of any one who dared to say that the Prophet was dead—the Prophet could not be dead—it was by a gentle reminder of what the Prophet himself had always taught that the venerable Abu Bakr, the earliest of the Prophet's friends, and his successor in the Kaliphate, calmed his excitement: "Is it then Mohammed, or the God of Mohammed, that we have learned to worship?"

LECTURE III.

FEBRUARY 28, 1874.

MOHAMMEDANISM.

"Allahu Akbar"—God is great; there is no god but God, and Mohammed is his prophet.

IN the concluding part of my last Lecture I discussed at length the question of the character of Mohammed, and we arrived, I think, at the conclusion that, on the one hand, he had grave moral faults, which may be accounted for, but not excused, by the circumstances of time, by the exigencies of his situation, and by the weaknesses of human nature. And on the other we saw reason to believe that he was not only passionately impressed with the reality of his divine mission in early life, but that the common view of a great moral declension to be traced in his latter years is not borne out by the evidence; and that to the end of his career, amid failures and successes, in life and in preparation for death, he was true to the one principle with which he started. He became indeed, by the force of circumstances, general and ruler, lawgiver and judge, of all Arabia; but above all and before all, he was still a simple prophet delivering God's message in singleness of heart, obeying, as far as he could, God's will, but never claiming to be more than God's weak and erring servant.

And now, perhaps, it is time to ask what was the essence of Mohammed's belief, that which made him what he was, which has given his religion its inexhaustible vitality? How did it resemble, and how did it differ from, the religions which it overthrew, and one of which at least we are accustomed to look upon, and shall, in its pure form as it came from Christ's own lips, and can still be read in Christ's own acts, and even to some extent in the character of his servants, always continue to look upon, as immeasurably superior to Mohammedanism?

The essence of Mohammedanism is not merely the sublime belief in the unity of God, though it is difficult for us to realize the tumult of the feelings and the intensity of the life which must be awakened in a Polytheistic people, who are also imaginative and energetic, when, on a sudden, they recognize the One in and behind the Many. Mohammed started indeed with the dogmatic assertion that there was but one God, the Creator of all things in heaven and earth, all powerful, knowing all things, everywhere present. He reiterates this in a thousand shapes as the forefront of his message ;* and, sublimely confident that it need only be stated to insure ultimate acceptance, he deigns not to offer proof of that which, in his judgment, must prove itself.

But it was more than the unity of God, and the attributes which flow from that conception, which Mohammed asserted. A theoretic assent to this might have had but little influence on practice. What is by its nature immeasurably above man may also be immeasurably removed from him; and accordingly Mohammed reasserted that which had been the life of the old Hebrew nation, and the burden of the song of every Hebrew prophet—that God not only lives, but that he is a righteous and a merciful ruler; and that to his will it is the duty and the privilege of all living men to bow.† Nor was the sublimity of this doctrine marred in its application by the old Hebrew exclusiveness. The Arabian nation was first

---

* See especially Suras i. and cxii., the beginning and end of the Koran in the orthodox arrangement; also Sura xxxv., 41-44. Cf. also Sura ii., 19-20, 109; vi., 1-6; xiii., 10, 11; xvi., 12-17; liii. and xcvi.

† See this well drawn out in Maurice's "Religions of the World," p. 21-24. The passage is a most suggestive one. I owe much to it; and it seems to me that here, and in many other passages of his writings, Mr. Maurice did far more, and penetrated far deeper, than is allowed in a very brilliant passage of a recent work (see "Literature and Dogma," p. 345). When the unacknowledged debts of the nineteenth century to its great writers come to be added up, I am convinced that it will be fully recognized that the mental powers of Mr. Maurice rank as high as did the purity and nobility of his life; and more can hardly be said.

called indeed; but as in Christianity, and as it was not in Judaism, the obligations of the Arabs were to be measured by their privileges, and the call was to be extended through them to the world at large. The Jew surrendered his birthright if he imparted his faith to other peoples. The Arab surrendered his if he did not spread his faith wherever and however he could.

But Mohammed's assertion of the unity of God, and of his rule over every detail of man's life, was no mere plagiarism from an older faith. The Jewish people at large had, even in their best days, rushed wildly after the worship of alien gods; at last, indeed, the iron of the Captivity had entered into their souls; they learned much during their sojourn in the East, but they unlearned more —they unlearned there, once and forever, the sin of idolatry. But though they never henceforward worshiped other gods, the higher teaching of their prophets they still too much ignored, and the period which might have been the culmination of their glory ended in that tragedy of tragedies which was the immediate precursor of their fall. The sceptre departed from Judah, but the Jewish exiles in Arabia still clung desperately to the phantom of those proud religious privileges when all which had given some claim to them had disappeared. Christians too—such Christians as Mohammed had ever met—had forgotten at once the faith of the Jews, and that higher revelation of God given to them by Christ which the Jews rejected. Homoousians and Homoiousians, Monothelites and Monophysites, Jacobites and Eutychians, making hard dogmas of things wherein the sacred writers themselves had made no dogma, disputing fiercely whether what was mathematically false could be metaphysically true, and nicely discriminating the shades of truth and falsehood in the views suggested to bridge over the abysmal gulf between them; turning figures into facts, rhetoric into logic, and poetry into prose, had forgotten the unity of God while they were disputing about it most loudly with their lips. They busied themselves with every question about Christ except those which might have led them to imitate Christ's life. Now Mohammed came to make a clean sweep of such unrealities. Images: what are they? "Bits of black wood, pretending to be God;"* philosophical theories, and theological cobwebs. Away with them all! God is great, and there is nothing else great. This is the Mussulman creed. "Islam," that is, man must resign his will to God's, and find his highest happiness in so doing. This is the Mussulman life. And I would remark here, and would particularly beg those who are doing me the honor to attend these Lectures to bear in mind, that though I have, in

---

* Carlyle, "Heroes," p. 226.

compliance with European custom, often spoken of Mohammedanism and Mohammedans, the name was never used by Mohammed himself or by his earlier disciples, and, in spite of the reverence paid to their Prophet, it has always been rejected by his followers themselves as a rightful appellation. To quote once more the noble words of Abu Bakr, it was not Mohammed, but the God of Mohammed, that the Prophet taught his followers to worship. The creed is "Islam," a verbal noun, derived from a root meaning "submission to" and "faith in God," and the believers who so submit themselves are called Moslems, a participle of the same root, both being connected with the words "Salam," or "peace," and "Salym," or "healthy."* There was nothing, therefore, theoretically new in what I have described as the central truth of Islam, for it was this belief that lay at the root of the greatness of the Jewish nation, and their separation from all other nations. Certain forms of Christianity have asserted it as strongly as did Mohammed. This principle has been the strength of Calvinism and of Puritanism; and in this direction perhaps lies the explanation of the fact that those forms of religion which have been theoretically most fatalistic have by their acts given the strongest practical assertion of free-will. This was

---

* Sprenger, vol. i., p. 69.

the spark from heaven which lit the train. In his assertion of this lay the religious genius of Mohammed. This gave the Arabs " unity as a nation, discipline and enthusiasm as an army."* This sent them forth in their wild crusade against the world; and, armed with this, they swept away before them every creed, or memory of a creed, which did not then contain any principle so inspiring.

Such then were the two leading principles of the new creed: the existence of one God, whose will was to be the rule of life, and the mission of Mohammed to proclaim what that will was. The one doctrine as old, if not older than the time when the father of the faithful left his Chaldean home in obedience to the divine will; the other sanctioned, indeed, in its general assertion of the prophetic office, by the traditionary belief of both Jews and Arabs; but startling enough in the time at which the revelation came, in the instrument selected, and in the way in which he proclaimed it. In this consists the real originality, such as it is, of Mohammedanism. The other articles of faith, added to the two I have already discussed—the written revelation of God's will, the responsibility of man, the existence of angels and of Jinn, the future life, the resurrection, and the final judg-

---

* Maurice, loc. cit.

ment—are to be found, either developed or in germ, in the systems either of Jews or Zoroastrians or Christians. Even in the times of ignorance, the camel tethered to a dead man's grave was an indication that the grave was, even to the wild Arab, not the end of all things.*

Nor was there any thing much more original in the four practical duties of Islam—in prayer and almsgiving, in fasting and in pilgrimage.† Prayer is the aspiration of the human soul toward God, common to every religion, from the rudest Fetichism to the most sublime Monotheism. Almsgiving is the most easy and obvious method of evidencing that love to man which leads up to and is, in its turn, the result of love to God. Fasting is an assertion, though a superficial one, of the great truth that self-denial is a step toward God; but it is peculiarly liable to abuse as fostering the belief, so common among the ruder of the Semitic nations, and still commoner among ascetics in modern times, that God is to be feared rather than loved, and that there is something pleasing

---

* Sprenger says (vol. i., p. 4, 301) that the reason why Mohammed refers so often, *e. g.*, in the very first Sura in chronological order, to the "clot of blood" from which man was created, is because he looked upon it much as Christians have done to the emerging of the butterfly from the chrysalis as a proof or illustration of the resurrection. In Sura liii. Mohammed says he took not the doctrine merely, but the illustration also, from the roll of Abraham. Cf. Sura lxxv., entitled "The Resurrection," ad fin.: "Is not the God who formed man from a mere embryo powerful enough to quicken the dead?"

† Cf. Milman, "Latin Christianity," vol. i., p. 453.

to him in pain as such—pain, that is, apart from its effect upon the will, and so upon the character. Pilgrimage is a concession to human feelings, not to say to human weakness, common again, in practice, to all the religions of the world. But this last calls, perhaps, for some special remark here, since its actual influence has been so great, while in theory and in reality it is alien alike to Mohammedanism and to Christianity.

"The hour cometh when ye shall neither in this mountain nor yet in Jerusalem worship the Father." "God is a spirit, and they that worship him must worship him in spirit and in truth." But from the time the words were spoken, even to this day, a continuous living stream has poured toward the Holy Land. For nineteen centuries Christian pilgrims have been seen to leave their homes and kindred, facing, now privations, now dangers, and now ridicule, that they might enjoy the sacred luxury, the ineffable religious rapture, of beholding the city over which the Saviour wept, of standing on the spot which gave him birth, of gazing on the lake whereon he taught, and of worshiping in the shrine which covers the rock wherein his body lay. And far be it from me to say—spite of the invention of the true cross, spite of St. Andrew's lance and the relics of the Apostles, spite of the Crusades themselves, spite of the keys of the Holy Sepulchre, and even of the imposture of the holy fire—

that the evils belonging to this reverence for places have altogether predominated over the good. A scientific and unimaginative age laughs at the weaknesses and the follies involved, but it forgets the dauntless faith and heroic endurance, the sacrifice of self, and the romance of danger; it forgets that it is the office of religion to deal with these very human weaknesses and follies, and make the best of such materials as it has to work upon.

Christ swept away some of the abuses of the Temple worship, and looked forward to its ultimate abolition; but he did not sweep away the Temple itself. He rather paid it its customary honors. Mohammed saw the dangers of the Kaaba worship, and, once and again, proposed to destroy it altogether; but he had to deal with an historical faith, and with a shrine of immemorial antiquity, one which Diodorus Siculus, a hundred years before the Christian era, tells us was even then "most ancient, and was exceedingly revered by the whole Arab race." The traditions of the Kaaba ran back to Ishmael and Abraham—nay, even to Seth and Adam;* and, as its very name, "Beit Allah," shows, it

---

* Cf. Sura iii., 90. "The first temple that was founded for mankind was that in Becca (place of resort, *i. e.*, Mecca)—Blessed, and a guidance to human beings. In it are evident signs, even the standing-place of Abraham, and he who entereth it is safe. And the pilgrimage to the temple is a service due to God from those who are able to journey thither." This sentence is still woven into the covering of the Kaaba sent annually by the Sultan.

might, in its first rude shape, have been erected by some such ancient patriarch as he who raised a pillar of rough stone where in his sleep he had seen the angels ascending and descending, and called it "Bethel, or Beit Allah: this is the house of God, and this the gate of heaven." Mohammed cherished also all the family associations of a Haschimite,* and all the local affections of a Meccan patriot; and the family, and the place, and the country, the historical lore and the religious imagination, combined to save the sacred shrine. Mohammed swept away the idols of the Kaaba; he abolished the nude processions† and the other abuses of its worship, but he retained the Kaaba itself; and the quaint rites, which were old in Mohammed's time, are still religiously observed by the whole Mohammedan world. Seven times the pilgrim walks around the sacred mosque, seven times he kisses the Black Stone; he drinks the brackish water of the sacred well Zemzem, buries the parings of his nails and the hair he has at length shaved in the consecrated ground; he ascends Mount Arafat, and showers stones on the three mysterious pillars.‡ Nor is the Kaaba

---

* See a curious conversation between Mohammed and Ayesha on the Kaaba, illustrating the strong family feelings of the Prophet. Sprenger, vol. i., p. 315.

† Sura vii., 27, seq. Cf. xxii., 27-40.

‡ A plan of the Kaaba, as taken by Ali Bey, and a full description of

present to the mind at those times only when the prescribed pilgrimage is near at hand, in prospect or in retrospect. The first architectural requisite of every Mussulman house is the niche or arch which points with mathematical precision to the sacred pile; and, guided by this, every devout Mussulman turns five times a day toward the Kiblah of the world in earnest prayer to God. "That man," says Dr. Johnson, "has little to be envied whose patriotism would not gain force on the plains of Marathon, or whose piety would not grow warm among the ruins of Iona." The ceremonies of the Kaaba may perhaps seem to us ridiculous, but the shrine is one which kindled the feelings of the Arab patriot, and roused the hopes of the Bedouin of the desert, ages before Miltiades fought, and tens of ages before Columban preached. It has been consecrated in its later history by its connection with the grandest forward movement that the Eastern world has ever known; and, in spite of the mummeries and the abuses which have grown around the pilgrimage of the Hadj in the course of ages, I should be slow indeed to assert that the feelings which still draw, year

---

the pilgrim ceremonies, which he himself went through, may be seen in Burton's "Pilgrimage," vol. iii., p. 61. Burckhardt and Burton have both described the Black Stone minutely from personal observation; and a picture of it, the size of the original, is given in Muir, vol. ii., p. 18.

after year, Mussulmans by myriads from the burning sands of Africa, from the snows of Siberia, and the coral reefs of the Malays, toward a barren valley in Arabia, do not, on the whole, elevate rather than depress them in the scale of humanity. In their own rough and imperfect way, they raise the mind of the nomad and the shepherd from the animal life of the present to the memories of the distant past, and the hopes of the far future. They are a living testimony to the unity of God, and a homage paid by the world to that Prophet who softened the savage breast and elevated the savage mind, and taught them what, but for him, they had never learned at all.

It will be apparent, from what I have already said, that of the previous faiths existing in the world, the one which influenced Mohammed most was, beyond all question, Judaism. Insomuch that one who probably, with the single exception of Dr. Sprenger, knew more of the literature of the two faiths than any living man —one whose loss all who take interest in Eastern questions are now deploring, and one who, had he lived, would probably have done ampler justice to Islam and its founder than perhaps any one else has done or can do—the late Emanuel Deutsch, summed up the connection between them in the celebrated dictum, that " when the Talmud was gathered in, the Koran began

—post hoc ergo propter hoc." And he went on to indorse and to develop what Dean Milman had hinted before him, that Islam was little else than a republication of Judaism, with such modifications as suited it to Arabian soil, *plus* the important addition of the prophetic mission of Mohammed.* The gifted author was, perhaps, from the very extent of his knowledge of Talmudical literature, prone to trace its influence everywhere; and the proposition is, perhaps, stated a little too nakedly, and, as he, no doubt, would have been the first to admit, needs some important qualifications; but nobody would deny that it is substantially true. Indeed, the general connection between race and creed has been proved by the Science of Comparative Religion to be so intimate, that it could hardly in any case have been otherwise. It seems a cruel destiny that allows a man of great original genius to accumulate such vast stores of recondite learning, and then snatches him away before he has had time to do more than leave the world dimly and sadly conscious of what it has lost in losing him!

Anyhow, the Koran teems with ideas, allusions, and

---

* It must be remembered also that the ceremonialism of the Jews for the time almost entirely disappeared. For a full account of the influence of the Essenic communities and their doctrines on the rise of Islam, see Sprenger, vol. i., p. 17-21, and p. 30-35; and for that of the Ebionites or Judaizing Christians to the east of the Jordan, p. 21-28.

even phraseology, drawn not so much from the written as from the oral Jewish law, from the traditions that grew around it, and the commentaries on it. The Talmud, in its two divisions of Halacha and Haggada, sums up the intellectual and social and religious life of the Jews during a period of nearly a thousand years. It is the meeting-point of the three Monotheistic creeds of the world; and, even with the imperfect information that Eastern scholars have yet given respecting it, it has done much to throw light upon them all. Mohammed was never backward to acknowledge the intimate connection between his faith and that of the Jews. And in more than one passage of the Koran he refers with equal respect to their oral and to their written law. Nor did Christ really draw so broad a distinction between these two as might be imagined from the sweeping way in which he sometimes denounces the Scribes and Pharisees. "Whatsoever they that sit in Moses's seat bid you observe, that observe and do."* And it is incontestable that the Pharisees, as a body, contained some of the best and noblest—Hillel and Shammai, Gamaliel and St. Paul—as it contained some of the worst and meanest, of their nation.

---

* St. Matt. xxiii., 2–3. See this well argued in an article on the Talmud, *Edinburgh Review* for July, 1873.

And, accordingly, Mohammed, during the early years of the Hegira, struggled hard, and, as it might have seemed to him, with every prospect of success, to secure the adhesion of the Jewish tribes who dwelt around Medina. He appealed to their Scriptures, which, he said, he came not to destroy, but to fulfill, and which, as he argued, for those who had eyes to see, pointed to him. "A prophet shall the Lord your God raise up unto you of your brethren like unto me; to him shall ye hearken." "Was he not like unto Moses?" he asked again and again; "and did he not spring from their brethren, the children of Ishmael?" He adapted the fasts and the feasts of the new religion to their model. He took from them the law of usury and the law of inheritance. He owes to them some of his regulations respecting ablutions and unclean animals. He even, till he could hope no longer, made Jerusalem the Kiblah of the world for the five daily prayers.

It must have surprised Mohammed, with his half-knowledge of their history, that the Jews should be unable to enter into his views of a great catholic creed, or Religion of Humanity—the creed of Abraham—embracing Jews, Arabs, and Christians in one body. But it can surprise no one who has ever in any degree entered into the religious genius of the Jewish race, or who has reflected on the almost insuperable difficulties

G

which lay in the way of the Jews accepting that higher creed, the Author of which it is their eternal honor to have produced, and their tragic destiny to have rejected. And the Bani Kainucaa, and the Bani Nadhir, the Bani Koreitsa, and the Jews of Kheibar, bitterly experienced in Mohammed's subsequent treatment of them the truth of the now all-too-familiar maxim in ecclesiastical history that they who differ least in religious matters hate the most.

It is impossible to gain for one's self, and almost equally so to give to others within a short space of time, any thing like an adequate idea either of the form or of the contents of the book of which Mohammed, whatever the general influences brought to bear upon his mind, was the undisputed author, and which still underlies the life of the vast fabric of the Mohammedan world. In my first Lecture I compared and contrasted the Koran with the Bible; but it is necessary, perhaps, to say something more of its leading characteristics, or the want of them. The Koran defies analysis, for that presupposes something like method in the thing to be analyzed. It can hardly be characterized by any one epithet, for there is not a single Sura of any length which sustains a uniform character throughout. It has often been remarked that there is no more striking proof of the discrepancies of national taste than the diametrically opposite opinions held by the cultivated classes of East and West on the literary merits of the Koran. Having performed repeatedly, for the purpose of these Lectures, a task which Bunsen and Sprenger and Renan all pronounce to be almost impossible—that of reading the Koran continuously from beginning to end, both in the orthodox and chronological order—I have acquired a better right, perhaps, than most people to indorse the superficial opinion that dullness is, to a European who is ignorant of Arabic, the prevailing characteristic of the book as a whole until he begins to make a minute study of it. The importance of the subjects it handles, the unique interest attaching to the speaker, and the unaffected reverence with which every utterance is still regarded by so large a portion of the world, are insufficient to redeem it from this general reproach.

Endless assertions as to what the Koran is, and what it is not, warnings drawn from previous Arabian history, especially the lost tribes of Ad and Thamud; Jewish or Arab legends of the heroes of the Old Testament—stories told, and, it must be added, often spoiled in the telling of them; laws, ceremonial and moral, civil and sumptuary; personal apologies; curses showered upon Abu Lahab or the whole community of the Jews; all this alternates with sublime revelations of the attributes of the Godhead, bursts of admiration for Christ himself—though not for the views held of him by his so-called followers—flights of poetry, scathing rebukes of the hypocrite, the ungrateful, the unmerciful.

That the book as a whole is a medley, however it may be arranged, will seem only natural when we remember the way in which it was composed, preserved, edited, and stereotyped. Dictated from time to time by Mohammed to his disciples, it was by them partly treasured in their memories, partly written down on shoulder-bones of mutton or on oyster shells, on bits of wood or tablets of stone, which, being thrown pell-mell into boxes, and jumbled up together, like the leaves of the Cumean Sibyl after a gust of wind, were not put into any shape at all till after the Prophet's death by order of Abu Bakr. The work of the editor consisted simply in arranging the Suras in the order of their respective lengths—the longest first, the shortest last; and, though the book once afterward passed through the editor's hands, this is substantially the shape in which the Koran has come down to us. Various readings, which would seem, however, to have been of very slight importance, having crept into the different copies, a revising committee was appointed by order of the Kaliph Othman, and an authorized edition having been thus prepared "to prevent the texts differing, like those of the

Jews and Christians," all previous copies were collected and burned.

Nor is it to be wondered at that the principle of arrangement, combined with the impossibility of keeping the rhyme or rhythm in any translation, have prevented European critics, as a body, from indorsing the judgment, not merely of Mohammed himself, for that, if it had stood alone, might be looked upon as partial, but also of the whole Eastern world.

"If ye be in doubt as to our revelation to our servant, then produce a Sura like unto it, and summon your witnesses, God and all, if ye be men of truth."*

And again, "If men and genii were assembled together that they might produce a book like the Koran, they must fail."†

It is to be remarked that Mohammed and Mohammed's enemies are quite at one as to the merits of the book. The Arabs said that the Koran could not be Mohammed's work because it was too good. Mohammed replied to the effect that they were both right and wrong. They were right, for it was too good for Mohammed uninspired; they were wrong, for it was too good to have come originally from any one but the All-Merciful.‡

---

* Sura ii., 21. † Sura xvii., 90.
‡ Sura xvi., 103, compared with xxv., 5, etc.

Of course, by the existing arrangement, even such psychological development as there was in the Koran has been obscured; for, as a rule, what the editor put last comes really first. These are the burning utterances of the Prophet, who knows no influence but the inspiration pent within him; in these are the pith and poetry of the whole; while the elaborate and labored arguments, the *apologiæ pro vitâ suâ*, are the product of the mind which the force of circumstances and the love of spiritual power—that most exquisite and most dangerous of fascinations—had driven to become conscious of itself. The very titles of the earlier Suras, the imprecations with which they abound, the imagery they employ, suggest the shepherd of the desert, the despised visionary, the poet and the prophet. "The folding up," "the cleaving in sunder," "the celestial signs," "the unity," "the overwhelming," "the striking," "the inevitable," "the earthquake," "the war-horses," tell their own story. There are passages in these, though it must be admitted they are rare, which may be compared in grandeur even with some of the sublimest passages of Job, of David, or of Isaiah.

Take, for instance, the vision of the last day with which the eighty-first Sura, "The folding up," begins:

"When the sun shall be folded up,
 And when the stars shall fall,
 And when the mountains shall be set in motion,

And when the she-camels with young shall be neglected,
And when the wild beasts shall be huddled together,
And when the seas shall boil,
And when souls shall be joined again to their bodies,
And when the female child that had been buried alive shall ask for what crime she was put to death,
And when the leaves of the Book shall be unrolled,
And when the Heavens shall be stripped away like a skin,
And when Hell shall be made to blaze,
And when Paradise shall be brought near—
Every soul shall know what it has done."

Allusions to the monotony of the desert; the sun in its rising brightness; the moon in its splendor; are varied in the Koran by much more vivid mental visions of the Great Day when men shall be like moths scattered abroad, and the mountains shall become like carded wool of various colors, driven by the wind. No wonder that Labyd, the greatest poet of his time, forbore to enter the poetic lists with Mohammed when he recited to him the description of the infidel in the second Sura:

"They are like one who kindleth a fire, and when it hath thrown its light on all around him, God taketh away the light and leaveth him in darkness, and they can not see."

"Deaf, dumb, blind, therefore they shall not retrace their steps."

"They are like those who, when there cometh a storm-cloud out of heaven big with darkness, thunder, and lightning, thrust their fingers into their ears because of the thunder-clap for fear of death. God is round about the infidels."

"The lightning almost snatcheth away their eyes: so oft as it gleameth on them, they walk on in it; but when darkness closeth upon them, they stop; and if God pleased, of their ears and of their eyes would he surely deprive them: verily God is almighty."

And at the end of the same Sura, which, it is to be remembered, appeared quite late in the Prophet's life, at a period when it might have been expected that the cares of government would dim the brightness of the Prophet's visions, we find the sublime description of Him whom it had been the mission of his life to proclaim, and which is still engraved on precious stones, and worn by devout Mussulmans:

"God! there is no god but he, the Living, the Eternal. Slumber doth not overtake him, neither sleep; to him belongeth all that is in heaven and in earth. Who is he that can intercede with him but by his own permission? He knoweth that which is past and that which is to come unto them, and they shall not comprehend any thing of his knowledge but so far as he pleaseth. His throne is extended over heaven and earth, and the upholding of both is no burden unto him. He is the Lofty and the Great."

Almost equally well too, as a proof of his poetic

inspiration, Mohammed might have quoted that other description of Infidelity, also produced late in his life, and pronounced by Sir William Muir and by Emanuel Deutsch to be one of the grandest in the whole Koran:

"As to the infidels, their works are like the Serab on the plain,* which the thirsty traveler thinketh to be water, and then, when he cometh thereto, he findeth it to be nothing; but he findeth God about him, and he will fully pay him his account; for swift in taking an account is God;

"Or as the darkness over a deep sea, billows riding upon billows below, and clouds above; one darkness on another darkness: when a man stretcheth forth his hand he is far from seeing it; he to whom God doth not grant light, no light at all hath he." †

Strange and graphic accounts have been preserved to us by Ayesha of the physical phenomena attending the Prophet's fits of inspiration. He heard as it were the ringing of a bell; he fell down as one dead; he sobbed like a camel; he felt as though he were being rent in pieces; and when he came to himself he felt as though words had been written on his heart. And when Abu Bakr, "he who would have sacrificed father and moth-

---

* That is, the Mirage of the Desert.
† Sura xxiv., 39, 40. See Muir, vol. iii., p. 308; and Deutsch, "Islam," in *Quarterly Review*, No. 254, p. 346.

er for Mohammed," burst into tears at the sight of the Prophet's whitening hair, "Yes," said Mohammed, "Hud and its sisters, the Terrific Suras, have turned it white before its time."*

But in order to make the general outline of Mohammed's system, which I am attempting to draw, as little imperfect as it is possible for me to make it within the limits I have prescribed myself, it is necessary to touch upon three difficult questions, which have acquired different degrees of prominence at successive periods in the history of Mohammedanism—questions which have been much misunderstood, and sometimes intentionally misrepresented, and which call more loudly even than other matters which we have been considering for a laborious investigation and a candid judgment. They need also above all things the historical sense, which does not apply the standard of the nineteenth century to the seventh, of Europeans to Asiatics, or of a high civilization to semi-barbarism; and which is content to balance the evil against the good, without requiring a verdict either for an absolute acquittal or an uncompromising condemnation. The three questions I refer to are the relation of Mohammedanism to Miracles, to Fatalism, and to wars for the sake of Religion. I

---

* Suras xi., Hud; lvi., "The Inevitable;" ci., "The Striking." See Muir, vol. ii., p. 88.

propose in the remainder of this Lecture to deal with these in succession; not I hope consciously shirking any difficulty, or glossing over what is unquestionably bad, but, of course, not professing in any degree to exhaust the subject.

I. First, then, Miracles. Mohammedanism is a system in many respects unique, but in none more so than in this, that alone of the great religions of the world it does not, in its authoritative documents, rest its claims to reception upon miracles; and yet the attitude of Mohammed toward the miraculous has been made the ground by different people of very conflicting accusations. Superficial observers up to the middle of the last century, and Christian missionaries of later times, whose zeal has not always been tempered by accurate knowledge of their subject, fastening on the fantastic character of the few miracles attributed to Mohammed by the pious credulity of his followers or the "successors," have triumphantly torn the mask from the "impostor;" and have gone on to contrast, as well they might from their point of view, the purposeless character and impossibility of his supposed miracles with the sober nature and the moral purpose which underlie the miracles of the New Testament, however supernatural they may be. Other writers—White in his "Bampton Lectures," and Paley in his "Evidences of

Christianity," and Butler in his "Analogy"—preferring to appeal to what Mohammed said of himself, rather than what was said of him by others, have driven home the contrast between Mohammedanism and Christianity by pointing out that Christianity is attested by supernatural manifestations, and is therefore divine, while Mohammedanism is neither the one nor the other. Let us inquire what the Koran itself, the only reliable authority on the subject, says, and then make one or two remarks on the general question.

In the thirteenth Sura we read:

"The unbelievers say, Unless a sign be sent down with him from his Lord, we will not believe. But thou art a preacher only, O Mohammed!"

Mohammed replies that God alone can work miracles; and, after specifying some of them, he says:

"God alone knoweth that which is hidden, and that which is revealed. He is the Great and the Most High."

In the seventh Sura the infidels ask why Mohammed had not been sent with miracles, like previous prophets? Because, replied Mohammed, miracles had proved inadequate to convince. Noah had been sent with signs, and with what effect? Where was the lost tribe of Thamud? They had refused to receive the preaching of the prophet Saled unless he showed them a sign, and caused the rock to bring forth a living camel. He did what they asked. In scorn they had cut off the camel's feet, and then, daring the Prophet to fulfill his threats of judgment, were found dead in their beds next morning, stricken by the angel of the Lord. There are some seventeen places in the Koran in which Mohammed is challenged to work a sign, and he answers them all to the same effect.

There are in the whole of the Sacred Book only two supposed exceptions to the attitude thus assumed by him; and those who know how large a part the Miraj, or miraculous journey on the Borak,* bears in popular conceptions of Mohammedanism, will learn with surprise, if they have not gone much into the matter, that there is only one passage in the Koran which can be tortured into an allusion to the journey to heaven:

"Praise be to Him who transferred his servant by night from the sacred temple to one that is more remote."†

To make this refer at all to the Miraj, we have to insert the word "Mecca" in one place, and "Jerusalem" or "seventh heaven" in another, and this, though in the sixtieth verse of the same Sura Mohammed tells us he

---

* "Borak" after all means only Lightning: the Barak of the Jews; the Barca of the Carthaginians.

† Sura xvii., 1.

was not sent with miracles, because people would not believe them; and in the sixty-second verse express mention is made of a vision he had had, beyond doubt of this very journey! So, too, in the verse, "The hour hath approached, and the moon hath been split in sunder:"* people were so anxious to see an allusion to the extravagant story of the moon's descending on the Kaaba, and entering Mohammed's sleeve, that they forgot that "the hour" means "the hour of judgment," and that the tense used is the prophetic preterite. To the eye of the Semitic "nabi," whether Jewish or Arab, the future is as the past.†

Without discussing the question of miracles at length, I would make three remarks on the general subject: First, that in a new religion the real cause for wonder is, not that it claims to be founded on miracles, but that it should ever be able to profess to do without them. In certain stages of the human mind there is no natural phenomenon which will not bear a supernatural interpretation. In fact, the supernatural is then the rule; the natural, the exception. Gibbon, I think, has somewhere asked whether there exists a single instance in

---

* Sura liv., 1.

† Cf. the past tense used in Sura xcviii., called "The Victory: "Verily, we *have* won for thee an undoubted victory"—believed to point to the conquest of Mecca two years later.

ecclesiastical history of a Father of the Church claiming for himself the power of working miracles, and I am not aware that the question has ever been answered in the affirmative. And yet we know that during many centuries there was hardly a Father of the Church who did not have miracles attributed to him by other men of equal, or even greater, reputed sanctity. Among many others, I need only mention the names of St. Benedict and St. Martin of Tours, of St. Bernard and St. Francis of Assisi. They attribute even to inanimate remains, and to relics, which were often fictitious, powers which they would never dream of claiming for themselves. St. Augustine, whose honesty is above suspicion, tells us gravely that he had ascertained, on certain evidence, that some small fragments of the disinterred relics of St. Stephen had, in his own diocese, within two years, performed no less than seventy miracles, and three of them raisings from the dead! St. Bernard was believed by his admirers to have excommunicated some flies which teased him, and "they straightway fell down in heaps." And if such be the mental atmosphere of a Church in its adolescence, *à fortiori* will an age which is capable of producing or receiving a new religion throw a mystic halo of supernaturalism around the supreme objects of its reverence. Even if the founder himself disclaims the power of working miracles, they will be thrust upon him in the most perfect good faith by the warm imagination of his disciples.

Second, and what would seem to follow from the first: In proportion as exact knowledge advances, the sphere of the supernatural is narrowed; and therefore a proof which is fitted for an imaginative and creative age is not best suited for a critical and scientific one. Many minds, no doubt, will always crave the supernatural, and they will always find plenty of it; but to many, also, in an age like this, miracles have been a stumbling-block, and have seemed a reason for rejecting the religion which is made to rest mainly on them. Where there is a choice, it is at least wise to select the strongest ground we have; nor is there any fear that Science will ever explain too much. Behind what she explains there will always remain the unexplained and the unexplainable. Let her classify and explain the phenomena of Mind and Matter as she will, but will she ever be able to tell us what Mind and Matter are themselves? Let her analyze the springs of human action, and dissect the complex anatomy of the human conscience; but the religious instinct will still remain, as an ultimate fact of human nature; and that instinct will find without, or supply from its own resources, the verities with which it deals—the verities which supplement and explain to it the facts of Nature, and are not explained by them; which assure us that this life is not the only life, nor death extinction; and that love, the main source of human happiness, is not given us to make all real happiness impossible; which, in a word, supply the soul with the supreme objects for its worship and its aspirations.

Third: I would remark that the answers given by Mohammed himself to those who demanded miracles—that God gave the power of working miracles to whom he pleased; that other prophets had wrought miracles, and had not been believed; that he who could not know even himself adequately could not know what God had hidden; that there were greater miracles in Nature than any which could be wrought outside of it; that the Koran itself was a miracle—find at least one line of thought in a greater than Mohammed, which is not opposed to, but identical with them. People have raised questions about the authenticity and meaning of much that is in the Gospels, but, by the rules of all critical interpretation, what they can least question is the genuineness and accuracy of those passages which the Disciples have, in their undoubted honesty, recorded, as it were, in spite of themselves, and which appear to run counter to other and loftier conceptions of that majestic character on whose partially preserved utterances all

Christendom still hangs. He who said he could of his own self do nothing; it was the Spirit which quickened —the flesh profiteth nothing; the words that he spake unto them, they were spirit and they were life; he who, when his disciples wondered at the withered fig-tree, told them that the trust in God which underlay his act would enable even them to do greater things; who, we are told, *could* not, in certain places, work miracles because of their unbelief; and when people declined to accept his teaching on higher grounds, told them, with a touch of scorn, that they might do so if they liked on the lower ground, for "his *very* works' sake;" and, lastly, who said it was an evil and adulterous generation which sought after a sign, and that no sign should be given it; and that if a man believed not Moses and the Prophets, not even would he repent though one arose from the dead: in one aspect, at all events, his teaching agreed with the Arabian Prophet whom Christians have so much discredited. He, at all events, treated the miraculous as subordinate to the moral evidences of his mission, and struck upon a vein of thought and touched a chord of feeling which, it seems to me, is reconcilable at once with the onward march of Science and all the admitted weaknesses of human nature.*

---

* Compare throughout "Literature and Dogma," caps. v. and vi., especially p. 129, 154.

II. Second, Fatalism. I have spoken above of the extraordinary impulse given to the earlier followers of Mohammed by their vivid sense of God's personal presence with them. Inspiring, indeed, this principle then was; for it must never be forgotten, as I hope now to prove, that the belief in an absolute predestination, which turns men into mere puppets, and all human life into a grim game of chess, wherein men are the pieces, moved by the invisible Hand of but a single Player, and which is now so general in Mohammedan countries, was, all appearances to the contrary, no part of the creed of the Prophet himself or of his immediate successors;* and I venture, therefore, to think that Gibbon is wrong in tracing the desperate valor of the primitive Mussulmans mainly to the notion that since there was no chance, there need be no fear: the germ, indeed, of fatalism was there, but its effects were as yet any thing but fatalistic.

It is of course true that there are many passages in the Koran which assert in the strongest way the foreknowledge of God. For instance, "The fate of every man have we bound about his neck;" and the relations of the slain at the battle of Ohud are comforted by the assurance that every one must die at his appointed time,

---

* Cf. *National Review* for July, 1858, p. 154.

whether it be in his own bed or on the field of battle. Nor is it possible to any religion to reconcile the conflicting dogmas of the foreknowledge of God and of the free-will of man. The New Testament does not try to do so. Most assuredly our own Articles of Religion, however successful they may be in finding a compromise between opposing views on other things, fail to effect a compromise here. Press to its logical result either the omnipotence or the omniscience of God, and what becomes of man's free-will? But logic is not the only criterion of truth, nor is it the only rule of life; and consequently there is hardly a religion which does not, in words at all events, assert as strongly as possible God's foreknowledge; in acts, at all events, man's freedom. Sometimes one will be the more prominent, sometimes the other.

The Prophet of Arabia naturally dwelt most on those attributes of God which, throwing the widest gulf between the Creator and his creatures, would, once and for all, rescue the Arabs from worshiping what their own hands had made.* He inculcates hope in adversity and humility in success, on the ground that there is a supreme Ruler who never leaves the helm; who knows what is really best for man when man himself

---

* Cf. Gobineau, "Les Religions et les Philosophies dans l'Asie Centrale." See the whole passage on this subject, p. 72, 73.

does not; and whose supreme will and power, where he asserts them, can not be crossed by the efforts of the creatures of his hand. But this is not the only side to his teaching. He asserts that man is a free agent—free to refuse or to accept the divine message; responsible for his acts, and therefore deserving, now of punishment, now of reward. The future, in fact, is in his own hands, and Mohammed incessantly urges him to use his opportunities. Ali, the most saintly, I would almost say the most Christian, of all Mussulmans, pronounces those who say the will is not free to be heretics.* There are at least four sects among Mohammedans that differ from one another on the one point of predestination and free-will. One of them, the Mutazalites, almost assert what philosophers have called the "liberty of indifference;" and there is little doubt that Mohammed himself, if the alternative had been clearly presented to him, would have had more in common with Pelagius than with Augustine, with Arminius than with Calvin.

It is difficult to believe that if Mohammed had been the consistent fatalist he is often represented to have been, he would have made prayer one of the four practical duties enjoined upon the Faithful, and that on an

---

* Quoted by Gobineau, loc. cit.

equal or even a higher footing than almsgiving, fasting, and pilgrimage. He is said to have called it the Pillar of Religion and the Key of Paradise. He told a tribe which, after its conversion, begged for a remission of some of the daily prayers enjoined upon them, that there could be no good in the religion in which there was no prayer; and, according to one of his successors, prayer of itself lifts men half way to heaven. Now, if all events are absolutely fixed by the divine will and foreseen by the divine mind, then there is no possibility, I do not say of altering the fixed laws of Nature— for that is a power which few would claim for prayer— but even of a man's improving in the smallest degree, by any acts or petitions of his, his own spiritual condition. Prayer would thus be a superfluity and delusion if explained in any other way than as an aspiration of the heart toward God, which, being an end in itself, necessarily brings its own answer with it. Now, whether this last is a true view of prayer or not, it was certainly not Mohammed's view. In neither case would he have been quite a consistent fatalist; but it is not likely that he could have overlooked the glaring inconsistencies involved between an absolute predestination, on the one hand, and material answers to prayer on the other. The prayers that he enjoined five times a day*

---

* It is worth noticing, in passing, that the five daily prayers, like the are still offered with full confidence in their efficacy by all devout Mussulmans; and the cry of the Muezzin, before daybreak, from a myriad mosques and minarets—"Prayer is better than sleep, prayer is better than sleep"—is a living witness, wherever the influence of the Prophet of Arabia has extended, more vivid than the letter of the Koran itself—overpowering even the lethargy and quietism of the East—to Mohammed's belief in God's providential government of the world, and in the freedom of man's will.

Mohammed, on one occasion, complains of the Jews that "if good fortune betide them, they say it is from God; if evil betide them, they say it is from Mohammed:" say rather, he suggests, all is from God. But what, he asks in the very next verse, has come to these people that they are not near to understanding what is told them?

"Whatever good betideth thee is from God, and whatever betideth thee of evil is from thyself."*

There are the two contradictories brought face to face, and left fronting one another for all time; and can any religion do more, and perhaps I may add less, than this?

---

rite of circumcision, though universally observed by Mussulmans, are not enjoined in the Koran itself. Circumcision is not even mentioned in the Koran: it is one of the many Pre-Islamitic practices which Mohammed tacitly sanctioned.

* Sura iv., 80, 81.

It is not difficult to see how one and the same doctrine of God's foreknowledge, on the one hand, and of his actual intervention in human affairs on the other, may have diametrically opposite effects in different natures, or in even the same natures under different circumstances.

> "There is a tide in the affairs of men
> Which, taken at the flood, leads on to fortune;
> Omitted, all the voyage of their life
> Is bound in shallows and in miseries."

The early Mussulmans, in the new burst of life breathed into them by Mohammed, it inspired with double energy and double enthusiasm, as in their best days it inspired the Puritans, the Covenanters, the Pilgrim Fathers. But to their descendants in their more normal state—the lethargic Soufy, the brooding Sepoy, the insensate Turk; I would add, to those religious people who refuse to prevent the miseries and the diseases which Nature they think has attached to guilt—it furnishes with a new excuse for that life of inactivity to which they are already too much disposed, since they believe that they are acquiescing, as in duty bound, in the immutable decrees of God.*

III. One more question remains to be discussed in this Lecture—the wars of Islam, and the relation they bear

---

* See an eloquent passage on this subject in an article of the *National Review* for October, 1861, entitled "The Great Arabian," p. 312.

to Mohammed's religion. It is true that it was not till the Prophet found himself, to his surprise, in a position of power at Medina, that we hear even a whisper of the sword as an instrument of conversion. It is then, and not till then, that we are told that other prophets have been sent by God to attest his different attributes in their own person and by their miraculous acts; but that men had closed their eyes to the character and denied the miracles even of Moses and of Christ. What remained to the last of the prophets except that he should try the last argument of the sword? Was the sword then an after-thought and an accidental appendage merely to Mohammed's religion, or was it an essential part? I am inclined to think that the nature of the case itself and the verdict of subsequent experience will tend to show that, however absent it was from Mohammed's thoughts at first, and however alien to his gentle and forgiving nature, it came in the progress of events, to some extent in his own life, and still more so in the lives of his successors, to be the latter. How this came about requires careful explanation.

Mohammed's notion of God had never been that of a great moral Being who designs that the creatures he has created should, from love and gratitude to him, become one with him, or even assimilated to him. Mohammed believed in God, feared, reverenced, and obeyed him after his light, as few Jews or Christians ever did; but he could hardly be said in the Christian, or even the Jewish sense of the word, to love God. It is possible that repeated acts of obedience to a God whom he always represents as compassionate and merciful might imply or result in love; but at all events with him love was not, as it is in Christianity, the fulfilling of the law, the inspiring motive to action, the sum of its theology as of its morality. Had it been so, Mohammed would have seen more reason to doubt whether the sword could ever be its best ally; but though he must in any case have seen that it was impossible to force men to love God, it may have crossed his mind that it was possible to force men to abstain from idolatry, to acknowledge one God with their lips, to fear and to obey him at all events in their outward acts.

Had Mohammed remained master of himself — had he remained, that is to say, the simple Prophet throughout his career—it is possible, on the one hand, that his message would never have spread in his lifetime beyond the walls of Mecca and Medina; and it is more than probable, on the other, that his character might now be held up to the world as that which we feel the founder of a religion ought to be; that which Confucius and Buddha were, and that which Mohammed himself, throughout his life at Mecca, unquestionably was—a perfect model of the saintly virtues. There is one glory of the founder of a religion, another of the founder of a nation, another of the founder of an empire. They are better kept distinct; and the limits of the human faculties are an adequate security against their being often found united in one person. It is the uncongenial mixture of earthly needs and heavenly aspirations which has made Mohammed at once a smaller and a greater man—at once more and less commanding than he would otherwise have been. What he gains as a ruler of men, he loses as a guide and as an example; and people are, naturally enough, led to condemn the prophet for the drastic energy of the leader, and the leader for the shortcomings of the prophet. It is, perhaps, inevitable that Christians should do so; for the image of Him whose kingdom was not of this world, who did not strive nor cry, whose servants were never to draw the sword in his defense, forces itself upon the mind, in silent and reproachful antithesis to the mixed and sullied character of the Prophet-soldier Mohammed. The trumpet-call is not the still, small voice; it is immeasurably below it: but there has been room for both in the development of humanity.

Now, on a sudden, Mohammed found himself in a position he had not courted, which was forced on him by his enemies; and the exigencies of his exiled followers—the need of sustenance, the appetite for plunder, the desire of revenge, and the longing for their homes, no less than the impending attack of the Koreishites—drove the Prophet for the first time to place himself at their head; and, for temporal purposes only, to unsheath the sword. Mohammed thus became a general by accident; and the extraordinary success of his first ventures deepened the impression, already half natural to an Arab, that the sword might be a legitimate instrument of spiritual warfare, and that God had put into his power a new means, where all other means, as in the case of previous prophets, had failed. At all events the sword, originally drawn for temporal purposes only, was found to have, half unexpectedly, answered another end as well. It was found that the religion, once started by the sword, was soon able to throw the sword away. The march of the Faith anticipated the march of the army of the Faithful, and the all but uniform success of the armies, when they had to fight, seemed to stamp the means used with the divine approbation; and so it was that Mohammed felt less and less scruple as to the use of the sword where it seemed to him to be wanted; and at the close of his life, in one of the last Suras of the Koran, we are hardly surprised to find the stern command and the "magnificent presentiment:"

"Fight on, therefore, till there be no temptation to idolatry, and the religion becomes God's alone."*

The early Kaliphs obeyed the precepts and imitated the example of the warrior-Prophet, and went forth on their enterprise in all the plenitude of autocratic power; there was no rivalry between Church and State to tie their hands, for the Kaliph was the head of both in one; the State, so far as it had any separate existence at all, being simply a creature of the Church. And let us here turn aside for a moment to examine the relation then subsisting between the spiritual and temporal power, first in the Western, and then in the Eastern Empire, and to contrast it with the extraordinary concentration of all the energies of a new-born enthusiasm placed in the hands of the Kaliph. We shall then see, on the one hand, from what a vantage-ground the Arabs, at that precise moment, entered the lists to contend with Christendom; but, on the other, we shall note how few are the men and how rare the occasions on which power of any kind can afford to dispense with those checks which are a condition of its permanence, and which alone can prevent it from developing into unbridled tyranny or dying of inanition.

The Christianity of the West then had, centuries be-

---

* Sura viii., 40. Cf. also xxii., 40, and ix., *passim;* perhaps the last Sura Mohammed composed.

fore this, organized an *imperium in imperio* which afforded a substantial check to the tyranny of the emperors, and, by its moral majesty, could restrain a savage barbarian even in the full career of conquest. Ambrose had sternly rebuked Theodosius; Innocent had mitigated the horrors of the sack of Rome by Alaric; Leo had turned back Attila, and half disarmed Genseric. The transference of the seat of empire to Constantinople forced the Bishops of Rome into a political prominence which would not otherwise have belonged to them; and, in process of time, the spiritual power thus fortified began to contend, on something like equal terms, with the temporal. Gregory the Great, whose pontificate ended shortly before the "call" of the Prophet of Arabia, was the virtual sovereign of Rome, able to protect it alike from the ferocity of the Lombards and from the pretentious weakness of the Exarchs. Before long the sacerdotal monarchs who reigned on the Tiber were to be seen deposing by right divine one Frankish dynasty which ruled upon the Rhine; setting up another of their own creation; and, finally, in the person of Charles the Great, giving new body to the phantom of the ancient Roman Empire which had never ceased to flit before the mind of Europe, and fancying, in their superb audacity, that a breath might overthrow what a breath had made. And by the time that the Eternal City itself heard the dreaded Tecbir at their gates, it was to a Pope and not a Cæsar—a Pope, too, elected in hot haste, without even the formal sanction of the Cæsar—that Rome owed her safety!*

But the religion of the Eastern Empire, to quote Gibbon's epigram, could teach men only " to suffer and to yield." The Patriarch of Constantinople, unlike the Patriarch of Rome, was the puppet of the emperor, indorsed his worst deeds, or was swept away if he objected to them.† And the Saracens who besieged the ceremonious Emperor of the East in his own capital must have enjoyed, if they could read, the form of service, prescribed by Church and State together, for the day on which the emperor should trample on the necks of the captive Mussulmans, while the singers were to chant, " Thou hast made mine enemies my footstool," and the people were to shout forty times the " Kyrie Eleeson."‡ The crusading spirit which

---

* Leo IV.

† See the history of the Iconoclastic Emperors generally, A.D. 717-841, and their dealings with the Patriarchs of Constantinople. Read especially, on the one hand, the account of the dastardly submission of the Patriarch Anastasius to Leo, and, on the other, the horrible cruelties inflicted on the Patriarch Constantine by Copronymus. Milman, vol. ii., chap. vii.

‡ See the " De Ceremoniis Aulæ et Ecclesiæ Byzantinæ " of Constantine Porphyrogenitus, vol. ii., p. 19 ; quoted by Gibbon, chap. liii., p. 116, and note.

might have been evoked by a proposition of the great Emperors, Nicephorus and Zimisces, to give a martyr's crown to those who fell in battle with the infidels, was checkmated by a counter-proposition of the Patriarch to exclude from the highest rites of the Church all those who took up arms, even in self-defense.* Had it been otherwise, the period of the Crusades might have been anticipated by more than a hundred years. We see, therefore, that in the West, by the time that the tide of Arab conquest had spread from Mecca to Gibraltar, the spiritual power was independent of temporal, and was often able to control or neutralize its action, even in temporal affairs; while in the East, on which the storm was first to burst, it was almost non-existent; and if ever it did cause its voice to be heard, the cry it uttered was that of Phocion, not of Demosthenes — of Jeremiah, not of Isaiah: that of submission to the inevitable, not of resistance to the bitter end.

But with the Saracens the case was different. The God of Mohammed, like the God of the wanderers of the wilderness, and unlike the God of Christendom, was pre-eminently the God of battles. The early Mussulmans shed tears when held back within their leashes from the battle; and the Emperor Leo, who condemned

---

* See Gibbon, loc. cit.

the Mohammedan idea of God, must have secretly envied the vigor that it brought. Military zeal under a tried leader is a strong passion, so is religious enthusiasm; and never probably in the history of the world have these two passions burned with so consuming a flame as they did in the breasts of the early followers of Mohammed. The civil, the religious, and the military were as indissolubly blended together in his system as they were in mediæval chivalry. It was not so much religion that became warlike, as war, the normal condition of the Arabs on a small scale, now itself became religious, with the whole world for its battle-ground. Probably in no army in the world, not even among the Scotch Covenanters, nor among Cromwell's Ironsides, did religious exercises so form part of the military discipline, and religious enthusiasm so infuse an *esprit de corps*.

The early battles of Islam—Bedr and Ohud, Kadesia and Nehavend, the Yermuk and Aiznadin; its early sieges—Bozra and Damascus, Jerusalem and Aleppo, Memphis and Alexandria—are more than Homeric in the reckless valor and the chivalrous devotion that they exhibit. And it is to be remembered that they are in the main historical. Kaled is the Achilles of the siege of Damascus, Amrou of that of Memphis, Dames of Aleppo. At Bedr, Omeir, a mere stripling, who, fearing that he might be rejected on account of his youth, had managed to join the small army of the Faithful unknown to Mohammed, flung away the dates he was eating with the vow that he would eat the next in the presence of God. " Paradise is before you, the devil and hell-fire in your rear," was the exhortation of the generals at the battle of Yermuk. The Faithful courted death with the ecstasy of martyrs, and received a martyr's reward. At Aiznadin, Derar maintained a flying fight single-handed against thirty infidels, and killed seventeen of their number. At the siege of Damascus, a Saracen heroine, who had followed her husband, Aban, to the holy war, saw him killed by her side, stopped to bury him, and then fought on in the post of danger till she slew the famous archer who had killed her husband. Nor is there any period in the history of Mohammedanism, late or early, in which the intensity of the crusading spirit does not on occasion manifest itself. It is God's battle that each Mussulman is fighting, and as God may will, he is ready for either event—for victory or defeat, for life or death. In the Crusades themselves, when Christendom seemed to be seized with a double portion of the Mohammedan spirit, by the confession of the Christians, the generosity, the reckless valor, the self-sacrifice, and the chivalry were not all on one side.

Richard of England and Frederick Barbarossa found their match in Saladin; and even the history of England's empire in India teems with proofs that the vital spark of fanaticism is latent only, not extinct.

Whenever hitherto in the history of Mohammedanism the belief has grown feeble that the Faithful hold a commission from on high to put down evil, wherever it shows itself, with a strong hand, it must be admitted that the religion itself has proportionately failed to do its proper work, both as a compelling and as a restraining power. In the Middle Ages the vitality and energy of Mohammedanism evidenced itself most clearly, not in Arabia or Persia or Africa, where its success was most complete, but in the Christian border lands—in Spain, in Palestine, in Asia Minor—where the crusading spirit was most evoked. Where there was no outlet for an active and even a material warfare, against what was believed to be evil, there corruption crept in, and stealthily paralyzed all the energies of Mussulman society. "*Corruptio optimi fit pessima.*" Ommiade and Abbasside and Fatimite Kaliphs; Ghaznevide and Seljukian and Ottoman Sultans, passed through the same dreary stages of luxury and decay; and the government that now represents, or misrepresents, the Kaliphate, and is by most people foolishly supposed to be the main support of Islam, originally, in the hands of men like Abu Bakr or Omar, the best, the simplest, and the most republican of all absolute governments, has, in the hands of the Ottoman Turks, ever since their faith ceased to be militant, become the most hopeless of despotisms, since the abject submission to the ruler remains, while all reason for submission has vanished.*

In the eyes of many the admission I have frankly made that the propagation of religion by the sword has been an essential part of Mohammedanism will serve to condemn it at once, and so in the abstract and from the highest point of view it ought. The sword is a rough surgical instrument in any case; but the doctrine that religion can ever be propagated by it, paradoxical as it sounds now, has seemed a truism in more ages than one; and though the Arabs were semi-barbarians, the conquered nations were constrained to admit that in their conquests they were not barbarous. Their wars were not mere wars of devastation, like those of Alaric or Genseric in earlier times, or of Zenghis Khan or Tamerlane in later. It was the savage boast of Attila, the genius of destruction, the "scourge of God," that the grass never grew where his horse had once trodden.

---

* See this line of thought developed by Maurice, "Religions of the World," p. 29, seq. I have done little more in this paragraph than condense and illustrate his argument.

But of the Mohammedan conquests it would rather be true to say that, after the first wave of invasion had swept by, two blades of grass were found growing where one had grown before; like the thunderstorm, they fertilized while they destroyed; and from one end of the then known world to the other, with their religion they sowed seeds of literature, of commerce, and of civilization. And as these disappeared, in the lapse of years, in one part of the Mussulman world, they reappeared in another. When they died out, with the dying of the Abbasside Kaliphate, along the banks of the Tigris and Euphrates, they revived again on the Guadalquivir and Guadiana. To the splendors and civilization of Damascus succeeded Bagdad; to Bagdad, Cairo; to Cairo, Cordova.

Mohammedanism has been accused of hostility to the growth of the human intellect. It may have been so in its earliest days, when Omar, as the story goes, condemned the Alexandrian Library to the flames by his famous dilemma: "If these books agree with the Book of God, they are useless; if they disagree, they are pernicious; and in either case they must be destroyed." It may be so whenever there is a passing outburst of fanaticism; but it is not so in its essential nature, nor has it been so historically, not even in its wars. The religion which has declared that "the ink of the learned is as precious as the blood of the martyrs,"* and which declares that at the Day of Decision a special account will be given of the use made of the intellect, can not fairly be accused of obscurantism. It was not so when, during the darkest period of European history, the Arabs for five hundred years held up the torch of learning to humanity. It was the Arabs who then "called the Muses from their ancient seats;" who collected and translated the writings of the Greek masters; who understood the geometry of Apollonius, and wielded the weapons found in the logical armory of Aristotle. It was the Arabs who developed the sciences of Agriculture and Astronomy, and created those of Algebra and Chemistry; who adorned their cities with colleges and libraries, as well as with mosques and palaces; who supplied Europe with a school of philosophers from Cordova, and a school of physicians from

---

* Quoted by Gobineau, p. 26. So, too, Abulpharagius, in his "Dynasties," says that Almamun, Kaliph of Bagdad, invited learned men to his court because they were the elect of God, whose lives were devoted to the development of the mind. (See Gibbon, vol. vii., p. 34.) Against the destruction of the Alexandrian Library by Omar may fairly be set the destruction by the Crusaders of an immense library at Tripoli, in Palestine. The general, finding that the first room of the library contained the Koran only, ordered the whole library to be burned. So, too, Cardinal Ximenes, on entering the Moorish capital, showed that a crass fanaticism is not the prerogative of one religion only, by his order to destroy the vast collection of Arabic MSS. there, with the exception of three hundred medical works, which he reserved for his own university.

Salerno. When we condemn the Mohammedan wars, let us at least remember what of good they brought with them.

Nor is Mohammedanism the only religion which has tried to propagate itself by the sword. It is true, of course, that a holy war waged by Christians is in direct contravention of the spirit of their Founder, while one waged by Mohammedans is in accordance with both the practice and the precept of the Prophet, and so far there is no parallel at all between the two religions. The means authorized by Christ for the spread of his religion were moral and spiritual only. The means authorized by Mohammed were persuasion and example first; but, failing these, the sword.

Yet, historically speaking, the contrast between the practice of Christians and Mohammedans has not been so sharp as is often supposed. The Saxon wars of Charles the Great were avowedly religious wars, and differed chiefly from the Syrian wars of Omar and of Ali, from the African wars of Amrou and Akbah, and the Spanish wars of Moussa and of Tarik, in that they were much more protracted and vastly less successful. Otto the Great, the best of Charles's successors, used the sword with vigor to extend the external profession of Christianity among the Sclavonian tribes who dwelt along the shores of the Baltic. The Mediæval Papacy, whatever its other services to progress, was never backward to unfurl the standard of a religious war, whether against the common enemy of Christendom, or, as more often happened, against a sect of heretics—the Albigenses or the Waldenses—nearer home. Nor, in point of ferocity, is it clear that religious wars waged by Christians will compare favorably with those of Mohammedans. The Mohammedan wars were never internecine. Even on the field of battle the conquering Mussulman allowed his conquered foe the two other alternatives of conversion or of tribute. When Abu Bakr first invaded Syria, he charged his troops not to mutilate the dead, not to slay old men, women, or children, not to cut down fruit-trees, not to kill cattle unless they were needed for food; and these humane precepts served like a code of laws of war during the career of Mohammedan conquest. And this, be it remembered, among Orientals, who had always been remarkable for their disregard of human life. When we remember, on the other hand, the massacre of four thousand five hundred pagan Saxons in cold blood by Charles the Great—when we remember the famous answer by which the Papal Legate, in the Albigensian war, quieted the scruples of a too conscientious general, "Kill all; God will know his own"—when we recall the Spanish Inquisition, the conquest of Mexico and Peru, the massacre of St. Bartholomew, and the sack of Magdeburg by Tilly, we shall be disposed, never, indeed, to justify religious wars, but to point out that, of the religious wars which the world has seen, the Mohammedan are certainly not the worst—in their object, in their methods, or in their results.

Nor is the extermination of moral evil in all cases an unworthy object of war. There are occasions even in our modern civilization, and in an era of non-intervention, when one longs to feel that the sword a nation wields may be, in their eyes at all events, the sword of the Lord and of Gideon. An unselfish war to put down the slave-trade or the opium-traffic, to counteract some "Holy Alliance" of emperors against the rights of peoples, to prevent a giant iniquity like the partition of Poland, is perhaps the only kind of war, except those of self-defense, to which the spirit of Christianity is not opposed. Christianity *is* opposed to wars of aggression, to dynastic wars, and, above all, to religious wars; for a religious war rests upon the irreligious assumption that one fallible man holds a fiat from Omnipotence to step between another human soul and God; and to enforce his partial views of truth upon a fellow-mortal, who, for aught he knows, may have as wide a prospect and as deep an insight as he has himself. "*Deorum injuriæ Deis curæ.*" The sword may silence; it can not convince: it may enforce hypocrisy; it can never force belief. But this has not always seemed so self-evident; and I say it deliberately and with all the force of conviction, compared with the war of the Confederate States in the nineteenth century for the perpetuation of slavery, compared with England's Japanese wars for the extension of her trade, her Chinese wars for the sale of her opium, and her miserable African wars waged for the possession of a territory which she bought, and had no moral right to buy, from those who sold what they had no moral right to sell,* the Mohammedan wars for the propagation of a comparatively pure religion and a higher morality were, in their time and according to their light, inasmuch as they were not purely selfish, I do not say excusable, but they were at least intelligible and natural.

Here I must close this Lecture. What of good and what of evil the world owes to Mohammed; what is the condition and what the prospects of Mohammedanism now; what, as a matter of fact, is the historical connection between Mohammedanism and Christianity —its points of difference as well as of resemblance; finally, and most important of all, how that connection ought to be regarded by Christians, and under what

---

* See Appendix to Lecture III.

conditions or modifications the two great creeds may work together, or, if needs be, apart, for their common object, the general good of humanity—these are some of the points I hope to be able to discuss in my fourth and concluding Lecture.

LECTURE IV.

March 7, 1874.

MOHAMMEDANISM AND CHRISTIANITY.

Say unto the Christians, their God and my God is one.—The Koran.

Ὁ δὲ Ἰησοῦς εἶπε, Μὴ κωλύετε αὐτόν· ὃς γὰρ οὐκ ἔστι καθ᾽ ἡμῶν, ὑπὲρ ἡμῶν ἐστιν.—St. Mark.

It may have been observed that in attempting, in my last Lecture, to deal with some of the questions connected with Mohammedanism—such as miracles, fatalism, religious wars—which have much perplexed the Christian mind, I omitted to say any thing on a point which, more even than any of these, has scandalized those who view Mohammedanism from a distance: I mean the notions Mohammedans have formed of a future state. The omission was not altogether accidental, for I am inclined to think that too much stress has been laid upon these notions, no less by Mohammed's apologists than by his critics; more stress than the Koran itself, and more even than the current Mohammedan belief, will warrant. But, remembering a remark of

Sprenger's* that, although Islam has been described in many books, yet educated people have not got much farther in the knowledge of it than that the Turks are Mohammedans and allow polygamy, I think it will be well to add a few words to counteract the common notion, which I should be disposed to place on a par with this, that the Paradise of the Mohammedans is nothing more than the enjoyment of polygamy, with its earthly drawbacks and limitations removed.

So much has been said and written about the gross nature of Mohammed's Paradise, the black-eyed Houris, the perfumes and the spices, with which his imagination furnished it, that ordinary people may be excused for believing that it was mainly, if not wholly, sensual. But this is not, in the main, a true, and still less is it an adequate, account of the matter. The passages are few in number in which Mohammed dwells much on these aspects of the future, and, even in these, much of what is said is explained by orthodox Mohammedans to be merely Oriental imagery, while some of it is especially suitable — the bubbling fountains and the shady gardens above all — to the inhabitants of a dry and thirsty land, such as Arabia is.†

---

* Sprenger, vol. ii., p. 18.
† See Sale's "Introduction," p. 73; and Lane's "Modern Egyptians," vol. i., p. 84.

Few people now put a literal interpretation upon the gorgeous imagery and the glowing colors used in the Book of Revelation to describe the Celestial City; and every one will admit that in all religions, even the most spiritual, the circumstances of this life must necessarily, to some extent, lend both form and color to the views of the life to come. The Red Indian dreams of a heaven behind the cloud-topped hills, embosomed in woods, wherein his faithful dog will bear him company. The fierce Norseman hoped to be admitted after death to the Hall of Odin, and there, reclining on a couch, to drink ale forever from the skulls of his enemies whom he had slain in battle. The earnest Methodist pictures to himself a place

> "Where congregations ne'er break up,
> And Sabbaths never end,"

for the simple reason that he finds his highest spiritual happiness in these things on earth. A polygamous people could hardly have pictured to themselves a heaven without polygamy. It would never even have occurred to them that such a thing was possible, since few of them had ever known a society on earth which was without it; nor do I suppose that any individual Christian who has ever known the luxury of home affection has been able to accept in any literal sense the doctrine that in the future world there are to be no exclusive attachments,* for the simple reason, again, that without individual love no human heart can conceive of the possibility of any happiness as complete or real.

Again, it is to be remembered that much that is material or even gross in the Mohammedan conception of a future life is due, not to Mohammed, but to Mohammed's successors; and it is not the least of the enigmas that attach to the extraordinary and unique character of the Prophet that his views of a future state are never more spiritual than at the time when, according to the common theory, he had most entirely, and, in fact, he had to some extent, fallen away from his austerely moral life. Contrast the tone of the Suras, referring to this subject, which were written at Mecca early in his life,† with the third, for instance, which was written at Medina many years later.

"Fair," says he, "in the sight of men are the pleasures of women and children; fair are the treasured treasures of gold and silver; and fine horses; and flocks; and corn-fields! Such is the enjoyment of this world's life. But God! goodly is the home with him!

"Shall I tell you of better things than these, prepared for those who fear God in his presence? Theirs shall be gardens beneath which the rivers flow, and in which

---

* St. Matt. xxii., 30.
† Sura lv., 44–58; lvi., 17–36; lxxvi., 12–22.

they shall abide for aye, and wives of stainless purity, and acceptance with God, for God regardeth his servants.

"They who say, O our Lord, we have indeed believed, pardon our sins, and keep us from the torment of the fire.

"The patient are they and the truthful, the lowly and the charitable, and they who ask for pardon as each day breaks."*

Surely here, as elsewhere, and increasingly so as the Prophet drew near his end, it is the presence of God, the knowledge of him, the eternal Salaam or Peace with which they shall salute one another, the purity of love, and not its sensuality, which are the most prominent ideas.

Heaven and hell, indeed, were realities to the Mohammedan mind in a sense in which they have hardly ever been to any other nation. With a more than Dantesque realism, Mohammed saw the tortures of the lost no less than the bliss of the faithful.

"They shall dwell," he says, "amid burning winds and in scalding water, under the shade of a black smoke which is no shade, neither cool nor grateful, . . . and they shall surely eat of the fruit of the tree Ez-Zakkoum, and shall fill their bellies therewith, and they

---

* Sura xiii., 12-15.

shall drink thereon boiling water, even as a thirsty camel drinketh."*

And again he says:

"They shall have garments of fire fitted unto them, their bowels shall be dissolved thereby, and also their skins, and they shall be beaten with maces of iron." †

And once more, in one of his very early Suras, which, if it is memorable for nothing else, is memorable for its superb audacity, when we recollect that as yet Mohammed's prophetic claims were treated only with contemptuous indifference, and he himself was a mere outcast:

"Woe be," he says, "on that day to those who accused the prophets of imposture!

"It shall be said unto them, Go ye into that which ye denied as a falsehood.

"Go ye into the shadow of the smoke of hell, which, though it ascend in three columns,

"Shall not shade you from the heat, neither shall it be of service against the flames;

"But it shall cast forth sparks as big as towers,

"And their color shall be like unto that of red camels.

"Woe be on that day unto those who accuse the prophets of imposture." ‡

---

* Sura lvi., 41–56.   † Sura xxii., 20–21.

‡ Sura lxxvii , 29, to end. The "Woe be," etc., is a refrain which recurs ten times in the Sura.

"What shall be our reward," asked his earliest followers of Mohammed, "if we fall in battle?" "Paradise," said the Prophet, without the slightest hesitation. In the war of Tabuk his men demurred to marching because it was harvest-time. "Your harvest, it lasts for a day," said Mohammed; "what will come of your harvest through all eternity?" They complained of the burning sun. "Hell is hotter," said the Prophet, and on they went.*

That it was desirable to dwell with so much persistence upon the enormous issues involved as regards the future life, in every act and thought of this, I am far from asserting; since self-interest, however enlightened and however refined, however even spiritualized it may be, is self-interest still. But at all events it was stern reality to Mohammed and to his followers. The future was all as real and as instant to him as it was to the Apostles when, expecting, as they did, from the interpretation they put upon Christ's words, to see him in their own lifetime coming in the clouds of heaven, they drove home their warnings by bidding men flee from "the wrath to come." In every successive crisis of the Christian Church it has been the belief of Christians

---

* Carlyle's "Heroes," p. 239; and Sura ix., 82, etc. In this expedition water was so scarce that the fainting troops were obliged to kill the camels and drink the water out of their stomachs.

that the darkest hour is that before the dawn, and it has been used, however mistakenly, yet with effect and with sincerity, to comfort the depressed, to awaken the sleeping, and to arouse the dead. "*Finem suum mundus jam non nunciat solum, sed ostendit,*" says St. Gregory amid the devastations of the Lombards. "*Appropinquante jam mundi termino,*" is the heading of even legal documents amid the deeper depression of the tenth century caused by the ravages of the Hungarians by land and the Norsemen by sea. This is the burden of St. Bernard's hymns, of Savonarola's preachings, of Bunyan's allegories. Truly, if Mohammed sinned at all in this respect, he sinned in good company.

But the future world, ever present though it was to the minds of the early Mohammedans, did not supply the motive by which they were really inspired. A selfish hope of heaven and a slavish fear of hell may act as a "negative stimulus"—may possibly teach passive resistance to temptation; but it does not nerve the arm to strike or quicken the eye to see. Perhaps, indeed, the highest heroism of all, that which consists in absolute conscious self-sacrifice or self-annihilation for the good of others—the heroism of the ideal just man in the second book of Plato's "Republic;" the heroism of Moses when he prayed to be blotted out of the Book that God had written; the heroism of a greater than

Moses when He died upon the cross—is impossible to those who believe firmly in a future life, the happiness or misery of which is to be exactly determined by the life here. But there may be true heroism even short of the truest; and all true heroism, even if it can not deny or forget its reward, is stimulated not so much by the reward as by the difficulty of obtaining it. The reward, to use an Aristotelian phrase, is an ἐπιγιγνόμενόν τι τέλος, something thrown in—an after-thought and accessory merely; and this is what a future life was to the primitive warriors of the Crescent.

Nor is it true, in any sense of the word, that Mohammed's is an easy or sensual religion. With its frequent fasts, its five prayers a day, its solitudes, its almsgivings, its pilgrimages, even in the tortures of Indian fakirs and the howlings of Mecca dervishes, which are the abuse, and not the use, of the religion — it certainly does not appeal much to the laziness or the sensuality or the selfishness of mankind.

In his capacity even of temporal ruler, Mohammed rarely gave material rewards to his followers. Abu Bakr, Ali, Omar, Hamza, when in his early days they ranged themselves as friends around the then friendless enthusiast, sacrificed, as it must have appeared to them, all their worldly hopes; they little thought that they were enrolling themselves in that most select band of heroes who may be said to have made History. On one occasion, late in his life, Mohammed did give some material rewards to recent and perhaps half-hearted converts, but the exception only proved the rule, and that in the most memorable manner. The Helpers of Medina were naturally dissatisfied, but Mohammed recalled them to their allegiance by words which went straight from his heart to theirs: that he had given things of the world to those who cared for such things, but to them he had given himself. Others returned home with sheep and camels, the Helpers with the Prophet of God. Verily, if all the men of the earth went one way, and the Helpers of Medina another, he would go the way of the Helpers of Medina.* The Helpers burst into tears, and exclaimed that they were more than satisfied with what he had given them. And, just before his death, Mohammed commended these same Helpers of Medina to the protection of the exiles who had accompanied him from Mecca. "Hold in honor," said he, "the Helpers of Medina; the number of believers may increase, but that of the Helpers never can.† They were my family, and with them I found

---

* Alluded to in Sura lix., 8, 9; viii , 42. See Muir, vol. iv., p. 151–154.

† Cf. Herodotus, iii., 119: ὦ βασιλεῦ, ἀνὴρ μέν μοι ἂν ἄλλος γένοιτο, εἰ δαίμων ἐθέλοι, καὶ τέκνα ἄλλα, εἰ ταῦτα ἀποβάλοιμι· πατρὸς δὲ καὶ μητρὸς οὐκ ἔτι μευ ζωόντων ἀδελφεὸς ἂν ἄλλος οὐδενὶ τρόπῳ γένοιτο. Cf. also Soph., *Antigone*, 909–912.

a home; do good to those who do good to them, and break friendship with those who are hostile to them."

Perhaps there is no remark one has heard more often about Mohammedanism than that it was so successful because it was so sensual; but there is none more destitute of truth, as if any religion could owe its permanent success to its bad morality! I do not say that its morality is perfect, or equal to the Christian morality. Mohammed did not make the manners of Arabia, and he was too wise to think that he could either unmake or remake them all at once. Solon remarked of his own legislation that his laws were not the best that he could devise, but that they were the best the Athenians could receive; and his defense has generally been accepted as a sound one. Moses took the institutions of a primitive society as he found them—the patriarchal power, internecine war, blood feuds, the right of asylum, polygamy, and slavery—and did not abolish any one of them; he only mitigated their worst evils, and so unconsciously prepared the way in some cases for their greater permanence, in others for their eventual extinction.

In like manner the religion of Christ did not sweep into oblivion any national or political institutions. He contented himself with planting principles in the hearts of his followers which would, when the time was ripe for it, work out their abolition. Willing to sow if others could reap, to labor if others could enter into his labors, he cast into the ground the grain of mustardseed, and was content, with the eye of faith alone, to see it grow into the mighty tree whose branches should overspread the world, and whose leaves should be for the healing of the nations. With sublime self-restraint and self-sacrifice, governed by his thought for the boundless possibilities of the future of his Church, rather than by the impulse of the moment, he forbore to denounce in so many words the inveterate evils of the Roman Empire, which must have gone to his soul's soul—foreign conquest, tyranny, the amphitheatre, slavery. He even used words which have been wrongly construed to mean that at all times passive obedience is a duty, and that the people have nothing to do with the laws but to obey them. Nor has the Christian Church—sections of which have for strange and various, but intelligible, reasons canonized a Constantine and a Vladimir, a Cyril and a Charles the Great, a Dunstan and a Becket —ever attached the name of Saint to some who, in the fullness of time, have carried out far more fully and in spirit Christ's work, albeit in seeming contradiction to the letter of the law which inculcated submission to existing powers and institutions—to a Telemachus or a Theodoric, to an Alfred or a Wilberforce. And yet no Christian will deny that the monk Telemachus, who threw himself between the swords of the gladiators, and, braving the fury of the spectators athirst for blood, accomplished by his death what his life could never have won, did a deed which all the "Acta Sanctorum" could be searched to parallel.

Now Mohammed was a legislator and a statesman, as well as the founder of a religion; and why is the defense which we allow to Solon, and the praise we bestow upon the limited scope of the Mosaic legislation, denied to Islam?

Polygamy is, indeed, next to caste, the most blighting institution to which a nation can become a prey. It pollutes society at the fountain-head, for the family is the source of all political and of all social virtues. Mohammed would have more than doubled the debt of gratitude the Eastern world owes to him had he swept it away; but he could not have done so, even if he had fully seen its evils. It is not fair to represent polygamy as a part of Mohammedanism any more than it is fair to represent slavery as a part of Christianity. The one co-exists with the other without being mixed with it, even as the muddy Arve and the clear Rhone keep their currents distinct long after they have been united in one river-bed. Perhaps it is strange that they ever could have co-existed, even for a day; but we have to deal with facts as they are; and it is a fact that slavery has co-existed with Christianity—nay, has professed to justify itself by Christianity — even till this nineteenth century. Mohammed could not have made a *tabula rasa* of Eastern society, but what he could do he did. He at least put strict limitations on the unbounded license of Eastern polygamy* and the facility of Eastern divorce.† If the two social touchstones of a religion are the way in which, relatively to the time, it deals with the weaker sex, and the way in which it regards the poor and the oppressed, Mohammed's religion can stand the test.‡ He improved the condition of women by freeing them from the arbitrary patriarchal power of the parents or the heirs of their husbands, by inculcating just and kind treatment of them by their husbands themselves, by giving them legal rights in case of unfair treatment, and by absolutely prohibiting the

---

* Sura iv., 3, etc.

† Sura iv., 39 and 127; xxxiii., 48, 52, etc.

‡ Among many other illustrations of this see (*a*) the oath taken early in his life with other Koreishites, "to defend the oppressed so long as a drop of water remained in the ocean," an act the remembrance of which Mohammed said "he would not exchange for the choicest camel in Arabia;" (*b*) the account given by Jafar to the Najashy of Abyssinia of the change wrought by Mohammed among his followers; perhaps the noblest and truest summary we have of the moral teaching of the Prophet; (*c*) the pledge of Acaba, A.D. 621, taken by his first converts from Medina; (*d*) Sura ii., 170: "'There is no piety in turning your faces toward the East or the West, but he is pious who believeth in God; . . . who for the love of God distributeth his wealth to his kindred, and to the orphans, and the needy, and the wayfarer."

incestuous marriages which were rife in the times of ignorance, and the still more horrible practice of the burying alive of female infants.* Nor was this all, for besides imposing restrictions on polygamy, by his severe laws at first, and by the strong moral sentiment aroused by these laws afterward, he has succeeded, down to this very day, and to a greater extent than has ever been the case elsewhere, in freeing all Mohammedan countries from those professional outcasts who live by their own misery, and, by their existence as a recognized class, are a standing reproach to every member of the society of which they form a part.

Mohammed did not abolish slavery altogether, for in that condition of society it would have been neither possible nor desirable to do so; but he encouraged the emancipation of slaves; he laid down the principle that every slave that embraced Islam should be *ipso facto* free, and, what is more important, he took care that no stigma should attach to the emancipated slave in consequence of his honest and honorable life of labor. In Islam the emancipated slave is actually, as well as potentially, equal to a free-born citizen, and he often rises to one of the highest posts in the empire.† As to those

---

* Sura vi., 138, 141, 152.

† Zeid, the freedman of the Prophet, often took the command in war. Captain Burton mentions ("Pilgrimage," vol. i., p. 89) that the pacha

who continued slaves, he prescribed kindness and consideration in dealing with them.* "See," he said, in his parting address at Mina, the year before his death—"see that ye feed them with such food as ye eat yourselves, and clothe them with the stuff ye yourselves wear; for they are the servants of the Lord, and are not to be tormented." The equality of all men before God was a principle which Mohammed every where maintained; and which, taking, as it did, all caste feeling from slavery, took away also its chief sting. To Mohammed's mind labor could never be degrading, and the domestic slavery of the Arabs, under which, thanks to him, parents were never to be separated from their children, nor indeed relations from each other at all, though always to be condemned in the abstract, became, under the Prophet's hands, a bond closer and more lasting, and hardly more liable to abuse, than domestic service elsewhere.

The orphan, too, is the subject of his peculiar care, for he had been an orphan himself; and what God

---

of the Syrian caravan with which he traveled to Damascus had been the slave of a slave. Sebuktegin, the father of the magnificent Mahmoud, and founder of the Ghaznevide dynasty, was a slave; so was Kutb-ud-din, the conqueror and first king of Delhi, and the true founder, therefore, of the Mohammedan Empire in India. (See Elphinstone's "India," p. 320, 363, 370.)

* Sura xxiv., 34, 57.

had done for him, he was anxious, as far as might be, to do for others.* The poor were always present with him, and their condition never absent from his mind. In one of his early Suras, " the steep," as he calls it— that is to say, the straight and narrow way—is said to be to release the captive, to give food to the poor that lieth in the dust, and to stir up one another to steadfastness and compassion.† And in another Sura, Jews and Arabs are alike warned in their exclusive pride in their common progenitor, Abraham, that verily the nearest of kin to Abraham are they who follow him in his works.‡

Nor does Mohammed omit to lay stress on what I venture to think is as crucial a test of a moral code, and even of a religion, as is the treatment of the poor and the weak—I mean the duties we owe to what we call the lower animals. There is no religion which has taken a higher view of animal life in its authoritative documents, and none wherein the precept has been so much honored by its practical observance. "There is no beast on earth," says the Koran,§ "nor bird which flieth with its wings, but the same is a people like unto you—unto the Lord shall they return;" and it is the current belief that animals will share with men the

---

* Sura viii., 42, and xciii., 6, to end.
† Sura xc., 12, 15, and *passim*.
‡ Sura iii., 61.   § Sura vi., 38, and Sale's note *ad loc.*

general resurrection, and be judged according to their works. At the slaughter of an animal, the Prophet ordered that God should always be named, but the words "the Compassionate, the Merciful," were to be omitted; for on the one hand such an expression seemed a mockery to the sufferer, and, on the other, he could not bring himself to believe that the destruction of any life, however necessary, could be altogether pleasing to the All Merciful. "In the name of God," says a pious Mussulman, before he strikes the fatal blow—"God is most great; God give thee patience to endure the affliction which he hath allotted thee!"* In the East there has been no moralist like Bentham to insist in noble words on the extension of the sphere of morality to all sentient beings, and to be ridiculed for it by people who call themselves religious; there has been no naturalist like Darwin to demonstrate by his marvelous powers of observation how large a part of the mental and moral faculties which we usually claim for ourselves alone we share with other beings; there has been no Oriental "Society for the Prevention of Cruelty to Animals;" but one reason of this is not far to seek. What the legislation of the last few years has at length attempted to do, and, from the mere fact that it is legis-

---

* Lane's "Modern Egyptians," vol. i., p. 119.

lation, must do ineffectually, has been long effected in the East by the moral and religious sentiment which, like almost every thing that is good in that part of the world, can be traced back, in part at least, to the great Prophet of Arabia.* In the East, so far as it has not been hardened by the West, there is a real sympathy between man and the domestic animals; they understand one another, and the cruelties which the most humane of our countrymen unconsciously inflict in the habitual use, for instance, of the muzzle or the bearing-rein on the most docile, the most patient, the most faithful, and the most intelligent of their companions, are impossible in the East. An Arab *can not* ill-treat his horse; and Lane bears emphatic testimony to the fact that in his long residence in Egypt he never saw an ass or a dog (though the latter is there looked upon as an unclean animal) treated with

---

* The sympathy of the Prophet for his domestic animals is well known. There is a great variety of traditions respecting his horses, his mules, his milch and riding camels, and his goats. It would be easy to write a complete biography of his favorite she-camel, Al Kaswa. Her eccentricities and perversities exercised an influence on some critical occasions in the Prophet's life—*e. g.*, on his entrance to Medina, and at Kodeiba. Among the phenomena attending Mohammed's fits, it is recorded that if one came on him while riding, his camel itself became first wildly excited, and then fixed and rigid! And I have little doubt that the story arose from the almost electric sympathy that exists between an intelligent animal that is kindly treated and its master.

cruelty, except in those cities which were overrun by Europeans.*

By absolutely prohibiting gambling and intoxicating liquors, Mohammed did much to abolish, once and for all, over the vast regions that own his sway, two of the worst and most irremediable evils of European society: evils to the intensity of which the Christian governments of the nineteenth century are hardly yet beginning to awake.† Can any one then deny what I have already hinted above, that, looking at him merely as a moral reformer, and apart from his great religious revolution, Mohammed was really doing Christ's work, even if he had reverenced Christ less than in fact he did?

And this brings me to the most important question that I shall touch upon in this Lecture; and one but for which, in its various bearings, I do not know that I should have written these Lectures: I mean the attitude that Christianity ought to bear to Mohammedanism now. To say that in spite of the theoretic intolerance of Mohammedanism, it ought, unless its theory is put into practice, itself to be tolerated, is happily now a mere truism. But it ought not to be treated with a merely contemptuous or distant recognition, or to be inserted *tanquam infamiæ causâ*—" Jews, Turks, Infidels, and

---

* Lane, vol. i., p. 359-361. † Sura v., 92.

Heretics"—in a collect, once a year, upon that day of all others upon which the universality of Christ's self-sacrifice is brought before us. When the draft of a treaty was brought to the General of the armies of revolutionary France, the first clause of which contained a formal recognition by the Emperor Francis of Austria—the representative of legitimacy, absolutism, and divine right—of the existence of the French Republic, "Strike that clause out," said Napoleon; "the French Republic needs no recognition from him—it is as clear as the sun at noonday." Mohammedanism needs no formal recognition of its existence by a faith with which it has so much in common. The immemorial quarrel between Mohammedanism and Christianity is, after all, a quarrel between near relations; and, like most immemorial quarrels, is based chiefly on mutual misunderstandings. Without any appearance of extraordinary condescension, we should recognize the fact which Mohammedans themselves might at present certainly be inclined to deny, that Islam is the nearest approach to Christianity—I would almost call it, remembering Mohammed's intense reverence for Christ, the only form of Christianity—which has proved itself suited to the nations of the East. Even Dante placed Mohammed in the "Inferno," not as a heathen, but as a heretic; and is there any reason who our notion of Christianity should be less comprehensive than his?

Mohammedanism is the one religion in the world, besides our own and the Jewish, which is strictly and avowedly Monotheistic. "Dispute not," said Mohammed to his followers, "against those who have received the Scriptures, that is, Jews and Christians, except with gentleness; but say unto them we believe in the revelation which hath been sent down to us, and also in that which hath been sent down to you; and our God and your God is one."* And again he says in another place, "Verily the Believers, and those who are Jews, those who are Christians and Sabeans, whoever believeth in God, and the last day, and doeth that which is right, they shall have their reward with their Lord—there shall come no fear upon them, neither shall they be grieved."† The three creeds are branches from the same parent stock, not different stocks; and they all alike look back to the majestic character of Abraham

---

* Sura v., 73.

† Sura ii., 59. There is a still more striking passage in v., 52-53: "Unto every one have we given a law and a way. Now if God had pleased, he would surely have made you one people, but he hath made you to differ that he might try you in that which he hath given to each, therefore strive to excel each other in good works. Unto God shall ye all return, and he will tell you that concerning which ye have disagreed."
—Cf. Acts x., 35. These are passages on which the comparative mythologist, the Mussulman reformer, and the Christian missionary would alike do well to dwell. It is noteworthy also that the fifth Sura, from which two of them come, is placed by Rodwell and others last in the chronological order.

as the first teacher of the unity of God. Mohammed says, again and again, that the belief he inculcates is no new belief—it is the original creed of El-Khalil Allah, the Friend of God. The heroes of the Old Testament history, Isaac and Jacob, Joseph and Joshua, David and Solomon, are heroes of the Mohammedan religion as well as of the Jewish and Christian.

I remarked in my second Lecture that Mohammed may have thought himself justified in breaking the moral law he himself imposed, because a somewhat similar concession had been made to Moses. This is not a mere conjecture on my part, for it is certain that Mohammed had, for one who was so careless of facts, acquired somehow a full and fairly accurate knowledge of the history of the great Lawgiver. He relates it at length,* and recurs to it with a passionate fondness from an early period in his career, evidently dwelling mentally on the striking parallels between himself and Moses, the shepherd life, the call to the Prophet's office, the rejection by their own countrymen, no less than—be it always remembered to Mohammed's credit that he does not disguise it—the main point of difference, the prodigality of miracles performed by the one, and the inability to work them in the other. One most sa-

---

* See especially Suras vii., xviii., xxvii., xxviii., lv.

cred spot actually connects the two Prophets together. There is a tradition, to some extent authenticated, that Mohammed drove the camels of Kadijah to the very place where Moses had tended the flocks of Jethro. Moses and Mohammed may have reposed on the same rock, watered their cattle at the same springs, looked upon the same weird mountains.* And it is a redeeming point, perhaps the only redeeming point, in the melancholy history of St. Catharine's Monastery, that from age to age, within the convent walls, mosque and church have stood side by side, and Mussulmans and Christians have knelt together worshiping the same God; and there, if only there in the world, venerating with a kindred, if not with an equal reverence, the same prophets, Moses and Mohammed, and One who is infinitely greater than them both.†

Again, Mohammedanism is essentially a spiritual religion. As instituted by Mohammed it had "no priest and no sacrifice;"‡ in other words, no caste of sacri-

---

* Sura ii., 57; vii., 160.

† See the account of St. Catharine's and its degradation in "The Desert of the Exodus," by E. H. Palmer; and in Stanley's "Sinai and Palestine," p. 53, 54. It is said that at Nijni Novgorod the same phenomenon, mosque and church as near and not unfriendly neighbors, may be observed; but there no doubt it is commerce rather than religious sympathy which we have to thank for it.

‡ The sacrifice at the Annual Pilgrimage is a mere relic of the Pagan practice; it has little religious significance, and does not imply priest-

ficing priests were ever to be allowed to come between the human soul and God: forbidding the representation of all living things alike, whether as objects of use or of admiration, of veneration or of worship, Mohammedanism is more opposed to idolatry even than we are ourselves. Mohammed hated images more sternly even than the Iconoclasts of Constantinople or the soldiers of Cromwell. Every mosque in the world of Islam bears witness to this. Statuary and pictures being forbidden, variegated marbles, and festoons of lamps, and geometric shapes, and tortuous inscriptions from the Koran have to supply their place as best they can, and form that peculiar species of ornamentation, strictly confined to the inanimate world, which we call Arabesque; and which is still to be traced in the architecture of so many churches and so many mosques along the frontier line of four thousand miles which divides the realm of the Crescent from that of the Cross.*

---

craft; it indicates only the belief that sin deserves death. In orthodox Mohammedanism there is no priestly caste, and therefore no fictions of apostolical succession, inherent sanctity, indissoluble vows, or powers of absolution. See Palgrave's "Essays," p. 82.

* Cf. Stanley's "Lectures on the Eastern Church," p. 273. Without discussing the general question at length, I may remark here that Gothic architecture, though it is not very ready to acknowledge the debt, owes much to Moorish architecture—in particular the Horse-shoe or Crescent Arch. The pointed arch itself is to be found in many early mosques, and some of the most famous Venetian buildings, St. Mark's among them, owe much to Saracenic architecture.

This hatred of idolatry has been found even among the most uncivilized followers of the Prophet. The gorgeous ritual, the gaudy pictures, and the pious frauds which play so large a part in the conversion of the Sclavonian nations to Christianity seem only to have alienated these semi-barbarians. Mahmoud, the Ghaznevide, the son of a slave and the conqueror of Hindoostan, was offered a sum of ten millions sterling if only he would spare the famous idol in the pagoda of Somnat. Avarice is said to have been his besetting fault, but he replied in the memorable words, "Never shall Mahmoud be handed down to posterity as an idol seller, rather than an idol destroyer;" and broke it into pieces.*

Finally: Mohammedanism, in spite of centuries of wars and misunderstandings, looks back upon the Founder of our religion with reverence only less than that with which the most devout Christians regard him.

So far from its being true, as is commonly supposed, that Mohammedans regard Christ as Christians have too often regarded Mohammed, with hatred and with contempt, Sir William Muir remarks that devout Mussulmans never mention the name of Seyyedna Eesa, or

---

* Ferishta's "History of Mohammedan Power in India" (Briggs's translation), vol. i., p. 72; and Elphinstone's "History of India," p. 336.

Our Lord Jesus, without adding the words "on whom be peace." The highest honor that a Mussulman can conceive is given to Christ in the grave reserved for him by the side of the Prophet himself in the great mosque at Medina. Mohammedans expect that he will one day return to earth, and having slain Antichrist, will establish perfect peace among men. And Mr. Hunter* tells us that the Indian Sheeahs avowedly look forward to his reappearance simultaneously with that of the last of their twelve Imams, and to an amalgamation of the two creeds: of Islam as the followers of Ali hold it, and of Christianity, not as it is, but as they believe it was taught by Christ himself.†

If it be asked, why then did Mohammed not accept Christianity, I apprehend that the reasons are threefold; and that it appears, from the chronological order lately assigned to the Suras of the Koran, that at one period, that of the Fatrah, Mohammed did consider whether first Judaism, and secondly Christianity, as he knew it, contained the message he had to give.

I. The first explanation I would suggest is, that the Christ known to him was the Christ, not of the Bible,

---

* "Our Indian Mussulmans," p. 120, by W.W. Hunter.

† For a curious discussion on the return of the Messiah to earth held at Timbuctoo, see Barth's "Travels in Central Africa," vol. v., p. 4.

but of tradition; the Christ, not of the Canonical, but of the Apocryphal Gospels, and even these only from general tradition. The wonder is, Mohammed's information being confined to the incoherent rhapsodies and the miraculous inanities of the Gospels of the Infancy, the Acta Pilati and the "Descensus ad Inferos," not that he reverenced Christ so little, but so much. In the whole of the Koran there are only three passages which look like any direct acquaintance with the Evangelists; and one of these, the well-known passage about the Paraclete, he misunderstands himself, and accuses Christians of intentionally perverting from its proper meaning a prediction of the coming of the Periclyte, the Greek form of Mohammed, the Illustrious, or the Praised.*

II. Secondly, the worship of saints and images, and the shape which certain floating ideas had taken when they were stereotyped in the formulas of the Christian Church, seemed to Mohammed to conflict with his fundamental doctrine of the unity of God. The mysteries of the Trinity were to be appraised and handled by every one who called himself a Christian, not merely as a test, but as the test of his Christianity. Mohammed accuses even the Jews of having lost sight of their pri-

---

* Sura lxi., 6.

mary truth, which was also his, in calling Ezra the Son of God;* and what wonder if he rejected a religion the essence of which he understood, and too many Christians of his time understood, to be, not a holy life, but, as it is still represented in the Athanasian Creed, an elaborate and unthinkable mode of thinking of the Trinity?†

Let us hear on these points Mohammed himself, remembering all the while how slight was his knowledge of the doctrine which he travestied, and how dim the outline of the majestic character which yet filled his imagination:

"They surely are infidels who say God is the third of three, for there is no god but one God."‡

"Say not three; forbear, it will be better for thee; God is only one God."§

Christ was with Mohammed the greatest of Prophets.‖ He had the power of working miracles; he spoke

---

* Sura ix., 30.

† It is doubtful whether a people that has once become monotheistic in any other form than the Christian can ever be brought to accept, I do not say Christianity altogether, but the doctrines that are often supposed to be of its very essence. Among such a people the missionary invariably finds that the doctrine of the Trinity, however explained, involves Tritheism, and their ears are at once closed to his teaching. To a Pagan who accepts Christianity the change no doubt is one from Polytheism to Monotheism, but to the Jew or Mohammedan, except in very rare instances, it is the opposite.

‡ Sura v., 77.   § Sura iv., 6.   ‖ Sura ii., 254.

in his cradle; he made a bird out of clay. (Incidents drawn from the Gospels of the Infancy or of St. Thomas.) He could give sight to the blind, and even raise the dead to life.* He is the Word proceeding from God; his name is the Messiah. Illustrious in this world and in the next, and one of those who have near access to God.† "He is strengthened by the Holy Spirit," for so Mohammed, in more than one passage, calls the Angel Gabriel.‡ Mohammed all but believes in the Immaculate Conception of the Virgin,§ and certainly in the miraculous nature of the birth of Christ, to which he recurs repeatedly.‖ But that Jesus ever claimed, as is affirmed by the writers of the New Testament, and as we know he did, to be the Son of God, still less that he ever claimed to be equal with God, Mohammed could not bring himself to believe.

"It becometh not a man that God should give him the Scriptures, and the Wisdom, and the spirit of Prophecy, and that then he should say to his followers, Be ye worshipers of me as well as of God; but rather, Be

---

* Sura iii., 41–43.   † Sura iii., 40.   ‡ Sura ii., 81.

§ Sura iii., 30. There was a well-known sect of Christians called Collyridians in Arabia who paid the Virgin divine honors, and offered her a twisted cake (κόλλυρις). Thence, no doubt, came Mohammed's idea that the Virgin was one of the Persons of the Trinity.

‖ Sura xix., 20.

ye perfect in things pertaining to God, since ye know the Scriptures, and have studied them."*

And again, "For the Messiah himself said, O children of Israel, worship God, my Lord and yours."†

And once more, "Those who say that Jesus, the Son of Mary, is the Son of God, are infidels, for who could stop the arm of God if he were to destroy the Messiah and his mother, and all who are in the earth together?"‡

Neither can Mohammed ever believe that Jesus could have been crucified. "It is so long ago, let us hope that it is not true," said an old Cumberland woman when she heard for the first time in her life the story of the Crucifixion. "If I and my brave Franks had been there, we would have avenged his injuries," was the exclamation of the fierce barbarian Clovis when he received his first lesson in the Christian life. The Dreamer of the Desert sympathized rather with the first of these. As Stesichorus§ believed that the Greeks and Trojans fought for the phantom of Helen, and not for Helen herself; as the Docetists held that the phantom of Jesus and not Jesus had been crucified; so Mohammed rebels at the thought that God can ever have allowed such a tragedy to take place. Some one else, he curiously supposes, who deserved such a death—perhaps

---

* Sura iii., 73.
† Sura v., 76.
‡ Sura v., 19.
§ Plato, "Republic," ix., 386.

it was Judas himself—may have been substituted for Christ; and Christ being taken up to heaven, must have felt that the deception thus practiced on the Jews was a kind of punishment to himself for not having taken greater pains to prevent men calling him the Son of God.* And at the resurrection Jesus will himself testify against both Jews and Christians; the Jews for not having received him as a prophet, the Christians for having received him as God.

There is a short chapter in the Koran which Mussulmans look upon as equal to a third of the whole in value:

> "Say there is one God alone—
> God the Eternal;
> He begetteth not, and he is not begotten,
> And there is none like unto him."†

And once more, "They say the Merciful hath gotten offspring. Now have ye done a monstrous thing; almost might the very heavens rend thereat, and the earth rend asunder, and the mountains fall down in fragments, that they ascribe a son to the Merciful, when it becometh not the Merciful to beget a son. Verily there is nobody in the heavens nor in the earth that shall approach the Merciful but as a servant." ‡

I have dwelt thus at length upon Mohammed's views

---

* Sura iii., 49; iv., 156. † Sura cxii. ‡ Sura xix., 91-94.

of Christ, partly because of the intrinsic interest and importance attaching to the views held by one so great of one so infinitely greater; partly because they show how little Mohammed, and indeed how little Christians themselves, understood the real nature of Christianity; partly also because the strictures of Mohammed, however exaggerated and however mistaken, seem to me to suggest a caution necessary for us all. Christ came to reveal God, not to hide him; to bring him down to earth, not to shroud him in an immeasurable distance; to tell us that God is not primarily Justice, or Truth, or Power, but Love. Do Christians always remember this? Are our views of Justification, of Original Sin, of a Future Life, when drawn out in the forensic and almost legal language in which some churches foolishly delight to clothe them, always consistent with it? Do our prayers always pre-suppose a God who, in his own intrinsic nature, is anxious to receive them? Are we not apt to forget the unity of God while we dogmatize on the Trinity? Do we not sometimes place Christ, as it were, in front of God, thinking so much of the Son who sacrificed himself that we ignore the Father who "spared him not"—forgetting the Giver in the very magnitude of the gift?

III. And the third reason, and perhaps the most important of all, for Mohammed's rejection of Christianity, is the fact that Christianity as he knew it had been tried and had failed. It had been known for three hundred years in Arabia, and had not been able to overthrow, or even weaken, the idolatry of the inhabitants.

It is strange, with this fact and the whole course of history before him, with which evidently few are more familiar, that a great writer can conclude a review of Mohammedanism, which is otherwise fair and able, by indorsing the charge made against it that it has kept back the East by hindering the spread of Christianity. The charge has been often made before,* but it rests on so slender a basis that I should not have thought it necessary to discuss it here had I not found at the last moment that one who is apparently so high an authority has lent the weight of his name to it. That I may do him no injustice, I quote his own words:

"Mohammed in his own age and country was the greatest of reformers—a reformer alike religious, moral, and political. . . . But when his system passed the borders of the land in which it was so great a reform, it became the greatest of curses to mankind. The main cause which has made the religion of Mohammed exercise so blighting an influence on every land where it has been preached, is because it is an imperfect system

---

* As, for instance, by Sir W. Muir, vol. iv., p. 321.

standing in the way of one more perfect. Islam has in it just enough of good to hinder the reception of greater good. . . . Because Islam comes nearer to Christianity than any other false system, because it comes nearer than any other to satisfying the wants of man's spiritual nature, for that very reason it is, above all other false systems, pre-eminently anti-Christian. It is, as it were, the personal enemy and rival of the Faith, disputing on equal terms for the same prize!"*

This indictment is so well drawn, at first sight it so carries conviction with it, and yet, if true, it is so fatal to any favorable or any fair judgment of Mohammedanism, that I am compelled, while I gladly acknowledge the author's fair and sympathetic treatment of the subject in every page that precedes and follows those I have quoted, to contest, from my point of view, as strongly as I can, upon this question, alike his facts and his inferences.

Upon what single fact, then, either before or after Mohammed's time, does the writer ground this charge? If the purest Christianity of all, preached by Christ and his Apostles, did not make way in the Eastern world; if the few Christian churches which did exist among the half Roman or Hellenic inhabitants of Syria and of

---

* *British Quarterly Review*, Jan., 1872, p. 132–134.

Africa had sunk to the condition in which we know they were when Mohammedanism swept them away, what reason have we, either *à priori* or *à posteriori*, for supposing that the Christianity of any later time would have been more successful? Have Christian nations been so energetic or so successful in converting any of those African or Asiatic nations which Mohammedanism has never reached, as to entitle us to turn round upon the religion which has remoulded so large a portion of the human race, and tell it that it is a curse to humanity because, forsooth, while we admit it was in its time a grand forward movement and has been a higher life to untold millions since, we wish that Fetich worship should have lasted on perhaps till now, that Christianity may now have the chance of doing the work somewhat better? If this is Christianity, I only say most certainly it is not of Christ. It is not of the spirit of him who said that those who were not against him were with him; and rejoiced that good was done by others, even if it seemed an infringement of his own divine commission. Christ was not like the Prætorian prefect of Tacitus, "*Consilii, quamvis egregii, quod non ipse afferret inimicus,*" though some Christians would have it that he was. The only monopoly of good that Christianity, if it is of the spirit of its Founder, may claim, is the monopoly, not of doing good, but of rejoicing at it whenever it is done, and whoever does it; of showing, if it carries out its Founder's intentions, that it is wide enough to recognize as its own and to embrace within its ample bosom all honest "seekers after God," and all true benefactors of humanity. The most "anti-Christian" religion is not that which comes nearest to Christianity, but that which is furthest removed from it; and the religion which after Christianity comes nearest to "satisfying the wants of man's spiritual nature" is really not its most deadly enemy, but its best ally. To say otherwise, liberal and tolerant as the author unquestionably is, is to encourage weaker men under the shadow of his name,* not merely to indulge in the *odium theologicum*, but to assert that the *odium theologicum* itself is Christian.

>"Non tali auxilio nec defensoribus istis
>   Tempus eget."

Can it be forgotten that the churches planted by the great Apostle were, without exception, to the west of Palestine—that star-worship and fire-worship were unaffected by Christianity then, even as Brahminism and Buddhism are unaffected by it now? Can we point to a

---

* This has actually been the case, for the passage I have quoted was the only one in an otherwise most temperate essay upon which religious periodicals pounced, and, by quoting apart from its context, fanned the flame of misconception and prejudice which, even when read with every thing which tends the other way, it would, in my judgment, be likely to kindle.

single Oriental nation which has been able to accept and to retain Christianity in its pure form, or to a single religion to be named with Mohammedanism in point of purity and sublimity, which has ever been able to overthrow any national Oriental faith? And, if we can not, what right have we to say that it is Islam, and not Nature, that has hitherto stood in the way of Christianity in Arabia and Persia, in Africa and India? The triumphs of the Cross have indeed been far purer, far wider, far sublimer than those of the Crescent; but they have been hitherto confined to the higher races of the world. Uncivilized nations of the higher stock—Ostrogoths and Visigoths, Vandals and Lombards, Franks and Northmen, the Celt, the Teuton, and the Sclavonian—invaded Christianity only to be conquered by it. But upon the Oriental barbarians of a lower race who invaded Europe, with the one exception of the Magyars, whose case is special *—Huns and Avars, Turks and Tartars—it has

---

* The Magyars, whatever their original home—and it seems that they were of the Finnish stock—are probably the most mixed race on the Continent of Europe, and were so even before they settled within the limits of the present Hungary. In their march toward Europe they were joined by hosts of Chazars, Bulgarians, and Sclavonians. During their ravages, which lasted for some fifty years, and spread from the Oural Mountains to the Pyrenees, they transported women and children wholesale from the countries they overran to their head-quarters on the Danube; and it is probable that at the time of their avowed conversion by Adalbert, about A.D. 1000, they had at least as much German and Italian as they had Tartar blood in their veins. St. Piligrinus (quoted by Gibbon,

had no influence. Shall Christians, then, complain of Mohammedans for having succeeded in some measure in doing for the East what they have failed to do; or would Christ have rejected what good service Mohammed did because his credentials were not precisely those of the Apostles? What superficial appearance of truth there is in the charge is this—that no Mohammedan nation has hitherto accepted Christianity, while some nations that were nominally Christians have accepted Mohammedanism. But to establish the charge it would, of course, be necessary to show that the East, if it had not accepted Mohammedanism, would have accepted a real Christianity, or any religion so much like Christianity as Mohammedanism unquestionably is; and to do this we must read history backward.

Now Mohammed offered to the Arabs an idea of God less sympathetic and less lovable, indeed, but as sublime as the Christian, and perhaps still more intense, and one, as it turned out, which they could receive. Christianity was compelled to leave its birthplace—the inhabitants and subsequent history of which it has scarcely affected, except indirectly—to find its proper home in the Western world, among the inhabitants and progressive civil-

---

vol. vii., p. 172), the first missionary who entered Hungary, says that he found the "majority of the population to be Christians," *qui ex omni parte mundi illuc tracti sunt captivi.*

ization of Greece and Rome. The lot of Mohammedanism has been different; "it is the religion of the shepherd and the nomad, of the burning desert and the boundless steppe." So admirably suited was it to the region in which it was born, that it needed no foreign air or change of circumstances to develop it.*

In its simple grandeur it has been able, without tampering with that which is its Alpha and Omega—the belief in one God, who reveals himself by his prophets —to leave the most essential elements of national life to the various nations which made up the Arabian Empire; and to adapt itself to every peculiarity, mental and moral, of the inhabitants of Central and Western Asia. The rapid intuition and the wild flights of imagination; the vivid mental play around the antinomies of the reason, and the craving for the supernatural in the utmost particularity of detail; the fervid asceticism of the Dervish, and the mystic Pantheism of the Soufy, have each found in Islam something to meet their wants.

But, on the other hand, Mohammedanism has never passed into countries of a wholly different nature, and held them permanently. Spain is not a case in point, though it was never so well governed as under the Mohammedans; for the Spaniards themselves never became

---

* Compare throughout this paragraph, M. Barthélemy St. Hilaire, p. 230, seq.

Mohammedan, and the Moorish settlement there was only like a Greek ἐπιτείχισμα or a Roman colonia—an outpost in the heart of the enemy's country. Much the same may be said of Turkey, where the subject population has always remained Christian. I can not, therefore, "*pace tanti nominis*," follow Gibbon in his picture of the probable consequences to European civilization had Charles Martel been conquered at Tours—of Mussulman preachers demonstrating to a circumcised audience, in the mosques of Paris and of Oxford, the truth of the religion of Mohammed! The wave of conquest might have spread over Europe; but it would have been but a wave, and few traces would have been left when it had swept on. In Africa the case was different; the Greek colonists and Roman conquerors—the higher races, in fact—were driven out by the Saracens, and, "in their climate and habits, the wandering Moors who remained behind already resembled the Bedouins of the desert."* Mohammedanism is the only form in which the knowledge of the true God has ever made way with the native races of Africa; and the form of Christianity which it supplanted in the North—the Christianity of the Donatists and of the Nitrian monks; of Cyril, strangely called a saint; and of the infamous George of

---

* Gibbon, vol. vi., p. 473.

Cappadocia, still more strangely transformed into St. George of England, the patron of chivalry and of the Garter—was infinitely inferior to Mohammedanism itself.

I fully admit that Mohammedanism, if indeed it had succeeded in conquering the most civilized races of the world and the Christianity of the West, as it succeeded in conquering the Eastern nations and their various forms of belief, would have conquered something that was potentially better than itself, and then it would have been what Christian writers are so fond of calling it—a curse to the world rather than a blessing. It would have stepped beyond what I conceive to have been its proper mission; but I maintain that it stopped short of this, and that it destroyed nothing that was not far inferior to itself. I should hesitate to say that even its conquest of Spain was not, while it lasted, a blessing to Spain itself, and through Spain to the whole of Europe. Has Spain exhibited more order, more toleration, more industry, better faith, more material prosperity, under her most Christian Kings or under her Ommiade Kaliphs? The names of the three Abdal Rahmans, and of Almamun, suggest all that is most glorious in Spanish history, and much that has conferred benefit on the rest of Europe in the darkest period of her annals—religious zeal without religious intolerance, philosophy and literature, science and art, hospitals and libraries and universities.

It follows, from what I have said, that Mohammedanism is not a world-wide religion. The sphere of its influence is vast, but not boundless; in catholicity of application it is as much below the purest Christianity as the Semitic and Turanian nations which have embraced it are below the Western Indo-Germanic. I say the Western Indo-Germanic races, for among the Eastern branches of that great family, the inhabitants of Persia and of Hindoostan, Mohammedanism did establish itself.

The Persians are of a race and genius widely different from the Arabs; but the surroundings and the general mode of life are the same in each, and the exception, so far as it is an exception, to the rule I have laid down, tends rather, in its results, to prove its general truth, for the hold of Mohammedanism on them has been much modified by the difference of race. The religion which proclaimed the absolute supremacy of God was no doubt an infinite advance upon the "chilling equipoise" of good and evil to which the creed of Zoroaster had at that time sunk.* Nor was the national existence of Persia stamped out, as has been often said, by the Ka-

---

* See Elphinstone's "India," vol. v., p. 313.

liphs; for the Persian province of Khorasan was itself strong enough to place the Abbasside Kaliphs on the throne of Bagdad; and the Persian dynasties of the Samanides and Dilemites gave to' the nation a new lease of life, and a wholly new national literature; and it is to a Mohammedan Sultan of the Turkish race that Persia owes her greatest literary glory, her national epic, the "Shahnameh" of Ferdousi. Still it can not be said that the religion proved itself altogether suited to the people. In other countries the scimiter had no sooner been drawn from its scabbard than it was sheathed again. But in Persia the scimiter had not only to clear the way, but for some time afterward to maintain the new religion.* The Persians corrupted its simplicity with fables and with miracles; they actually imported into it something of saint-worship and something of sacerdotalism; and, consequently, in no nation in the Mohammedan world has the religion less hold on the people as a restraining power. The most stringent principles of the Koran are set at naught; beng and opium are common; the Ketman, or religious equivocation, is held to be as allowable as it has been by the Casuists or the Jesuits; and the nation which Herodotus tells us devoted a third of its whole educational curriculum to learning to speak

---

* See Sir John Malcolm's "History of Persia," vol. i., p. 277, etc.

the truth, now contains hardly an individual who will speak the truth unless he has something to gain by it.

In Hindoostan, amid the other branch of the great Aryan race which did not move westward, Mohammedanism has obtained finally a very strong footing; but it was slow in winning its way; and the thirty million Mussulmans over whom we rule — and a tremendous and but half-recognized responsibility it is* — devout as they are, have become so by long lapse of time, by social influences, and by intermixture with conquering Arabs, Ghaznevides, and Affghans, rather than by the sudden fervor of religious enthusiasm.†

Those who have followed me thus far will perceive that my main object in writing these Lectures has been, if possible, to render some measure of that justice to Mohammed and to his religion which has been all too long, and is still all too generally, denied to them. I have naturally, therefore, been led to dwell rather on the points in which Mohammedanism resembles Christianity than on the points in which it differs, and I have been led, also, to some extent, to compare the per-

---

* Since this was written the grievances of Mohammedans in India, so ably and temperately stated by Mr. Hunter, have been in part alleviated by the adoption of some of the remedies he suggests, at least as far as regards education.

† Elphinstone, vol. v., p. 314, and cap. iii. on the reign of the Sultan Mahmoud.

sons of their respective Founders. It is not possible to avoid this. Of the Founder of Christianity I have necessarily spoken only under that aspect of his character which Mussulman as well as Christian, friend as well as foe, will perforce allow him; and in which alone, by the nature of the case, he can be compared with any other founder at all. In like manner, in comparing the two creeds, I have insisted mainly on the points in which they approximate to each other; and to do this is more necessary, more just, and, I venture to think, more Christian, than to do the opposite.

But if, in order to prevent misconception, the two creeds must necessarily be contrasted rather than compared, nothing that I have said, or am going to say, will prevent my admitting fully—what, indeed, is apparent upon the face of it—that the contrasts are at least as striking as the resemblances.

The religion of Christ contains whole fields of morality and whole realms of thought which are all but outside the religion of Mohammed. It opens humility, purity of heart, forgiveness of injuries, sacrifice of self to man's moral nature; it gives scope for toleration, development, boundless progress to his mind; its motive power is stronger, even as a friend is better than a king, and love higher than obedience. Its realized ideals in the various paths of human greatness have been more commanding, more many-sided, more holy, as Averroes is below Newton, Haroun below Alfred, and Ali below St. Paul. Finally, the ideal life of all is far more elevating, far more majestic, far more inspiring, even as the life of the founder of Mohammedanism is below the life of the Founder of Christianity.

And when I speak of the ideal life of Mohammedanism I must not be misunderstood. There is in Mohammedanism no ideal life in the true sense of the word, for Mohammed's character was admitted by himself to be a weak and erring one. It was disfigured by at least one huge moral blemish; and exactly in so far as his life has, in spite of his earnest and reiterated protestations, been made an example to be followed, has that vice been perpetuated. But in Christianity the case is different. The words, "Which of you convinceth me of sin?" forced from the mouth of Him who was meek and lowly of heart, by the wickedness of those who, priding themselves on being Abraham's children, never did the works of Abraham, are a definite challenge to the world. That challenge has been for nineteen centuries before the eyes of unfriendly, as well as of believing, readers, and it has never yet been fairly met; and at this moment, by the confession of friend and foe alike, the character of Jesus of Nazareth stands alone in its spotless purity and its unapproachable majesty. We have each of us probably at some period of our lives tried hard to penetrate to the inmost meaning of some one of Christ's short and weighty utterances—

> "Those jewels, five words long,
> Which on the stretched forefinger of all time
> Sparkle forever."

But is there one of us who can say there is no more behind? Is there one thoughtful person among us who has ever studied the character of Christ, and has not, in spite of ever-recurring difficulties and doubts, once and again burst into the centurion's exclamation, "Truly this was the Son of God?"

Nor are the methods of drawing near to God the same in the two religions. The Mussulman gains a knowledge of God—he can hardly be said to approach him—by listening to the lofty message of God's Prophet. The Christian believes that he approaches God by a process which, however difficult it may be to define, yet has had a real meaning to Christ's servants, and has embodied itself in countless types of Christian character—that mysterious something which St. Paul calls a "union with Christ." "Ye are dead, and your life is hid with Christ in God."

But this unmistakable superiority does not shake my position that Mohammedanism is, after all, an approach to Christianity, and perhaps the nearest approach to it which the unprogressive part of humanity can ever attain in masses; and yet how large a part of the whole human race are unprogressive! Whatever we may wish, and however current conversation and literature may assert the contrary, progress is the exception, and not the rule, with mankind. The whole Eastern world, with very few exceptions, has been hitherto and is still stationary, not progressive. What Oriental society is now, it was in the time of Solomon—I might say, in the time of Abraham. Even those nations which, like the Chinese, have considerable powers of invention and mechanical skill, reach a certain height rapidly, and then stop short.*

Accepting, then, the non-progressiveness of a large part of the human race, when left to themselves, as a fact, can not we estimate other religions, not by our conception of what we want, but by their bearing on the life of those whom they affect, ennobling them so far as the other conditions of their existence may ren-

---

* I specify China; for I can not accept the changes relied upon by Dr. Bridges in his very able essay on China, in "International Policy," as being evidence of continuous and progressive change, which is the real point at issue. Of course this in no way affects the more important questions treated of in the essay, the moral elevation of which seems to me almost unequaled in the writings even of those who, like the contributors to the volume referred to, and the followers of Auguste Comte generally, have labored most earnestly to treat all political questions from a moral stand-point.

der possible? Judged by this relative standard—which is, as I conceive, the only true one—Mohammedanism has nothing to lose, and every thing to gain, by the keenest criticism.* I grant to the full every thing that can be said by travelers such as Burckhardt and Burton and Palgrave upon the degradation of the mass of the Bedouins and the Turks, and the want of all vital religion, sometimes of the very elements of religion, among them. But is the state of the Mohammedan world as a whole worse in proportion to its light than was that of Christendom when the cup of iniquity was full and a Luther was born? To take a particular instance, has religion less hold upon the Arabs than it had upon the English throughout the last century, till the evangelical revival of Wesley and Whitefield aroused it from its sleep? Has it less hold even upon the "Frenchmen of the East," as the Persians have been called — liars, drunkards, profligate though they are — than it has at this moment upon the Frenchmen of the West? What account do travelers in Russia give us of the state of religion among the masses there? And what judgment

---

* Abyssinia is a case in point for those who think that a religion, because it is better and purer in itself, is necessarily better than all other religions, wherever and whenever and in whatever degree of purity it may be found. Abyssinia has been nominally Christian since very early times, and yet it would puzzle the greatest enemy of Islam to name a single particular in which the inhabitants are superior to their Mussulman neigh-

must pious Mohammedans form of Christianity, if their knowledge of it is confined to the average lives of Europeans who profess it?

To say that gross abuses have crept into Mohammedanism—that the lives of many, or even of the majority, who profess it are a disgrace to their name—is only to say that it is not exempt from the common conditions of humanity.

Take one instance, drawn from the history of the Christian Church. Christianity was in its origin and in its essence a creed entirely spiritual; but Christians, forming, as they did, a new human society, were allowed by their Founder to symbolize this close union, and to bring it home more vividly to themselves and to the world, by two external rites. The mere fact that they were external, in a religion which was otherwise a matter of the heart, ought to have put men on their guard, lest they should assume in time a too prominent place; lest what was accidental and secondary and relative should dominate over what was absolute and primary

---

bors. Spain may suggest similar thoughts. We are apt to forget that there are two factors to be considered in testing the value of a religion in any given case—the creed itself and the people who receive it. There are of course good and bad men, and these of every degree of goodness and badness, to be found professing every creed; but the average morality of the followers of an imperfect creed may, in this very imperfect world, be better than the average morality of those who profess a higher one, and of course *vice versa*. Πάντων μέτρον ἄνθρωπος.

and eternal. Baptism was of considerable importance in the infancy of the Church, for it was a pledge of fidelity consciously and voluntarily given by a new recruit, in the face of the enemy, to a cause whose victories were yet in the future. It was, as it were, the uniform assumed by the small army which at its Master's bidding went forth against the world. The love-feast also was of special importance among the earliest Christians, as a constant reminder that those who had taken upon themselves the commission of the Cross, that crowning act of love, were bound to one another by the same enthusiasm of love which bound them to their common Master. Both did good service then, and in the history of the Christian Church have done good service since, in so far as they have acted upon the heart, and thence upon the conduct, through the medium of a powerful appeal to the religious imagination. But in so far as any mysterious or supernatural efficacy has been attached to the form of either, they have sapped the root of Christianity. They have done for Christianity what of good, no doubt, Mohammed thought—and half rightly, half wrongly thought—that pilgrimages to the holy places might do for Mohammedanism. Both were so far concessions to human weakness that they introduced formal, or even material, conceptions into a spiritual religion; both, in fact, were capable of being used to advantage; and experience has proved that they were both alike liable to the same kind of abuse.

Every human institution, therefore—religion itself, so far as man can affect it—is exposed to inevitable decay; and the purer the religion, the more inevitable the degradation which contact with the world, which is not of it, must bring.* Accordingly, a religion which is not waiting for a revival, is waiting only till it be swept away.

But, on the other hand, we must not judge of a religion by its perversions or corruptions; and it is as fair to take Turkish despots and maniac dervishes and Persian libertines as types of the Mohammedan life, as it would be to take Anabaptists or Pillar Saints or Jesuits as types of the Christian life. Most of the well-known vices of our Mohammedan fellow-subjects in India are Indian vices, and not Mohammedan. Max Müller has remarked with truth, that without constant reformation—that is to say, without a constant return to the fountain-head—every religion, however pure, must gradually degenerate. Christianity has always reformed itself, and will to the end of time continue to reform itself, by going back to the words and to the life of Christ. It is a maxim of the Buddhists that "what has been said by Buddha, that alone is well said;"† and it is currently be-

---

* Max Müller, "Chips," Preface, p. 23.
† Quoted by Max Müller, loc. cit., p. 23.

lieved that Mohammedanism is dying out because it has no such power of revival. But the very reverse of this is, rather, true. Probably no religion has produced, in the various parts of its vast empire, a more continuous succession of reformers, whose aim has been to bring it back to its original simplicity and purity. Such was one object, however wildly they set about it, of the Carmathians in the ninth century; and, to select one among many individual reformers, such was the career of Abdul Wahhab, the son of a petty Arabian sheik, a hundred and fifty years ago. The facts I take almost *verbatim* from an interesting and able essay on "Our Indian Mussulmans" by Dr. Hunter.*

Commencing by a moral attack upon the profligacy of the Turkish pilgrims and the mummeries which profaned the holy cities, Abdul Wahhab gradually elaborated a theological system which is substantially identical with the original creed of Mohammed. He taught, first, absolute reliance on one God, and the rejection of all mediators between man and God, whether saints or Mohammed himself; second, the right of private interpretation of the Koran; third, the prohibition of all forms and ceremonies with which the pure faith has been overlaid in the lapse of centuries; finally—and this is the

---

* See Hunter, p. 55-60; and for a further account of the Arab movement, see Burckhardt's "Notes on the Bedouins and Wahhabees."

only part to be regretted in the movement — he reasserted the obligation to wage war upon the infidel. In 1803 Wahhab's successors took the holy cities, and desecrated the sacred mosque at Mecca and the Prophet's tomb at Medina, to save them from the greater desecration, as it seemed to those Puritans of the Desert, involved in the almost divine honors lavished on them by ignorant or profligate pilgrims.

Here was an act upon the significance of which we may well dwell for a moment, and endeavor, by comparing it with somewhat parallel and better-known cases, to realize what it must have seemed like then, and what it proves about Mohammedanism now. Imagine the feelings of pious Jews when their most religious king broke into pieces the relic of relics, the memorial of the divine deliverance and of their desert life, and stigmatized it as a bit of brass! Imagine, if you can, the feelings of the Apostles when it dawned upon them that one of their number, even then, was a traitor in his heart! Imagine, to take a parallel case suggested by Mr. Hunter,* mediæval Christendom, when the news spread that Bourbon's cutthroats were installed in the Vatican, and that the head of the Christian Church had been taken captive by the Church's eldest son! Imagine Luther, when in the fervor of youthful enthusiasm he visited the Rome of

---

* Hunter, p. 59.

the Martyrs and of the Apostles, and found it to be the Rome of the Papacy, the Rome of impostures and indulgences, of the Borgias and the Medici! And we can then picture to ourselves the thrill of horror that must have passed through the orthodox Mussulman world when they heard that a sect of reformers, whose one idea of reform was a return to the life and doctrine of the Prophet, had rifled the mosque whose immemorial sanctity the Prophet had himself increased by making it the Kiblah of the world, and had even violated the Prophet's tomb. Imagine, on the other hand, what it must have cost the Wahhabees to have, like Luther, the courage of their convictions, to appear to stultify themselves, to dishonor their Prophet, and all that they might make their religion the spiritual religion that it had once been! And then say, if you can, that Mohammedanism has no power of self-reform, and is dying gradually of inanition!

Beaten down at last by the strong arm of Mehemet Ali, Pasha of Egypt, in 1812, helped, I regret to say, by Englishmen, the Wahhabees disappeared temporarily from Arabia,* only to reappear in 1821 in In-

---

* For a graphic and not very favorable account of the Wahhabee Empire, as it exists now in Arabia and its seat of government at Riad, see Palgrave's "Arabia," chap. ix.-xiii. There are one or two passages in this account, e.g., vol. i., p. 365-373, 427-437, in which I can not but think, with all my admiration for Mr. Palgrave's varied powers, that he has not been, even on his own showing elsewhere, altogether fair to Islam as a system.

dia, under the leadership of the prophet Sayyed Ahmad; and the despised sect of Wahhabees are now, perhaps, the real ruling spirit of Mussulman politics in India, and enjoy the singular honor of having, as much, no doubt, by their gloomy fanaticism as by their moral lives and their missionary zeal, attracted to themselves considerable attention even from their English rulers at home. Puritans of the Puritans of Islam, they are despised and hated by the so-called orthodox Mussulmans, as the Lutherans were hated by Leo, and the Covenanters by Claverhouse.

The extraordinary phenomena attending the great religious movement called Bâbyism now going on in Persia, the ecstatic martyrdoms and the prodigality of tortures submitted to amid songs of triumph by women and children, the followers of the "Bâb," are well worth the study of all who are interested in the history of religion; and, however we explain the facts, much that I said of Wahhabeeism may, *mutatis mutandis*, be said of it; and at all events its existence is a standing proof that Persian Mohammedanism possesses so much of vitality as is necessary to adapt an old creed to a new belief.*

When I first wrote the above paragraphs on the

---

* See Gobineau, "Les Religions et les Philosophies dans l'Asie Centrale," p. 141-215.

power of revival which I conceive to be inherent in Islam, I did not know that my words were at that very time being illustrated in the most striking way, not only in India and Persia and Arabia, upon which I then dwelt, but also throughout the Asiatic dominions of the Ottoman Sultans. Since then Mr. Palgrave's most interesting " Essays on Eastern Questions" have come into my hands; and I find in them both evidence to show that there is such a revival, and a graphic account of its leading symptoms.

Secular and denominational schools are every where giving place to schools of the most strictly Mussulman type. Mosques which were deserted are now crowded with worshipers; mosques which were in ruins are rebuilt. There is a general reaction, not perhaps to be wondered at, against the employment in public offices of the European and the Christian. Wine and spirit shops are closed, for their trade is gone except among the Levantine residents. Even opium and tobacco are becoming luxuries which are not only forbidden, but also forsaken.

Add to this, what Mr. Palgrave has also shown, that a new nation is as it were growing up under our eyes in Eastern Anatolia, rich with all the elements of a vigorous national and religious life, and we shall then have reason to believe that though the Ottoman supremacy may pass away, as Kaliphs and Sultans, Attabeks and Khans, Padishahs and Moguls, have passed away before them, yet Islam itself is a thing of indestructible vitality, and may thrive the more when rid of the magnificent corruptions and the illusory prestige of the Stamboul successors of the Prophet. In truth, Islam has existed for centuries in spite of Osmanlee rule, and not because of it; and this the embassadors lately sent to the Porte from the most distant parts of the Mussulman world—from Bokhara and Khotan, from the Sultan of Atchin and the Sultan of the Panthays—must have learned to their cost, when they found that the so-called Commander of the Faithful was sufficiently employed nearer home, and had neither the power nor the will to give them the help or even the advice they asked.

Mohammedanism, therefore, can still renew its youth, and it is possible that the present generation, in face of the advance of semi-barbarous and intolerant Russia, may see a revival of the old crusading spirit—an outburst of stern fanaticism, which, armed with the courage of despair, obliterating, as in the Circassian war,*

---

* See Baron Von Haxthausen's "Tribes of the Caucasus;" especially his interesting account of the rise of Muridism, and the heroic struggle of Schamyl, his personal influence, and his genius for military and political organization. Truly while Mohammedanism can throw off geniuses like Schamyl, it may well be able to dispense with such governments as that even the immemorial schism of Sonnee and Sheeah, may hurl once more the united strength of the Crescent upon the vanguard of advancing Christendom. It is a prospect formidable to every Christian Power—formidable above all to those who for good or for evil rule thirty millions of Mussulmans in India; but I can not think, even if the result were to be that a stop should be put to all further conquests of Europeans in the East, that the world would be altogether a loser thereby. In the East a revived Islam contains more elements of hope for the future than a corrupt Christianity —and Christianity in Asia has rarely been otherwise than dead ;* and the religious enthusiasm of some new Commander of the Faithful—of some heroic Schamyl or Abdel Kader on a vaster scale—than the dull, heavy tread of military despotism beneath the shadow of the Czars of all the Russias.

---

of the Turks. The Baron's prophecies of a general collapse of Mohammedanism are being signally falsified. The union of Sonnees and Sheeahs was one principle of Muridism as taught by Moollah Mohammed, and after him by Schamyl.

* For the marked superiority, for instance, of the tribes of the Caucasus which are Mohammedan, to those which are nominally Christian, see Freshfield's "Caucasus," p. 454-457 : " In the Caucasus the traveler will be compelled to contrast the truthfulness, industry, and courteous hospitality of the Mohammedans north of the chain with the lying indolence and churlishness of the Christians in the south ;" and for the general subject of Oriental Christianity as it is found in Armenia, Georgia, Syria, Egypt, etc., see Palgrave's essay entitled " Eastern Christians."

And here, perhaps, will be the place to make a few remarks upon a subject which can not have failed to attract the attention of the more thoughtful among us in recent years—I mean the attempt made to introduce Western manners and customs into Eastern countries.

We live in days when we hear of Khans and Khedives, Shahs and Sultans, giving up their immemorial passivity and seclusion, and even coming to Europe with the avowed intention of carrying back to Asia what they can of Western science and civilization. I should be slow, indeed, to complain of any steps taken by the Western Powers to do away with any institutions which, like the Suttee, the festivals of Juggernaut, the East African slave-trade, or the traffic in opium, are a curse to our common humanity, or are not grounded on any fundamental peculiarity of the Eastern world. But to attempt by force, or even by influence brought to bear upon Eastern rulers, to do away with any domestic or national institutions, such as the form of government or patriarchal slavery, or even polygamy, can do no good.

Eastern despotism is not what Western despotism is, nor is Oriental slavery like American. Nor is even polygamy in the East so intolerable an evil as it would be in the social freedom of the West. For example, an Eastern sovereign has all the power over his subjects that a father had in the most primitive times, and had even in Rome, over his children. His power is liable to the same abuses; but it has also some of its safeguards and redeeming points. To introduce into his government, as the Shah has been supposed to wish, a system of Boards and Parliaments, of checks and counter-checks, such as works fairly well in this country, because it has grown with our growth and is suitable to our instinct of compromise in every thing, would be to make many tyrants instead of one, and to cripple the power and lessen the responsibility of the only man in Persia whose interest it is to let no one commit injustice but himself. Asia, till its whole nature be changed, can probably never be better governed than it was by the early Kaliphs; and if an Abou Bakr or an Omar, or even a Haroun or a Mahmoud, a Baber or an Akbar, do not come twice in a century, it is probable that Nature has endowed Asiatics with precisely those qualities of patience, docility, and inertness which harmonize better with the evils of such a government than with those of any other.

Polygamy is a more difficult question, and it is impossible, for obvious reasons, to discuss it adequately here. It is a gigantic evil, worse even than slavery; for with its attendant mischiefs, so far as it extends, it does away with all real sympathy and companionship

L 2

between man and woman; it is unnatural in the fullest sense of the word, in a highly civilized nation, for Nature, by making the number of men and women equal, has declared decisively for monogamy. But, in a barbarous people, polygamy has this one redeeming point, that it is less likely that any woman will be left without a natural protector; and, as a matter of fact, it is almost universally allowed in primitive stages of civilization.* In the East it is the almost inevitable result of that fundamental institution of Eastern as well as of Moslem society, the absolute seclusion of women. There is an impervious bar to all social intercourse between the sexes before marriage. The husband's knowledge of his future wife is at second hand only, and rests on the report of a Khatibeh,† or professional match-maker. Such a marriage is more than a lottery; there can be no affection to begin with, and, except on rare occasions,

---

* In an uncivilized nation, split up, as Arabia was before Mohammed, into a number of hostile tribes, or overrun by its more powerful neighbors, as was Palestine in the time of the Judges, the number of births of men and women is no doubt about equal; but the male population is reduced by war to half its proper number; the preponderance of women in such a state of society renders polygamy possible, and the insecurity renders it from that one point of view allowable. Sir Samuel Baker, in his "Albert Nyanza," Introduction, p. 25, remarks that "in all tropical countries polygamy is the prevailing evil." He might have gone on to say much the same of slavery; but then what would become of the charge he so often makes against Islam—that it is responsible for polygamy and slavery?

† Lane's "Modern Egyptians," vol. i., p. 199.

it is not likely that it will turn out to be really happy. If it be thoroughly uncongenial, a man tries his luck once more in the same miserable lottery, and for his own happiness, and probably also for that of all concerned, annuls the previous bond. Hence polygamy implies freedom of divorce, and both together are the inevitable result of the seclusion of the female sex. But to abolish by law the two former, without dealing with the far more fundamental institution which is its root, would be to carry on a war with symptoms only, and to introduce evils worse than those it is wished to prevent. The only way of going to the root of the matter would be, if it were possible, to allow a freer intercourse between the sexes at all times; Sir William Muir allows that this could not be done at all with the present freedom of divorce.* It is a melancholy fact, but a fact still, that the strict checks imposed by Mohammed on married women, degrading though they are,† are essential to prevent what is still worse, and, be it remembered, what was far worse before the reforms and limitations which Mohammed himself imposed. It is a complete dead-lock; and the greatest reformers, Moses no less than Mohammed, have been unable to deal with the root of the evil. It is to be

---

* Muir, vol. iii., p. 234, and note.
† Sura xxxiii., 6, 56. Also Sura xxiv., 32.

remembered, on the other hand, that both Moses and Mohammed did what they could to restrain and modify its abuses; and at present neither polygamy nor divorce is so common as is often supposed. The humanity of human nature has asserted itself; and Lane, the most accurate observer, says that polygamy is in Egypt at all events very rare among the higher classes, and not common among the lower.*

Much the same may be said of slavery. The slavery of the East is a patriarchal institution, coeval with the very dawn of history. It is an institution allowed and modified by Moses, even as it was allowed and modified by Mohammed, for people in that stage of civilization which required it. In neither nation has it any thing in common with slavery as it was in America, or slavery as practiced at all by civilized nations. To do away with it by force, as has been the case in Khiva, though we naturally rejoice at it, will probably do little permanent good. It will revive in another, and probably a worse shape. Perhaps we have hit upon the one pos-

---

* Lane, vol. i., p. 231: "Not more than one husband in twenty has two wives at the same time." But divorce is very common. If it were not for Lane's proverbial accuracy, one would be inclined to suspect that in the passage referred to in the text he had transposed the words higher and lower. Certainly in other parts of the Mohammedan world polygamy is, for obvious reasons, much more common among the rich than among the poor. But the current of opinion, like the general conditions of society, seems to be every where setting against it, especially in India.

sible means of gradually getting rid of it, in making it impossible to recruit slavery from without by means of the slave-trade. Much will have to be done henceforward by free labor in Arabia, in Persia, and in Egypt, which has hitherto been done by slaves; and we need not fear but that the result will be so good that even in a stolid Oriental people the gradual movement will be one in the direction of abolition. The foreign slave-trade, in fact, is, owing to the remonstrances of Dr. Livingstone and the expeditions of Sir Samuel Baker and Sir Bartle Frere, already, for the time at all events, almost at an end, and it is a mistake to suppose that it ever received any sanction either from Moses or Mohammed. Moses ordered the man-stealer and the man-seller to be put to death.* Mohammed is reported by the "Sonnah" to have said, "The worst of men is the seller of man."†

Western science, with its railways, its canals, and its printing-presses, may, no doubt, do something for the material prosperity of Eastern countries, but by itself it

---

* Exodus xxi., 16.
† The slave-trade rests for its support on no religion at all, but only on that which is cruel and selfish in human nature. It is no more fair to tax Islam, as is often done, with the horrors of the East African slave-trade, than it would have been in the last century to tax Christianity with the still greater horrors of the West African traffic and its *sequelæ* in America. It has been remarked with truth that the cruel treatment of domesticated slaves is the shameful and exclusive prerogative of civilization.

will do little for their moral welfare; and a thin varnish of Western civilization, introduced by rulers who have been forced to admire the material power of the West, and have lost their own self-respect in the process, is earnestly to be deprecated. Those Orientals who have been most influenced by the Franco-mania of Stamboul are, beyond all comparison, the most degraded and profligate of their race, and no earnest observer can wish to see imported into other parts of the Mohammedan world that indescribable combination of all that is contemptible in human nature conveyed by the word Levantine.

The heroic and unselfish lives of a few such men as Livingstone—alas that it is now all too certain that his life is a thing of the past!—are the only legitimate means of introducing into semi-civilized countries such benefits as we think we have to bestow. A life and character like Livingstone's has done more to regenerate the African races than any amount of direct preaching, or any number of European settlements, with the miserable and immoral wars that so often follow in their train. Such men are the true pioneers of civilization and Christianity—of the only species of civilization and the only form of Christianity which we have any reason to expect will be a real benefit to the East.

But does it follow, from what I have said of the immobility of the East, that it is impossible for Islam to make any advance at all; that it is impossible for it to yield any thing to the progressive civilization of Christianity and of the West?

How Christianity and civilization should deal with Mohammedanism I have partly indicated already, and shall have a very few more words to say upon the subject presently. But, first, what can Islam do on its part? Where religion and law are indissolubly bound up together, as they are in the Koran, each loses and each gains something. What they gain in stability, they more than lose in flexibility. And yet it may be safely said that there is nothing more extraordinary in the whole history of Islam than the way in which the theory of the verbal inspiration of the Koran, and the consequent stereotyped and unalterable nature of its precepts, have, by ingenuity, by legal fictions, by the "Sonnah," or traditional sayings of Mohammed, and by *responsa prudentum*, been accommodated to the changing circumstances and the various degrees of civilization of the nations which profess it. When the Kadi fails to find in the law laid down for the nomad Arabs a rule precisely applicable to the more complex requirements of Smyrna or of Delhi, he places the sacred volume upon his head, and so renders homage to human reason and to the law of progress. He does what Puritans and Churchmen would alike do well to remember, when each professes to find in the varying or convertible expressions of the writers of the New Testament a divinely ordered and unalterable model of Church government.* It is not, therefore, quite so true as is commonly supposed that Islam is reconcilable with one narrow form of government or society only; and it is quite possible that where so much has been done already, more may be done in future, and means may be found for reconciling, for instance, the laws against taking interest for money with the requirements of modern society. The intolerant principles of the Koran have long since been reconciled, except where there is a passing outburst of fanaticism, with the utmost practical toleration; and the standard of the "Jihad," or holy war, will probably never henceforward be raised on an extensive scale except in a war of self-defense, and unless the lives and liberties of Mohammedans, as well as their religion, are at stake.

And, what is infinitely more important, it seems to me that while Mohammedans cling as strongly as ever to their rigid Monotheism, and to their unfaltering be-

---

* Compare Acts xx., 17, μετεκαλέσατο τοὺς πρεσβυτέρους τῆς ἐκκλησίας, with ver. 28, ὑμᾶς . . . ἔθετο ἐπισκόπους. The watchwords of the bitterest ecclesiastical jealousy and hatred are in this passage of the New Testament seen to be, after all, synonymous and convertible terms.

lief in the divine mission of their Prophet—and what serious person could wish them to do otherwise—to give up those beliefs which have made them what they are, which have given them a glorious history, and which have influenced half a world; to give up—

> ". . . Those first affections,
> Those shadowy recollections,
> Which, be they what they may,
> Are yet the fountain-light of all their day,
> Are yet a master-light of all their seeing;
> Uphold them—cherish—and have power to make
> Their noisy years seem moments in the being
> Of the eternal silence: truths that wake
> To perish never!"

while they cling, I say, to these as strongly, yes, more strongly than ever, they may yet be brought to see that there is a distinction between what Mohammed said himself and what others have said for him; and that there is a still broader distinction between what he said as a legislator and as a conqueror, and what he said as a simple prophet. There are some among them who see now, and there will be more who will soon see, that there may be an appeal to the Mohammed of Mecca from the Mohammed of Medina; that there may be an idolatry of a book, as well as of a picture, or a statue, or a shapeless mass of stone; and that the Prophet, who always in other matters asserted his fallibility, was never more fallible, though certainly never more sincere, than when he claimed an equal infallibility for the whole Koran alike. Finally, with the growth of knowledge of the real character of our faith, Mohammedans must recognize that the Christ of the Gospel was something ineffably above the Christ of those Christians from whom alone Mohammed drew his notions of him; that he was a perfect mirror of that one primary attribute of the Eternal of which Mohammed could catch only a far-off glance, and which, had it been shown to him as it really was, must needs have taken possession of his soul.

All this may or may not be in our own time; but in a sympathetic study even of Mohammedanism as it is, Christians have not a little to gain. There is the protest against Polytheism in all its shapes; there is the absolute equality of man before God; there is the sense of the dignity of human nature; there is the simplicity of life, the vivid belief in God's providence, the entire submission to his will; and last, not least, there is the courage of their convictions, the fearless avowal before men of their belief in God, and their pride in its possession as the one thing needful. There is in the lives of average Mohammedans, from whatever causes, less of self-indulgence, less of the mad race for wealth, less of servility, than is to be found in the lives of average Christians. Truly we may think that these things ought not so to be; and if Christians generally were as ready to confess

Christ, and to be proud of being his servants, as Mohammedans are of being followers of Mohammed, one chief obstacle to the spread of Christianity would be removed. And the two great religions which started from kindred soil, the one from Mecca, the other from Jerusalem, might work on in their respective spheres—the one the religion of progress, the other of stability; the one of a complex life, the other of a simple life; the one dwelling more upon the inherent weakness of human nature, the other on its inherent dignity;* the one the religion of the best parts of Asia and Africa, the other of Europe and America—each rejoicing in the success of the other, each supplying the other's wants in a generous rivalry for the common good of humanity.

A few words more about Mohammed himself, and I have done. The world, in its wisdom or unwisdom, has never thought proper to distinguish Mohammed from the millions of Mohammeds named after him by calling him "the Great." Perhaps he was too great for such an external distinction. People call the conqueror of Constantinople, eight centuries later, Mohammed the Second. But I do not think they ever speak of the Prophet as Mohammed the First; and perhaps the unconscious homage thus rendered to him by a world which

---

* Perhaps the two views are, after all, only different aspects of the same truth.

ostensibly, and till very lately, has done him such scant justice, is the highest tribute that can be given to his greatness. The Greeks paid the highest compliment they could to the surpassing splendor of the King of Persia when, consciously or unconsciously, they dropped the article before his name, and so put him on a level, grammatical and moral, with the sun, the moon, and the earth, which could by no possibility need any such distinguishing mark. Compare Mohammed with the long roll of men whom the world by common consent has called "Great;" while I admit that there is no one point in his character in which he is not surpassed by one or other, take him all in all, what he was, and what he did, and what those inspired by him have done, he seems to me to stand alone, above and beyond them all. A distinguished writer on the Holy Roman Empire has remarked of Charles the Great that, " like all the foremost men of our race, he was all great things in one."* But though Mr. Bryce does not illustrate the truth of his remark by Mohammed—nay, by not including him among the foremost men of the world whom he goes on to enumerate, he seems designedly to exclude him—I venture to think that of no one of them all is this remark more strictly true.

---

* Bryce's "Holy Roman Empire," p. 73.

Mohammed did not, indeed, himself conquer a world like Alexander or Cæsar or Napoleon. He did not himself weld together into a homogeneous whole a vast system of states like Charles the Great. He was not a philosophic king like Marcus Aurelius; nor a philosopher like Aristotle or like Bacon, ruling by pure reason the world of thought for centuries with a more than kingly power; he was not a legislator for all mankind, nor even the highest part of it, like Justinian; nor did he cheaply earn the title of "the Great" by being the first among rulers to turn, like Constantine, from the setting to the rising sun. He was not a universal philanthropist, like the greatest of the Stoics—

"Non sibi sed toti genitum se credere mundo;"

nor was he the apostle of the highest form of religion and civilization combined, like Gregory or Boniface, like Leo or Alfred the Great. He was less, indeed, than most of these in one or two of the elements that go to make up human greatness, but he was also greater. Half Christian and half Pagan, half civilized and half barbarian, it was given to him in a marvelous degree to unite the peculiar excellences of the one with the peculiar excellences of the other. "I have seen," said the embassador sent by the triumphant Koreishites to the despised exile at Medina—"I have seen the Persian Chosroes and the Greek Heraclius sitting upon their thrones, but never did I see a man ruling his equals as does Mohammed."

Head of the State as well as of the Church, he was Cæsar and Pope in one; but he was Pope without the Pope's pretensions, and Cæsar without the legions of Cæsar. Without a standing army, without a body-guard, without a palace, without a fixed revenue, if ever any man had the right to say that he ruled by a right divine, it was Mohammed; for he had all the power without its instruments and without its supports. He rose superior to the titles and ceremonies, the solemn trifling and the proud humility of court etiquette. To hereditary kings, to princes born in the purple, these things are, naturally enough, as the breath of life; but those who ought to have known better, even self-made rulers, and those the foremost in the files of time — a Cæsar, a Cromwell, a Napoleon — have been unable to resist their tinsel attractions. Mohammed was content with the reality, he cared not for the dressings, of power.* The simplicity of his private life was in keeping with his public life. "God," says Al Bokhari, "offered him the keys of the treasures of the earth, but he would not accept them."

Hagiology is not history; but the contemporaries of

---

* See "British Quarterly Review," Jan., 1872, p. 128.

Mohammed, his enemies who rejected his mission, with one voice extol his piety, his justice, his veracity, his clemency, his humility, and that at a time before any imaginary sanctity could have enveloped him. A Christian even, as is remarked by a great writer whom I have quoted above, with his more perfect code of morality before him, must admit that Mohammed, with very rare exceptions, practiced all the moral virtues but one; and in that one, as I have shown, he was in advance of his time and nation.

Assuredly, if Christian missionaries are ever to win over Mohammedans to Christianity, they must alter their tactics. It will not be by discrediting the great Arabian Prophet, nor by throwing doubts upon his mission, but by paying him that homage which is his due; by pointing out, not how Mohammedanism differs from Christianity, but how it resembles it; by dwelling less on the dogmas of Christianity, and more on its morality; by showing how perfectly that Christ whom Mohammed with his half-knowledge so reverenced came up to the ideal which prophets and kings desired to see, and had not seen, and which Mohammed himself, Prophet and King in one, could only half realize. In this way, and in this alone, is it likely that Christianity can ever act upon Mohammedanism; not by sweeping it into oblivion — for what of truth there is in it, and there is very much truth, can never die—but by gradually, and perhaps unconsciously, breathing into its vast and still vigorous frame a newer, a purer, and a diviner life.

By a fortune absolutely unique in history, Mohammed is a threefold founder—" of a nation, of an empire, and of a religion." Illiterate himself, scarcely able to read or write, he was yet the author of a book which is a poem, a code of laws, a Book of Common Prayer, and a Bible in one, and is reverenced to this day by a sixth of the whole human race as a miracle of purity of style, of wisdom, and of truth. It was the one miracle claimed by Mohammed—his "standing miracle" he called it; and a miracle indeed it is. But looking at the circumstances of the time, at the unbounded reverence of his followers, and comparing him with the Fathers of the Church or with mediæval saints, to my mind the most miraculous thing about Mohammed is that he never claimed the power of working miracles. Whatever he had said he could do, his disciples would straightway have seen him do. They could not help attributing to him miraculous acts which he never did, and which he always denied he could do. What more crowning proof of his sincerity is needed? Mohammed to the end of his life claimed for himself that title only with which he had begun, and which the highest philosophy and the truest Christianity will one day, I venture to believe, agree in yielding to him—that of a Prophet, a very Prophet of God.

The religion, indeed, that he taught is below the purest form of our own, as the central figure of the Mohammedan religion is below the central figure of the Christian — a difference vast and incommensurable; but, in my opinion, he comes next to him in the long roll of the great benefactors of the human race; next to him, *longo intervallo* certainly, but still next. He had faults, and great ones, which he was always the first himself, according to his light, to confess and to deplore; and the best homage we can render to the noble sincerity of his character is to state them, as I hope I have tried to do, exactly as they were. "It was the fashion of old," to quote once more the words of our greatest novelist and greatest psychologist—and so to conclude this course of Lectures, of the manifold imperfections and shortcomings of which no one of those who have so kindly listened to me week after week can be half so conscious as myself—"It was the fashion of old, when an ox was led out for sacrifice to Jupiter, to chalk the dark spots, and give the offering a false show of unblemished whiteness. Let us fling away the chalk, and boldly say—the victim *is* spotted, but it is not therefore in vain that his mighty heart is laid on the altar of men's highest hopes."

M

APPENDICES.

APPENDIX TO LECTURE I.

SIR BARTLE FRERE, in an interesting and able and catholic essay in "The Church and the Age" on Indian Missions, takes a hopeful view of the future of India as influenced by Western civilization and Christianity. He begins (p. 318) by showing, rightly enough, that almost every thing we do in India tends to break up old beliefs, and so to prepare the way for a new one, and is, therefore, more or less missionary work; "not only railways and printing-presses, education, commerce, and the electric telegraph; our impartial codes and uniform system of administration; but our misfortunes and our mistakes, our wars, our famines, and our mutinies." He then gives (p. 334–337) elaborate statistics of the missionary agencies at work in 1865 in Western India; they have enormously increased in the last thirty years, and he estimates the number of missionaries at work at about 105, and the number of converts at somewhere about 2200; and this, multiplied by six or seven, would probably, he thinks, give a general idea of the direct results of missionary work during that period throughout all India (I would remark here that an official statement published in 1873 gives a much more favorable account, estimating the number of communicants at 78,494); but when Sir Bartle Frere comes to deal with Mohammedanism (p. 354–356), he gives no statistics on the point we most desiderate—the number of converts, if it be at all appreciable, from Islam to Christianity; the general remarks, indeed, he does make, seem to me to go exactly contrary to the conclusions he draws from them—*e. g.*, Mohammedans study portions of the Bible more than they did formerly; but these portions unfortunately seem to be the prophetical writings, especially those of Daniel; and they find therein the denunciations of Christianity which Christians find in it against other creeds; they are humiliated by the fact that Mohammedanism is no longer the imperial creed of India; but the upshot of their depression is not Christianity, but Wahhabeeism, *i. e.*, a return to Islam in its simplest and sternest shape. Brahmoism, which is really Brahmanism as modified by Christianity—Brahmanism *minus* caste and *minus* idolatry of every kind—seems to be in some respects the beginning of a national movement, and, judging from the authoritative sermon (p. 346–352) delivered in Calcutta on the thirty-ninth anniversary of the Brahma Samaj, and entitled "The Future Church," seems to me to give real hope for the future, and to be very suggestive as to the way in which missionaries should go to work. "The answer," says the preacher, "of Jesus the immortal Son of God, Thou shalt love the Lord thy

God with all thy heart, and with all thy mind, and with all thy soul, and with all thy strength, and thy neighbor as thyself, is the essence of true religion simply and exhaustively expounded." "The composite faith of the future Church is to combine in perfect harmony the profound devotion of the Hindoo and the heroic enthusiasm of the Mussulman;" but, unfortunately, the simplicity and intelligibility of the Mohammedan creed render it incapable at present of actually coalescing with the eclectic spirit of Brahmoism. It is strange at first sight that Mohammedanism, originally the most eclectic of religions, should, in India at all events, prove itself to be the least capable of settling down on terms of equality with other creeds, or of combining with them. No doubt the fact that Mohammedanism has been the imperial creed and is so no longer, and the proud memories of Mahmoud and Akbar, of Baber and of Aurungzebe, are a formidable, though it is to be hoped a passing, difficulty. If the Mohammedan revival now going on in India under the influence of the Wahhabees, the Firazees, and the followers of Dudu Miyan, can only be accompanied by a great moral reformation, such as Sprenger himself does not seem to despair of (vol. i., p. 459—"the Arabs only want another Luther"), the result, partially at least, of Christian influences, the simplicity of Islam will no doubt in its turn give it a great advantage over the Brahma Samaj in the struggle to fill the void created by the crumbling fabric of Hindooism. It has another great advantage in being already to some extent in possession of the ground. I observe that one of the speakers at the recent Allahabad Missionary Conference says that thirty millions, the estimated number of Mussulmans in India, is much below the mark.

The unfavorable opinion expressed by Dr. Livingstone on the effects of Mohammedanism in Africa ("Expedition to the Zambesi," p. 513–516, and 602–603) appears opposed to the general view I have taken in the Lecture; and of course, so far as his personal experience goes, is unimpeachable and conclusive. But it is clear that Dr. Livingstone drew his general conclusions almost entirely from his acquaintance with the Arab slave-traders in the south and east of Africa, whom it was the main purpose of his noble and heroic life to put down. In the Lecture I have purposely not dwelt upon the extension of Islam along the coast to the south of the Equator, for the simple reason that the inhabitants are Mohammedans in nothing but the name. The Arabs there are of the most degraded type, and are engaged almost to a man in the brutalizing slave-trade, which by itself is a complete obstacle to every species of civilization and religion. No doubt, as Dr. Livingstone remarks, the native African there contrasts favorably with the Mohammedan—as favorably, I would add, as he does even with the Portuguese; but that Dr. Livingstone judged of the whole of Mohammedan Africa by his experience of its worst part is clear from his remark—opposed as it is to the unanimous testimony of travelers in Northern and Central Africa—"that the only foundation for the statements respecting the spread of Islam in Africa is the fact that in a remote corner of Northwest Africa the Foulahs and Mandingoes, and some other tribes in Northern Africa, have made conquests of territory; but that even they care so little for the extension of their faith, that after conquest no pains whatever are taken to indoctrinate the adults of the tribe" (p. 513). Captain Burton asserts that "Mohammedans alone make proselytes in Africa." Dr. Livingstone says as explicitly "in Africa the followers of Christ alone are anxious to propagate their faith." Here is a direct contradiction; and it is obvious that in a country of such vast extent as Africa no such sweeping statement can be absolutely true. Perhaps Sierra Leone, to which Dr. Livingstone paid a visit for the purpose of testing the results of missionary enterprise, and to which he specially refers (p. 663), will furnish us with the best materials for pointing out how far the two statements are reconcilable with each other, and with substantial accuracy. In Sierra Leone there is a large negro community, the members of which having been brought for many years into contact not only with direct Christian preaching, but, what is more important, with Christian education, government, and example, are both excellent citizens and sincere Christians, and, as one would expect, contrast favorably in point of morality even with the best Mohammedans. This is unquestionably true; and of the self-denying efforts of the missionaries, especially the native ones, within certain limits, it is impossible to speak too highly.

As to the exact number of Christians in the colony at this moment it is rather difficult to arrive at an accurate conclusion; but, to take Dr. Livingstone's figures, he remarks (p. 605) that in the census of 1861 the whole population of Sierra Leone itself was 41,000 souls, 27,000 of them being Christian, and 1774 Mohammedan—"not a very large proportion," he observes, "for the only sect in Africa which makes proselytes." It is not a large proportion, but what is the number now? Sierra Leone now affords the most striking proof that can be given of the extent to which on the one hand Islam is spreading in that part of Africa by the efforts of unassisted missionaries, and on the other of the absence of any such propagation of the Christian faith among the tribes beyond the limits of the settlement. When Dr. Livingstone visited Sierra Leone a few years ago, Islam was, as he says, hardly known there; since then Mohammedan missionaries have come thither from the Foulahs and from the far interior, and with what result? No one will say that it is the sword to which they owe their success, for the peace of Sierra Leone has been for years undisturbed. And now we have (Government Report of West African Colonies, 1873) the testimony of Mr. Johnson (p. 15), the able and excellent missionary whom I have quoted in my Lecture, indorsed as it would seem by the bishop of the diocese, that the Christian community at Sierra Leone, however flourishing itself, has exercised no influence on the large number of native Africans resorting annually to the town for the purpose of trade, and still less has it done any thing to propagate itself by sending out missionaries among adjoining tribes. On the other hand, a few active and zealous Mohammedan missionaries have carried their peaceful war into the enemy's country, and have produced great results even among the Christian and native population of Sierra Leone itself; insomuch that the religion of a large portion, the Governor says of the majority, of the Christians within the settlement has been actually changed by their preaching. There may be, and it is to be hoped there is, exaggeration as to the numbers; but there can be no doubt, looking to the *consensus* of testimony, that Islam is propagated in Western, Northern, and Central Africa; that it is propagated by simple preaching and with marked success, even where a Christian government, and, what is better, Christianity itself, is to a great extent in possession of the ground. One wishes that Dr. Livingstone, the greatest and most single-minded of all the friends of Africa, had himself come into contact with a few of these simple and single-minded Mohammedan missionaries. They come so near in many respects to his own ideal of what a Christian missionary ought to be, that one feels sure he would have been led to modify his judgment as to the system which produces them, and to the great teacher whom he rarely mentions but as the "false prophet."

The remarks I have made in the Lecture as to the attitude which it seems to me that Christian missionaries should adopt, wherever their efforts appear to have a chance of being successful—and surely there is too much evil in the world that is remediable to allow of a great expenditure of labor or money where there is no such prospect—have been suggested to me mainly by way of contrast to what I have read in most books devoted to the cause of Missions. Even so noble and self-sacrificing and single-hearted a man as Henry Martyn appears to have gone out as a missionary to India—nay, to have argued with Mohammedans—without having first read a word of the Koran, even in its English dress ("Memoir of Rev. Henry Martyn," by Rev. J. Sargent, p. 177: cf. 225); and throughout his career he treats it as an "imposture;" "the work of the devil." He is sent to fight "the four-faced devil of India"—*i. e.*, Hindoos, Mohammedans, Papists, and Infidels (p. 259); and see a summary of his written arguments against Mohammedans (on p. 335), which are quite enough by themselves to account for his ill success. See also the account by another devoted missionary, the Rev. C. B. Leupolt, of his mission at Benares ("Recollections of an Indian Missionary"), who takes much the same position. "The so-called Prophet of the Mohammedans;" "the Koran is an assemblage of facts and passages taken from the Bible, mixed with a great number of gross and cunningly devised fables;" "no Mohammedan who believes the whole Koran can have the notion of the true God;" "the Koran is calculated to lead man daily farther from God, and to unite him closer to the Prince of darkness;" "Satan holds them enthralled by a false religion," and so on. How not to deal with a different faith could hardly be better demonstrated than by the writings of two such admirable and devoted men. Surely the system has been to blame! Happily, as is shown from the general tone of the Allahabad Conference, and the explicit testimony of the Government of India in 1873, there has been a great advance in the right direction lately. Not to go beyond the limited circle of one's own acquaintance, such men as Bishop Cotton; the Rev. George and the Rev. Arthur Moule, now in China; and the Rev. James Johnson, native of Sierra Leone — though I would not venture to say that they would in any degree accept my point of view — yet in reality would have much in common with it; and all would certainly admit the immense amount of good that is to be found in the creeds which it is their duty to controvert. Alas, that those who knew Bishop Cotton well, and who therefore know what his catholic spirit might have done for India, can only now, when they think of him, repeat to themselves, consciously or unconsciously, the touching lament—

> "But oh for a touch of the vanished hand,
> And a sound of the voice that is still!"

APPENDIX TO LECTURE III.

THAT the assertions I have made in the third Lecture, as to the comparative ferocity of Christian and Mussulman religious wars, are within the mark, it would be easy to bring abundance of proof. I will adduce here one illustration only, drawn from the chief battle-ground of the contending forces, the Holy Land. Jerusalem capitulated to Omar, the third Kaliph, after a protracted blockade, in the year 637. No property was destroyed except in the inevitable operations of the siege, and not a drop of blood was shed except on the field of battle. Omar entered the city with the Patriarch, conversing amicably about its history; at the hour of prayer he was invited by the Patriarch to worship in the Church of the Holy Sepulchre, but he refused to do so for fear that his descendants might claim a similar right, and so the freedom of religious worship, which he wished to secure to the inhabitants by the articles of capitulation, might be endangered. In the year 1099 the Holy City fell before the arms of the Crusaders after a much shorter siege. It was taken by storm, and for three days there was an indiscriminate slaughter of men, women, and children; 70,000 Mussulmans were put to the sword, 10,000 of them in the mosque of Omar itself: "*in eodem templo decem millia de-*

collata sunt; pedites nostri usque ad bases cruore peremptorum tingebantur, nec feminis nec parvulis pepercerunt." This comes not from an enemy, but from the monkish historian, an eye-witness and a partaker of what he relates, Foulcher of Chartres. Raymond of Argiles and Daimbert, Archbishop of Pisa, give similar details, and all with approval. The city itself was pillaged; but the turn of the Saracens came once more in the year 1187. The breach was already forced, when the great Saladin retracted a hasty vow he had made to avenge the innocent blood that had been shed when the city had been sacked by the Crusaders, and took not Godfrey de Bouillon but Omar for his model. No blood was shed, and the captives were allowed to ransom themselves, the Frankish Christians leaving the city, the Eastern Christians continuing in peace.

As to humanity in war in general, the progress made has not been so great as is commonly supposed, even among those who pride themselves—and who to some extent pride themselves with reason—on being the pioneers of Christianity and civilization. Take the case of Africa. I am not aware that the Saracens in the full career of conquest deliberately burned a single city in the whole of the North of Africa, whether as a precautionary measure, or to support their prestige, or to glut their revenge. Can England say the same? If we assume—a large assumption—that the war on the Gold Coast in 1874 is wholly justifiable, if we also assume that the burning of the enemy's capital was indeed a necessity, it was a necessity for which a Christian nation should go into mourning, and should contemplate not with feelings of triumph, but with those of humiliation and regret. Is there any thing of the kind, or has one single ruler either in Church or State—now that the elections are over, and the moral iniquity of the war has been condoned by its success—been heard to raise his voice in condemnation of it, as even Omar or Saladin might have done? It is difficult to see how the English nation, which has abolished the slave-trade in the West of Africa, and is in its best portions profoundly philanthropic, can honestly believe that they are advancing the objects they have at heart when, in support of such a treaty as I have alluded to in the Lecture, they lead on a weaker barbarous nation, whom *pro hac vice* we designate as "our allies," against a more powerful one, and deliberately burn out of their homes a people who, barbarous and cruel as they were, have offended us not by their cruelty or by their human sacrifices, but by their honest belief that we had come to Africa to bar them from access to their own coast. It seems not to have occurred to any one that our "prestige" would have been sufficiently vindicated, and our future security sufficiently provided for, if we had burned down the palace of the king, the chief offender. But our "prestige" serves as an ample excuse for committing what we should condemn as crimes in any other nation. It is an entity that has juggled us into the belief that to destroy what we can not retain and can not use is the prerogative, not of barbarism, but of civilization and of Christianity. Had the war upon the Gold Coast been avowedly a war not for the spread of our influence, or for the security of a territory acquired by questionable means, but a moral crusade against human sacrifice, or for any purely unselfish object, the case would have been different. Truly this war will be a *damnosa hereditas* to posterity, alike whether we accept or disclaim the fearful responsibilities in which it has involved us.

There is an anecdote related of Mahmoud the Ghaznevide, the great Turkish conqueror of Central Asia, which seems to me to be suggestive. Soon after the conquest of Persia, a caravan was cut off by robbers in one of its deserts, and the mother of one of the merchants who was killed went to Ghazni to complain. Mahmoud urged the impossibility of keeping order in so remote a part of his territories, when the woman boldly answered: "Why, then, do you take countries which you can not govern, and for the protection of which you must answer in the Day of Judgment?" Mahmoud was struck with the reproach; whether it would have prevented all further conquests on his part we do not know, for he died soon afterward; but he liberally rewarded the woman, and took immediate and effectual steps for the protection of the caravans.

APPENDIX.

ISLAM.

BY
EMANUEL DEUTSCH.

ISLAM.*

THE Sinaitic Manifestation, as recorded in the Pentateuch, has become the theme of a thousand reflections in the Talmud and the Haggadah generally. Yet, however varied their nature — metaphysical, allegorical, ethical— one supreme thought runs through them all—the catholicity of Monotheism, its mission to all mankind. Addressed, apparently, to a small horde of runaway slaves, the "Law," those fundamental outlines of religious and social culture, revealed on Mount Sanai—"the lowliest of the range, to indicate that God's Spirit rests on them only that are meek of heart"—was indeed intended, the Masters say, for all the children of men. "Why," they ask, "was it given in the desert and not in any king's land?"—To show that even as the desert, God's own highway, is free, wide open to all, even so are his words

---

* This article appeared in the *Quarterly Review* for October, 1869, vol. cxxvii., No. 254, p. 293, and reviewed the following works: 1. "The Koran." 2. "The Talmud." 3. "The Sunnah." 4. "The Midrash." 5. "Mohammed." By Sprenger. Allahabad, 1851. 8vo. Berlin, 3 vols., 1861-65. 8vo. 6. "Life of Mahomet." By William Muir. 4 vols. London, 1858-61. 8vo.

a free gift to all; like the sun, the moon, and the stars. It was not given in the stillness and darkness of night, but in plain day, amid thunders and lightnings. Indeed, it had been offered to all nations of the world before it came to the "chosen one." But they, one and all, had pointed to some special national bent or "mission" with which one or the other of these commandments would have interfered, and so they declined them all. And intensely characteristic are some of the ethnological pleas put into their mouths by the, at times, humorous Haggadah. As for those trembling waifs and strays who, worn out with "anguish of spirit and cruel bondage," a short while since would not even listen to the message of Liberty, and who now, scared with terrors and wonders, cried, "We will obey and hear!"—obey, as the old commentators keenly point out, unconditionally, whatever we may hear—to them no choice had been left. Had they not accepted the "Law," that self-same mountain would have covered them up, and that desert would have become their grave—a dictum significantly echoed by the Koran.

But—the Legend continues—when this Law came to be revealed to them in the fullness of time, it was not revealed in their tongue alone, but in seventy: as many as there were nations counted on earth—even as many fiery tongues leap forth from the iron upon the anvil.... And as the voice went and came, echoing from Orient to Occident, from heaven to earth, all Creation lay hushed in awful silence. No bird sang in the air, the winds were still, the Seraphim paused in their three times "Holy!" "And all men," says Scripture, "heard and saw." They "heard" the voice—and to each it bore a different sound: to the men and the women, the young and the old, the strong and the weak. It appeared unto them like the voice of their fathers, their mothers, their children, all those whom they loved with their holiest and tenderest love. And they "saw." In that self-same hour God's Majesty revealed itself in its manifold moods and aspects: as Mercy and as Severity, as Justice and as Forgiveness, as Grace and Peace and Redemption. And through the midst of all these ever-varying sounds and visions there rolled forth the divine word, "I am the everlasting Jehovah, thy God, *One* God!" . . .

In these and similar strains the wide and all-embracing nature of the Monotheistic creed and call is set forth in those ancient documents to which we again venture to draw the attention of our readers, and from a new point of view. If, on a former occasion, we endeavored to sketch out of themselves their own aim and purport, their poetry and their prose, their law and their legend, we shall now endeavor to show how they may be, and must be, utilized for the investigation of phases of creed and thought apparently wide apart in time and tendency and place; how far they form one of the most important sources—the most important one, perhaps—of Islam.

We are not about to enter here into any "Origines Islamismi." This lies, at present, beyond our task. But those who would adequately work out the whole problem of the Talmud—as far as it lies within individual range—must needs look somewhat deeply into the story of these phases. And with regard to Islam, it seems as if the knowledge of its beginning and progress, its tenets and its lore, were not quite as familiar as they might be to the world at large, notably England, which "holds the gorgeous East in fee."

But before we proceed with our subject, we shall treat with all the reverence and all the freedom which belong to Science in these our days, let us look back—but a few centuries—and see what, for instance, the great theologians and scholars of the time of the Reformation thought and said of Islam; of its doctrine and the preacher thereof.

Daniel's "Little Horn" betokens, according to Martin Luther, Mohammed. But what are the Little Horn's Eyes? The Little Horn's Eyes, says he, mean "Mohammed's Alkoran, or Law, wherewith he ruleth. In the which Law there is naught but sheer human reason (*eitel menschliche Vernunft*)." . . . "For his Law," he reiterates, "teaches nothing but that which human understanding and reason may well like." . . . Wherefore—"Christ will come upon him with fire and brimstone." When he wrote this—in his "army sermon" against the Turks—in 1529, he had never seen a Koran. "Brother Richard's" (Predigerordens) "Confutatio Alcoran," dated 1300, formed the exclusive basis of his argument. But in Lent of 1540, he relates, a Latin translation, though a very unsatisfactory one, fell into his hands, and once more he returned to Brother Richard and did his Refutation into German, supplementing his version with brief but racy notes. This Brother Richard had, according to his own account, gone in quest of knowledge to "Babylon, that beautiful city of the Sarassins," and at Babylon he had learned Arabic and been inured in the evil ways of the Sarassins. When he had safely returned to his native land, he set about combating the same. And this is his exordium: "At the time of the Emperor Heraclius there arose a man, yea, a Devil, and a firstborn child of Satan . . . who wallowed in . . . and he was dealing in the Black Art, and his name it was Machumet." . . . This work Luther made known to his countrymen, by translating and commenting, prefacing and rounding it off by an epilogue. True his notes amount to little more than an occasional "Oh fie, for shame, you horrid Devil, you damned Mohammed!" or, "Oh, Satan, Satan, you shall pay for that!" or, "That's it, Devils, Sarassins, Turks, it's all the same!" or, "Here the Devil smells a rat," or, briefly, "O pfui Dich, Teufel!"—except when he modestly, with a query, suggests whether those Assassins, who, according to his text, are regularly educated to go out into the world in order to kill and slay all Worldly Powers, may not, perchance, be the Gypsies or the "Tattern" ("Tartars"); or when he breaks down with a "Hic nescio quid dicat translator." His epilogue, however, is devoted to a special disquisition as to whether Mohammed or the Pope be worse. And in the twenty-second chapter of this disquisition he has arrived at the final conclusion that, after all, the Pope is worse, and that he and not Mohammed is the real "Endechrist." "*Wohlan*," he winds up, "God grant us his grace, and punish both the Pope and Mohammed, together with their Devils. I have done my part as a true prophet and teacher. Those who won't listen may leave it alone." ...

In similar strains speaks the learned and gentle Melanchthon. In an introductory epistle to a reprint of that same Latin Koran which displeased Luther so much, he finds fault with Mohammed, or rather, to use his own words, he thinks that "Mohammed is inspired by Satan," because he "does not explain what sin is," and further, since he "showeth not the reason of human misery." He agrees with Luther about the Little Horn—though in another treatise he is rather inclined to see in Mohammed both Gog and Magog. And "Mohammed's sect," he says, "is altogether made up (*conflata*) of blasphemy, robbery, and shameful lusts." Nor does it matter in the least what the Koran is all about. "Even if there were anything less scurrilous in the book, it need not concern us any more than the portents of the Egyptians, who invoked snakes and cats. ... Were it not that partly this Mohammedan pest and partly the Pope's idolatry have long been leading us straight to wreck and ruin—may God have mercy upon *some* of us!" ...

Thereupon Genebrard, on the Papal side, charged the German Reformers, chiefly Luther, with endeavoring to introduce Mohammedanism into the Christian world, and to take over the whole clergy to that faith. Maracci is of opinion that Mohammedanism and Lutheranism are not very dissimilar—witness the iconoclastic tendencies of both! More systematically does Martinus Alphonsus Vivaldus marshal up exactly thirteen points to prove that there is not a shadow of difference between the two. Mohammed points to that which is written down—so do these heretics. He has altered the time of the fast—they abhor all fasts. He has changed Sunday into Friday— they observe no feast at all. He rejects the worship of the Saints—so do these Lutherans. Mohammed has no baptism—nor does Calvin consider such requisite. They both allow divorce—and so forth. Whereupon Reland— only 150 years ago—turns around, not without a smile on his eloquent lips, and wants to know how about the prayers for the dead, which both Mohammed and the Pope enjoin, the intercession of angels, likewise the visiting of the graves, the pilgrimages to the Holy Places, the fixed fasts, the merit of works, and the rest of it.

If there be any true gauge of an age or a nation, it is the manner in which such age or nation deals with religious phases beyond the pale. We shall not follow here the vicissitudes of that discussion of which we have indicated a few traits, nor the gradual change which came over European opinion with regard to Islam and its founder. How the silly curses of the Prideaux, and Spanheims, and D'Herbelots; how their "wicked impostors," and "dastardly liars" and "devils incarnate," and Behemoths and beasts and Korahs and six hundred and sixty-sixes, gave room, step by step almost, to more temperate protests, more civil names, less outrageous misrepresentations of both the faith and the man: until Goethe and Carlyle, on the one hand, and that modern phalanx of investigators, the Sprenger, and Amari, and Nöldeke, and Muir, and Dozy, on the other, have taught the world at large that Mohammedanism is a thing of vitality, fraught with a thousand fruitful germs; and that Mohammed, whatever view of his character (to use that vague word for once) be held, has earned a place in the golden book of Humanity.

There is, however, another view which, though more slowly, yet as surely, is gaining ground in the consciousness, if not of the world at large, yet of those who have looked somewhat more closely into this matter. It is this, that Mohammedanism owes more to Judaism than either to Heathenism or to Christianity. We would go a step further. It is not merely parallelisms, reminiscences, allusions, technical terms, and the like, of Judaism, its lore and dogma and ceremony, its Halacha and its Haggadah (words which we have explained at large elsewhere, and which may most briefly be rendered by "Law" and "Legend"), which we find in the Koran;* but we think

---

* Several of these have been pointed out from Maracci, Reland, Mill, Sale, to Geiger (1833)—the *facile princeps* on this field—Muir, Nöldeke, Rodwell, etc.

Islam neither more nor less than Judaism as adapted to Arabia—*plus* the apostleship of Jesus and Mohammed. Nay, we verily believe that a great deal of such Christianity as has found its way into the Koran, has found it through Jewish channels.

We shall speak of these things in due season. Meantime, we would turn for a moment to certain mediæval Jewish opinions both on Christianity and Islam, which will probably astonish our readers. They belong to very high authorities of the Judæo-Arabic Dispersion in Spain: Maimuni, generally called Maimonides, and Jehuda Al-Hassan ben Halevi. The former, at the close of his great "Digest of the Jewish Law," fearlessly speaks of Christ and Mohammed as heralds of the final Messianic times. In filling the world with the message of the Messiah, with the words of Scripture and its precepts, they have, he says, caused these exalted notions and sacred words to spread to the furthest ends of the earth. The latter—sweet singer as well as great philosopher—wrote a book, in Arabic, called "Kusari," wherein a Jew, a Christian, and a Mohammedan, are made to defend and to explain their respective creeds before the King of the Chazars—the king of the country now called the Crimea—who, in the tenth century of our era, had, together with his whole people, embraced Judaism. The Jewish speaker compares the religion founded by Moses to a seed-corn which, apparently dissolved into its elements, is lost to sight; while in reality it assimilates the elements around and throws off its own husk. And in the glorious end, both it and the things around will grow up together even as *one* tree, whose fruit is the Messianic time. The concise description of Islam which the author puts into the mouth of the Mohammedan interlocutor is so fair and correct that it might stand at the beginning of a religious Mohammedan compendium.

But in this they were but the exponents of the real feeling of the Synagogue from the earliest times, on this matter. For, startling as it may seem, what we are wont to consider the emphatically *modern* idea of the "three Semitic creeds"—being by their fundamental unity on the one hand, and their varying supplementary dogmas on the other, apparently intended to bring all humanity within the pale of Monotheism—is found foreshadowed in those Talmudical oracles. They who composed them were truly called the Wise, the Disciples of the Wise. They did not prophesy; they would have shrunk with horror from a like notion; but with a heart full of poetry they often combined marvelous keenness of philosophical insight. And thus while they develop the minutest legal points with an incisive logical sharpness, while they keep our imagination spell-bound by their gorgeous lore, they at times amaze us with views apparently wide apart from their subject; but views so large, so enlightened, so "advanced," that we have to read again and again to believe —even as the age of the Renaissance was amazed and startled when the long-buried song and wisdom of the Antique were made to open their divine lips anew.

Parallel with those transparent allegories of all mankind being addressed on Sinai; or those others of "God's name being inscribed in seventy languages on Moses's wonderstaff;" or of "Joshua engraving the Law in seventy stones on the other side of the Jordan;" there runs the clear and distinct idea of certain apostolic Monotheistic nations or phases. They are three in number. These three are our three "Semitic creeds."

We shall, out of the many Variants that in more or less poetical guise embody this thought, echoed and re-echoed by the highest authorities of the Synagogue, and as often used and misused in fierce mediæval Judæo-Mohammedan controversy, select what we consider the very oldest. It is found in the *Sifre*, a work, although of somewhat later redaction, anterior to the Mishnah, and often quoted in the Talmud as one of its own oldest sources.

A homiletic exposition of Numbers and Deuteronomy, it lovingly tarries at the last chapter—Moses's parting blessing. The Tanchuma introduces this chapter by the striking remark that while through all other blessings recorded in the Pentateuch—of Noah, of Abraham, of Isaac, of Jacob—there always rings some discord, some one harsh note, whereby the bliss foretold is concentrated upon some special heads to the exclusion of others, the dying song of Moses is one unbroken strain of harmony. Its golden blessings flow for all alike, and there is none to stand aside, weeping. And the *Sifre*, in a kind of paraphrase of the special verses themselves, literally continues as follows: "'The Lord came from *Sinai*,' that means the Law was given in *Hebrew*; 'and rose up from *Seïr* unto them,' that means it was also given in *Greek* (*Rumi*); 'and he shineth forth from Mount *Paran*,' that means in *Arabic*." . . .

There is a fourth language added—"'He came with the thousands of Saints,' and this means *Aramaic*." Even granting the typical nature of the three geographical names alluded to—and it is not to be denied that Sinai and Seïr are constantly used for Israel and Esau-Edom-Rome, while Faran plainly stands for Arabia, whether or not it be the name of the mountains around Mecca as contended—the connection of the "thousands of Saints" with Aram does not seem quite clear at first sight—unless it mean Ezra's Puritans. What, however, is quite clear by this time is this, that "Aramaic" is typical of Judaism; that Judaism which has supplanted both Hebraism and Israelitism, and which, having passed through its most vital reformation under Aryan, notably Zoroastrian auspices, during the Exile, subsequently stood at the cradle both of Christianity and Mohammedanism. Aramaic represents that phase during and since the Babylonish captivity whose legitimate and final expression is the "Oral Law," the Talmud: that Talmud, which with one hand—like those Puritans—reared iron walls around the sacred precincts of Faith and Nationality, and with the other laid out these inmost precincts with flowery mazes, of exotic colors, of bewildering fragrance—"a sweet-smelling savor unto the Lord."

When the Talmud was completed (finally gathered in, we mean—not composed), the Koran was begun. *Post hoc—propter hoc.* We do not intend to convey the notion that the Talmudical authors had foretold the Koran. On the contrary, had they known its nature they would scarcely have bestowed upon it the term of "Revelation." But here is the passage: a wondrous sign of their clear appreciation of the elements of culture represented by the nations and clans around them. Hellas-Rome and Arabia appeared to them the fittest preparatory mediums or preliminary stages of this great Sinaitic mission of Faith and Culture.

Post hoc—propter hoc. The Hebrew, the Greek, the Aramaic phases of Monotheism, the Old Testament, the New Testament, the Targum, and the Talmud, were each in their sphere fulfilling their behests. The times were ripe for the Arabic phase.*

In the year 571 was born Mohammed—or he who, together with his mission, appears with that significant name of the "Praised," under which he was supposed to have been foretold in the Old and New Testament.† It was

---

* [We must protest against the construction put upon this passage by some of our contemporaries. The historical sequence of events is merely described; it was not our object to discuss the claims and authority of Judaism, Christianity, and Islamism; and it is a complete misrepresentation of our words to assert that we placed the three religions upon an equal footing.—Note by the Author to the SECOND EDITION.]

† There exist very grave doubts as to whether this really was the Prophet's name. Originally called Kothan, he is held to have first adopted the epithet of Mohammed, either together with his mission or, perhaps,

but a few years after the death of that Byzantine Louis XIV., Justinian, who had aimed at creating one State, one Law, one Church throughout the world; who had laid the first interdict upon the Talmud; who most significantly gathered building materials from all the famous "heathen" temples—of Baal of Baalbeck and Pallas of Athens, of "Isis and Osiris" of Heliopolis and the great Diana of Ephesus, therewith to reconstruct the Hagia Sophia at Constantinople—the same Hagia Sophia wherein now the grave and learned doctors cease not to expound the Koran. In those days Arabia expected her own prophet. The Jews in Arabia are said to have watched for his appearance.

Few religions have been founded in plain day like Islam, which now counts its believers by more than a hundred millions, and which enlarges its domain from day to day, unaided. Most clearly and sharply does Mohammed stand

---

not even before the Flight. It is not easy to fix upon the exact passages, either in the Old or New Testament, to which the Prophet himself alludes, as foretelling him by name: as Mohammed in the Old, and as Ahmad, another form of the same name, in the New. Regarding the latter, probably John's Paraclete (amended by some into $περικλυτός$), which in Arabic might be Ahmad, is meant. As to the Old Testament, the Vulgate—that most faithful receptacle of Jewish tradition, as transmitted to Jerome by his Rabbies—will best help us. There is no doubt that, with that root *hamad* there is generally mixed up some kind of Messianic notion in the eyes of Targumists and Haggadists. And when in Haggai ii., 8, we find the word "Hemdah"=a precious thing, rendered, against grammar and context, by "*Desideratus—omnium gentium,*" we may be sure that the Synagogue did look upon this passage as Messianic, though there be no very direct evidence extant.

out against the horizon of history. Those who knew him, not for hours or days or weeks, but from birth to death, almost during his whole life, count not by units or dozens, but by thousands upon thousands, whose names and whose biographies have been collected; and his witnesses were men in the fullness and ripeness of age and wisdom, some his bitterest enemies. No religious code extant bears so emphatically and clearly the marks and traces of one mind, from beginning to end, as the Koran, though, as to materials and contents, there is, as we have hinted already, a passing strange tale to tell. It will therefore behoove us, in order that we may better understand how Mohammed made these materials entirely his own, how he moulded and shaped, and added unto them, to try and realize first the man himself and the vicissitudes that influenced his mind—its workings and its strugglings, its despairs and its triumphs.

This shall be done very briefly. And, though it seems next to impossible to separate the man from his book, we shall yet attempt to separate them. True, the more than twenty years which its composition occupied are embalmed in it with all their strange changes of fortune, with their terrors and visions, their curses and their prayers, their bulletins and their field-orders. The Koran does indeed illustrate and explain its author's life so well that hitherto every biographer (and there have been many and great ones) has suggested, in accordance with his own views, a different arrangement of that book. In its present shape a sheer chaos as regards chronological or logical order of chapters and even verses, it will lend itself admirably to all and any arrangement. You may work it, as it were, backward and forward. Something is supposed to have happened at a certain time: here is a verse looking like a vague allusion to it; therefore the verse belongs to that period, and confirms the previously doubtful fact. Here is a verse which alludes to some event or other of which nothing is known, and the event is solemnly registered, a fitting date is given to it, and the verse finds its chronological place. But we have nothing to arrange, and therefore, though it be less easy and less picturesque to consider the author and the book as independently as may be, we do so at Mohammed's express desire as it were, and in bare justice to him. He wishes the Koran to be judged by its own contents. "Hic Rhodus, hic salta," he seems to cry. The Book is his sign, his miracle, his mission. His own story is another matter. And without preconceived opinions—either as panegyrist or as Advocatus Diaboli—shall we try to tell it, and then be unfettered in our story of the Book. If we make use of the "Sunnah" for our purpose, no one will blame us. This Midrash of Mohammedanism, as we should call those traditional records of the Prophet's doings and sayings, both in the legendary and juridical sense of the word, has, albeit in exalted tones and colors often, told us much of his outer and inner life. Used with the same patient care with which all documents are used by the impartial historian, it yields precious information.

We have reason to discard much of what has long been repeated about Mohammed's early life. All we know, or think we know now for certain, is that he lost his father before his birth, and his mother when he was six years of age. His grandfather who had adopted him died two years later, and his poor uncle Abu Tâlib then took charge of him. Though belonging to a good enough family, the Koreish, though sickly, subject to epilepsy, Mohammed had early to work for his living. He tended the flocks —even as Moses, David, and all prophets had done, he used to say. "Pick me out the blackest of these berries," he cried once at Medina, when, prophet and king, he saw some people pass with berries of the wild shrub Arak. "Pick me out the blackest, for they are sweet—even such was I wont to gather when I tended the flock of Mecca at Ajyâd." But by the Meccans tending of flocks was considered a very low occupation indeed. In his twenty-fourth year, a rich widow of Mecca, Chadija, about thirty-eight years of age, and twice before married, engaged his services. He accompanied her caravans on several journeys, probably as a camel-driver. Of a sudden she offered him her hand, and obtained the consent of her father by intoxicating him. She bore Mohammed two sons, one of whom he called after a popular idol, and four daughters. Both boys died early.

This is the whole story of Mohammed's outer life previous to the assumption of his mission. The ever-repeated tale of his having accidentally been chosen, in his thirty-fifth year, as arbiter in a quarrel about the replacing of the Black Stone in the Kaaba, is at least very questionable, as are his repeated travels in Syria with his uncles, to which we shall return anent a certain monk who appears in many aliases, and who proves to be more or less a myth.

Mohammed's personal appearance, a matter of some import, chiefly in a prophet, is almost feature by feature thus portrayed by the best authenticated traditionists:

He was of middle height, rather thin, but broad of shoulders, wide of chest, strong of bone and muscle. His head was massive, strongly developed. Dark hair, slightly curled, flowed in a dense mass down almost to his shoulders. Even in advanced age it was sprinkled by only about twenty gray hairs—produced by the agonies of the "Revelations." His face was oval-shaped, slightly tawny of color. Fine, long, arched eyebrows were divided by a vein which throbbed visibly in moments of passion. Great, black, restless eyes shone out from under long, heavy eyelashes. His nose was large, slightly aquiline. His teeth, upon which he bestowed great care, were well set, dazzling white. A full beard framed his manly face. His skin was clear and soft, his complexion "red and white," his hands were as "silk and satin"—even as those of a woman. His step was quick and elastic, yet firm, and as that of one "who steps from a high to a low place." In turning his face he would also turn his full body. His whole gait and presence were dignified and imposing. His countenance was mild and pensive. His laugh was rarely more than a smile. " Oh, my little son !" reads one tradition, " hadst thou seen him, thou wouldst have said thou hadst seen a sun rising." " I," says another witness, " saw him in a moonlight night, and sometimes I looked at his beauty and sometimes I looked at the moon, and his dress was striped with red, and he was brighter and more beautiful to me than the moon."

In his habits he was extremely simple, though he bestowed great care on his person. His eating and drinking, his dress and his furniture, retained, even when he had reached the fullness of power, their almost primitive nature. He made a point of giving away all " superfluities." The only luxuries he indulged in were, besides arms, which he highly prized, certain yellow boots, a present from the Negus of Abyssinia. Perfumes, however, he loved passionately, being most sensitive of smell. Strong drinks he abhorred.

His constitution was extremely delicate. He was nervously afraid of bodily pain—he would sob and roar under it. Eminently unpractical in all common things of life, he was gifted with mighty powers of imagination, elevation of mind, delicacy and refinement of feeling. " He is more modest than a virgin behind her curtain," it was said of him. He was most indulgent to his inferiors, and would never allow his awkward little page to be scolded, whatever he did. " Ten years," said Anas, his servant, " was I about the Prophet, and he never said as much as ' uff' to me." He was very affectionate toward his family.

One of his boys died on his breast, in the smoky house of the nurse, a blacksmith's wife. He was very fond of children. He would stop them in the streets and pat their little cheeks. He never struck any one in his life. The worst expression he ever made use of in conversation was, "What has come to him?—may his forehead be darkened with mud!" When asked to curse some one, he replied, "I have not been sent to curse, but to be a mercy to mankind." "He visited the sick, followed any bier he met, accepted the invitation of a slave to dinner, mended his own clothes, milked his goats, and waited upon himself," relates summarily another tradition. He never first withdrew his hand out of another man's palm, and turned not before the other had turned. His hand, we read elsewhere—and traditions like these give a good index of what the Arabs expected their prophet to be—was the most generous, his breast the most courageous, his tongue the most truthful; he was the most faithful protector of those he protected, the sweetest and most agreeable in conversation; those who saw him were suddenly filled with reverence, those who came near him loved him, they who described him would say, "I have never seen his like either before or after." He was of great taciturnity, but when he spoke it was with emphasis and deliberation, and no one could ever forget what he said. He was, however, very nervous and restless withal, often low-spirited, downcast as to heart and eyes. Yet he would at times suddenly break through those broodings, become gay, talkative, jocular, chiefly among his own. He would then delight in telling amusing little stories, fairy tales, and the like. He would romp with the children, and play with their toys—as, after his first wife's death, he was wont to play with the dolls his new baby-wife had brought into his house.

The common cares of life had been taken from him by the motherly hand of Chadija; but heavier cares seemed now to darken his soul, to weigh down his whole being. As time wore on the gloom and misery of his heart became more and more terrible. He neglected his household matters, and fled all men. "Solitude became a passion to him," the traditions record. He had now passed the meridian of his life. No one seemed to heed the brooder, no one stretched out the hand of sympathy to him. He had nothing in common with the rest, and he was left to himself.

Much chronological discussion has arisen as to the date of the event of which we are going to speak. So much, however, seems certain, that Mohammed was at least forty years of age when he went, according to the custom of some of his countrymen, to spend the Rajab, the month of universal armistice among the ancient Arabs, on Mount Hirâ, an hour's walk from Mecca. This mountain, now called Mount of Light, consists of a huge barren rock, torn by cleft and hollow ravine, standing out solitary in the full white glare of the desert sun, shadowless, flowerless, without well or rill. On this rock, in a small, dark cave, Mohammed lived alone, and spent his days and his nights, according to unanimous tradition, in "*Tahannoth.*"

The weary guesses that have been made from the days of these very traditions to our own, as to the meaning and derivation of this word, can not be told. It has been put on the rack by lexicographers, grammarians, commentators, translators, investigators, of all hues and ages, and, we are sorry to add, with no satisfactory result. To the general meaning the context gave some cue, but the etymology of the word, and its technical signification, have remained a mystery, notwithstanding many various readings of its single letters suggested by sheer despair. One of the latest and greatest investigators, Sprenger, numbers it as one of the most "indigestible morsels" among the many strange and obsolete words that occur in connection with Mohammed and the Koran.

We do not intend to do more than throw out suggestions—though very carefully weighed—for we must, to our regret, leave all our philological scaffoldings behind. Regarding this most mysterious word, we have a notion that it might be explained, like scores of other tough morsels in the Koran, by the Jewish, Hebrew, or Aramaic parlance of the period, as it is preserved most fortunately in the Talmud, the Targum, the Midrash. The word Tahannoth need not be emendated into *Tahannof*, or any other weird form, to agree with its traditional meaning, because we think that it is only the Hebrew word *Tehinnoth*, which occurs bodily in the Bible, and means "Prayers, Supplications." The change of vowels is exactly the same as that from the Hebrew *Gehinnom* (New Testament *Gehenna*) to the Koranic *Johannam*. Among the Jews the word became technical for a certain class of devotional prayers, customary, together with fastings, throughout the month preceding the New-Year's Day. It is known more generally as a term for private devotions throughout the year, chiefly for pious women. This, however, only by the way.

To devotions and asceticism, then, Mohammed gave himself up in his wild solitude. And after a time there came to him dreams "resplendent like the rosy dawn." When he left his cave to walk about on his rocky fastness, the wild herbs that grew in the clefts would bend their heads, and the stones scattered in his way would cry, "Salâm! Hail, O Prophet of God!" And horrified, not daring to look about him, he fled back into his cave. That same cave has now become a station for the Holy Pilgrimage, and on it that early predecessor of our Burckhardts and Burtons, "Hajj Joseph Pitts, of Exon," the runaway sailor boy, delivered himself of the judgment that "he had been in the cave, and observed that it was not at all beautified, at which he admired."

Suddenly, in the middle of the night—the "blessed night Al Kadar," as the Koran has it—"and who will make thee understand what the night Al Kadar is? That night Al Kadar, which is better than a thousand months.... which bringeth peace and blessings till the rosy dawn"—in the middle of that night, Mohammed awoke from his sleep, and he heard a voice. Twice it called, urging, and twice he struggled and waived its call. But he was pressed sore, "as if a fearful weight had been laid upon him." He thought his last hour had come. And for the third time the voice called—

"CRY!"

And he said, "What shall I cry?"

Came the answer: "CRY—in the name of thy Lord!"...

And these, according to well-nigh unanimous tradition, followed by nearly every ancient and modern authority, are the first words of the Koran. Our readers will find them in the ninety-sixth chapter of that Book, to which they have been banished by the Redactors.

We hasten to add that when we said that the above sentence would be found in the ninety-sixth chapter of the Koran, we were not quite accurate. The word which we have ventured to translate *Cry* they will find rendered in as many different ways as there were translators, investigators, commentators, old and new. They will find Recite, Preach, Read, Proclaim, Call out, Read the Scriptures—namely, of the Jews and Christians—and a weary variety of other meanings which certainly belong to the word, though the greater part of them is of obviously later date and utterly out of the question in this case.

Our reasons for deviating from these time-honored versions were of various kinds. In the first place, the Arabic root in question is *identical* with our own, and in this primitive root lie hidden all other significations. " Cry " is one of those very few onomatopoetic words still common to both Semitic and Indo-European. Its significations are indeed manifold; from the vague sound given forth by bird or tree, as in Sanskrit, to our English usage of silent weeping; from the Hebrew "deep *crying* unto deep" to the technical Aramaic "reading the Scriptures" —in contradistinction to "reading the Mishnah"—from the weird German *Schrei* to the Greek herald's solemn proclamation—it is always the same fundamental root: biliteral or triliteral.

Secondly, because the principal words of this tradition are startlingly identical — another fact not hitherto noticed, as far as we are aware—with a certain passage in Isaiah: "The Voice said Cry, and I said, What shall I cry?"—a passage in which no one has yet translated the leading verb by Recite, Read, Read the Scriptures, though there was never a doubt as to whether Isaiah knew the Scriptures and could read, while Mohammed distinctly denied being a "scholar."

And, thirdly, because from this root is also derived the word *Koran.* Derived: for it was in the very special Jewish sense of *Mikra*, Scripture, that Mohammed gave that name to every single fragment of that book, until it became, even as the word Mishnah, its collective and general name.

We now resume our recital of that first revelation and

its immediate consequences, as tradition has preserved it. It is of moment.

When the voice had ceased to speak, telling how from minutest beginnings man had been called into existence and lifted up by understanding and knowledge of the Lord, who is most beneficent, and who *by the pen* had revealed that which men did not know, Mohammed awoke from his trance and felt as if "a book" had been written in his heart. A great trembling came upon him, so that his whole body shook, and the perspiration ran down his body. He hastened home to his wife, and said, "Oh, Chadija! what has happened to me!" He lay down, and she watched by him. When he recovered from his paroxysm he said, "Oh, Chadija! he, of whom one would not have believed it [meaning himself], has become either a soothsayer [Kahin*] or one possessed [by Djins]—mad." She replied, "God is my protection, O Abu-'l-Kasim! [a name of Mohammed derived from one of his boys], He will surely not let such a thing happen unto thee, for thou speakest the truth, dost not return evil for evil, keepest faith, art of good life, and kind to thy relations and friends. And neither art thou a talker abroad in the bazaars. What has befallen thee? Hast thou seen aught terrible?" Mohammed replied, "Yes." And he told her what he

---

* The Hebrew "Cohen," priest, in a deteriorated sense like the German "Pfaffe." In the time of Mohammed it meant a low fortune-teller, an ever-ready interpreter of dreams, who had, like Daniel, to find out both the dreams and their solutions.

had seen. Whereupon she answered and said, "Rejoice, O dear husband, and be of good cheer. He in whose hands stands Chadija's life is my witness that thou wilt be the prophet of this people." Then she arose and went to her cousin Waraka, who was old and blind, and "knew the Scriptures of the Jews and Christians." When she told him what she had heard, he cried out, "*Koddus, Koddus!*—Holy, Holy! Verily this is the *Namus* which came to Moses. He will be the prophet of his people. Tell him this. Bid him be of brave heart."

We must here interpose for a moment. This Waraka has given rise to much and angry discussion—chiefly as to his "conversion." He was long supposed to have been first an idolater, then a Jew, finally a Christian. It has been shown, however, by recent investigations, that whatever he was at first, he certainly lived and died a Jew. To our mind this one sentence goes a long way toward settling the point. *Koddus* is simply the Arabicized Hebrew *Kadosh* (Holy). And while we need not prove that a Christian would scarcely have used this exclamation (any more than he would have spoken of the "Namus"), we are reminded of the story in the Midrash of the man whose heart was sore within him for that he could neither read the Scripture nor the Mishnah. And one day when he stood in the synagogue, and the precentor reached that part of the liturgy in which God's holy name is sanctified, this man lifted up his voice aloud and cried out with all his main: "*Kadosh! Kadosh! Ka-*

dosh!" (Holy! Holy! Holy!) And when they asked him what made him cry out thus, he said, "I have not been deemed worthy to read the Scriptures, or the Mishnah, and now the moment has come when I may sanctify God, shall I not lift up my voice aloud?" "It did not last a year, or two, or three," the legend adds, "but it so fell out that this man became a great and mighty general, and a founder of a colony within the Roman empire."

As to the "*Namus*," it is an hermaphrodite in words. It is Arabic, but also Greek. That it is Talmudical, need we say it? It is in the first instance νόμος, Law, that which "by custom and common consent" has become so. In Talmudical phraseology it stands for the Thorah or Revealed Law. In Arabic it further means one who communicates a secret message. And all these different significations were conveyed by Waraka to Mohammed. The messenger and the message, both divine, had come together, even as Moses had been instructed in the Law by a special angel—not, as former commentators, to save Waraka's Christianity, used to explain, because to Mohammed, as to Moses, a new Law was given, while Christ came to confirm what had been given before.

Not long after this the two men met in the street of Mecca. And Waraka said, "I swear by him in whose hand Waraka's life is, God has chosen thee to be the prophet of this people. The greatest *Namus* has come to thee. They will call thee a liar; they will persecute thee, they will banish thee, they will fight against thee.

Oh, that I could live to those days! I would fight for thee." And he kissed him on his forehead. The Prophet went home, and the words he had heard were a great comfort to him, and diminished his anxiety.

After this Mohammed, in awe and trembling, waited for other visions and revelations. But none came; and the old horrible doubts and suspicions crept over his soul. He went up to Mount Hirâ again — this time to commit suicide. But, as often as he approached the precipice, lo, he beheld Gabriel at the end of the horizon whithersoever he turned, who said to him, "I am Gabriel, and thou art Mohammed, the Prophet of God." And he stood as entranced, unable to move backward or forward, until anxious Chadija sent out men to seek him.

We must interrupt the course of the story for a moment respecting this "Voice," which is called in the Koran, Gabriel, *or* the Holy Ghost. We have on a previous occasion spoken of the strange metamorphoses of angels and demons, as they migrated from India to Babylonia, and from Babylonia to Judæa. Their further migration to Mecca did not produce much change, since the process of Semitizing them and making them subservient to Monotheism had been wrought already by the Talmud. Yet this strange identification of Gabriel with the Holy Ghost which we find here is a problem not fully to be solved, either by the Talmud or the Zend Avesta.

The Holy Ghost, an expression of most common occurrence in the Haggadah, is thus summarily explained by the Talmud—as an emphatic answer probably to the popular tendency of taking transcendental terms in a concrete sense. "With ten names," says the Talmud, "is the Holy Ghost named in Scripture. They are—Parable, Allegory, Enigma, Speech, Sentence, Light, Command, Vision, Prophecy." In the Angelic Hierarchy of the Talmud it is Michael (Vohumanô), and not Gabriel, who takes first rank. He stands to the right of the Throne, Gabriel to the left; he represents Grace; Gabriel, stern Justice; and though they are both intrusted with watching over God's people, yet it is Michael who stands forth to fight for them, who brings them good tidings, and who, as heavenly High-Priest, "offers up the souls of the righteous upon God's Altar." Yet he is often accompanied by Gabriel, who is, be it observed, particularly active in the life of Abraham. It is he who saves Abraham from the fiery furnace into which Nimrod had cast him; in the message of Isaac's birth he is one of the three "men," and his place is to Michael's right hand. In all other respects he is the exact counterpart of the Persian Çraôshô, and his principal office is that of revenging and punishing evil, while he acts as a merciful genius to the good and elect. Hence, probably, he became in later Persian mythology, as well as in the Talmud, the Divine Messenger. He is thus replete with all knowledge, and—alone of all angels—is versed in all human tongues. Islam has made a few transparently "tendencious" changes. Gabriel here stands to the right hand of the throne, and Michael to the left, *i. e.*, the former becomes the Angel of Mercy, and the latter that of Punishment. Omar, it is said, once went into a Jewish academy and asked the Jews about Gabriel's office. He, they mockingly answered, is our enemy; he betrays all our secrets to Mohammed, and he and Michael are always at war with each other—an answer which, taken seriously by Omar, so shocked him that he cried out, "Why, you are more unbelieving than the Himyarites!" But might this strange identification of Gabriel and the Holy Ghost possibly be accounted for by the fact that the mystic office with regard to the birth of Christ, ascribed to the Holy Ghost by the Church, is ascribed in Islam to Gabriel also, who, as in the New Testament, announces the message to Mary, and that thus the two have become fully identified in the minds of the traditionists?

We have left Mohammed in the terror-stricken state of a mind conscious of its mission, and vainly trying to struggle against it. The grim, lonely darkness within, the horrible dread lest it all be but mockery and self-deception, or "the Devil's prompting;" the inability of uttering, save in a few wild, rhapsodic sounds, that message which is silently and agonizingly growing into shape—and death seems the only refuge and salvation—who shall describe it? It was through these phases of a soul struggling between Heaven and Hell that Mohammed went in those days, and the thought of suicide came temptingly near. But, lo! Gabriel on the edge of the horizon, crying:

O

I am Gabriel, and thou art Mohammed, God's Messenger. . . . Fear not!

It is not easy to say how long that state of doubt and terror lasted. Tradition, wildly diverging here, is, of course, of little use. Probably he was not quite free from it to the day of his death. But, by degrees, and as he no longer had to carry that dread burden in his lonely heart, he gathered strength. His confidence in himself and in his mission rose. No demoniac, no contemptible soothsayer, no possessed madman he—the voice within urged. And at times a blissful exultation took the place of the former horror. His heart throbs with grateful joy. "By the midday splendor, and by the stilly night," he cries, " the Lord does not reject him, and will not forsake him, and the future shall be better than the past. Has he not found him an orphan and given him a home, found him astray and guided him into the straight path, found him so poor and made him so rich?" "Wherefore," he adds, "do not thou oppress the orphan, neither repel thou him who asketh of thee—but declare aloud the bounties of thy Lord!" . . .

And the revelations now came one after the other without intermission during a space of more than twenty years—revelations, the central sun of which was the doctrine of God's Unity, Monotheism, of which he, Mohammed, was the bearer to his own people.

Yet these revelations did not come in visions bright, transcendent, exalted. They came ghastly, weird, most horrible. After long, solitary broodings, a something used to move Mohammed, all of a sudden, with frightful vehemence. He "roared like a camel," his eyes rolled and glowed like red coals, and on the coldest day terrible perspirations would break out all over his body. When the terror ceased, it seemed to him as if he had heard bells ringing, "the sound whereof seemed to rend him to pieces"—as if he had heard the voice of a man—as if he had seen Gabriel—or as if words *had been written in his heart*. Such was the agony he endured that some of the verses revealed to him well-nigh made his hair turn white.

Mohammed was epileptic, and vast ingenuity and midical knowledge have been lavished upon this point, as explanatory of Mohammed's mission and success. We, for our own part, do not think that epilepsy ever made a man appear a prophet to himself, or even to the people of the East; or, for the matter of that, inspired him with the like heart-moving words and glorious pictures. Quite the contrary. It was taken as a sign of demons within—demons, "Devs," devils, to whom all manner of diseases were ascribed throughout the antique world, in Phœnicia, in Greece, in Rome, in Persia, and among the lower classes in Judæa after the Babylonian Exile. The Talmud, which denies a concrete Satan, or rather resolves him rationally into "passion," "remorse," and "death"—stages corresponding to his being "Seducer," "Accuser," and "Angel of Death"—speaks of these demons as hobgoblins, or special diseases, and inveighs in terms of contempt against the "exorcisms" in vogue* in Judæa about the period of the birth of Christianity. Those "possessed" loved solitary places, chiefly cemeteries; they tore their garments, and were altogether beyond the pale. On the special nature of the possessing demons, the "Shedim" of the Talmud, the "Devils" of the New Testament, the Jin, or Genii, of the Koran, as different from and yet alike to the Devas, and as forming the intermediate beings between men and angels, as in Plato (*Sympos.*), we may yet have to speak. That they were all "pure, holy, everlasting angels from the beginning," and only came to be degraded (as were the Devas by "Zoroastrianism," and the gods of Hellas and Rome by Christianity) into wicked angels in the course of religious reformation or change—is unquestionable, even if the Book of Enoch did not state it expressly. They are "fallen angels"—fallen through pride, envy, lust. The two angels Shamchazai (Asai) and Azael (Uziel) of the Targum, the Midrash, and the Koran (Márut and Hárut), are thrown from heaven because of

---

* True, Simon ben Yochai, the fabulous author of the Zohar, to whose rather badly kept shrine at Merom, a few hours from Tiberias (where also Shammai and Hillel are believed to be buried), the Faithful of Palestine, and even of Persia and India, make their annual pilgrimage to this day, did once, and apparently with the approval of the authorities, drive out a devil from the Emperor's daughter at Rome. But then this devil had good-naturedly offered his services himself, and the object of Simon's embassy, the rescinding of an oppressive decree, was considered so praiseworthy in the main that these authorities rather shut their eyes to the performance.

their desiring the daughters of man, even as Sammael himself loses his most high estate, because he seduces Adam and Eve. True, there is a peculiar something supposed to inhere in epilepsy. The Greeks called it a sacred disease. Bacchantic and chorybantic furor were God-inspired stages. The Pythia uttered her oracles under the most distressing signs. Symptoms of convulsion were even needed as a sign of the divine mania or inspiration. But Mohammed did not utter any of his sayings while the paroxysm lasted. Clearly, distinctly, most consciously, did he dictate to his scribe what had come to him—for he could not write, according to his own account. But it may well be, and it speaks for Mohammed's thorough honesty, that he believed himself, in the very first stages, to have been "inspired" during his fits by Jin. According to Zoroastrotalmudical notions, which had penetrated into Arabia, these Jin listened "behind the curtain" of heaven, and learned the things of the future. These they were then believed to communicate to the soothsayers and diviners. But it was dangerous eavesdropping enough. When the heavenly watchers perceived these curious goblins, they hurled arrows of fire at them—in which men saw falling stars. Mohammed soon, however, rejected this notion of "demoniac" inspiration: while from the Byzantines to Luther, and from Luther to Muir, it was the devil who prompted the Prophet. Muir has indeed instituted several minute comparisons between Satan tempting Christ and Mohammed. Whereat Sprenger somewhat irreverently observes, that since there be a devil, he must needs have something to do.

Tempted as we feel, before we proceed to describe the mental and religious atmosphere around Mohammed when he came to proclaim " the faith of Abraham," that first bearer of the emphatically Semitic mission, to enlarge upon that great question of the day, the mission of the Semitic races in general, we must confine ourselves to one or two points touching their religious development. A brilliant French *savant* has of late, in somewhat rash generalization, asserted that Monotheism is a Semitic instinct. On which another, one of the most profound scholars—since, alas! dead—observed that the assertion was perfectly correct, if you exclude all the Semitic races save the Jews; and these, it might be added, at a very late period indeed, notwithstanding all the teachings of Moses and the Prophets, not after a thousand judgments had come upon them, all the horrors of internecine war, misery, captivity, and exile. The Phœnicians were idolaters, the Assyrians were idolaters, the Babylonians were idolaters, and the Arabs were idolaters. And yet, perhaps, the truth lies, as usual, in the middle. If, according to Schelling, who goes much further, a vague Monotheism is the basis of all religions, there certainly does seem to be an abstract idea of absolute power of rule and dominion hidden in the universal Semitic name of the All-Powerful Supreme God, to whom all the other natural powers, in their personified mystic guises, are subject, and in whom they, as it were, are absorbed. Baal, El, Elohim, Allah, Elion, denote not merely the Light, the bright Heaven, as Zeus, Jupiter (subject in his turn to Fate, or that "which had once been spoken"), but Might, Almightiness—absolute, despotic, that created and destroyed, did and undid according to its own tremendous Will alone, and by the side of which nothing else existed; while Jehovah-Jahve seems to point to the other stage and side of absolute Existence, the Being from all times and for all times, the *Ens*, the First Cause. And what is especially characteristic of the Shemites is this, that while, as Jewish and Arabic tradition has it, the sons of Japhet (Indo-Germans) are kings, and those of Ham slaves, the sons of Shem are prophets. A thousand times lulled into sweet dreams of beauty, they are aroused a thousand times by the wild cry of the Prophet in their midst, who points heavenward, "Behold who hath created all these!" But what is a Prophet? In the Hebrew term *Nabi*, which Islam adopted, there does not indeed appear to inhere that foretelling faculty with which from the time of the Septuagint we are wont to connect it. For it is the Septuagint which first translates it by προφήτης, foreteller; while others render it by "Inspired," or simply "Orator." The manifold equivalents used in the Bible, such as watchman, seer, shepherd, messenger, one and all denote emphatically the office of watching over the events, and of lifting up the voice of warning, of reproving, of encouraging, before all the people at the proper hour. Hence the

Haggadah has been called "the prophetess of the Exile," though no Haggadist was ever considered "inspired." The Prophet was above all things considered as the popular preacher and teacher, gifted with religious enthusiasm, with an intense love of his people, and with divine power of speech: whence alone the possibility of prophetic schools. And most strikingly says the Midrash of Abraham that he was a Prophet, a *Nabi*, but not an "Astrologer," one whose calling it is not to forecast, but one who lifts men's minds heavenward. In this sense — all transcendentalism apart—Mohammed might well be called a prophet even by Jews and Christians.

We can but guess at the state of Arab belief and worship before Mohammed. For though the Arabs enter the world's stage as long after the first joyous revelation of humanity in Hellenism as the Assyrians and Babylonians, not to speak of the Phœnicians, had entered it before, they have left us but little record of their doings in the period of "Ignorance"—as with proud humility they called the time before Islam. From what broken light is shed by a few forlorn rays, we may conclude this, that they worshiped—to use that vague word—the Hosts of Heaven, and that with this worship there was combined a partial belief in resurrection among some clans. Others, however, seem to have ascribed every thing to "Nature," and to have denied a guiding Creator. We further find traces of an adoration of fetiches: bodily representatives of certain influences to be avoided, feared, and conciliated, or to be loved and gratefully acknowledged. The Sun and the Moon, Jupiter and Venus, Canopus and Sirius and Mercury, had their stony mementos, their temples, their priests, and, be it well understood, the power of protecting those who fled to their altars. Herodotus speaks of the Arabs as worshiping only Dionysos (whom Strabo changes into Jupiter) and Urania, "whom they call" Orotal (probably Nur-Allah=God's light), and Alilat—a feminine form of Allah, the Phœnician Queen of Heaven, Tanith-Astarte. Of a worship of heroes in the form of statues there are vague traces, but so vague and so mythical that they can not be counted historical material. Trees and stones are further mentioned as objects of primitive Arab worship, and on this point Maimonides has given, as is his wont, clear and transparent explanations, into which we can not, however, enter. Among the latter the famous Black Stone of the Kaaba, that primeval temple ascribed to Abraham, stands foremost; next we know of a White Stone (Al Lat), at Taïf, still seen by Hamilton, and one or two more immovable tokens of some great event, such as the Shemites were wont to erect—Jacob, among others, at Bethel (the general Phœnician term for these stone erections)—mementos which the Pentateuch emphatically protests against: "For *I* am Jehovah, your God." Vaguer still are the records of the Oracle-Trees, one of which stood near Mecca, while the other, dedicated to Uzza, the Mighty Goddess, the Queen of Heaven, seems to have spread all over the land, with its due complement of priests and soothsayers, male and female. That there were the usual accompaniment of Lares and Penates, more or less coarse and bodily, such as always have been necessary for the herd, need not be added. Thus it is recorded of one tribe that they worshiped a piece of dough, which, compelled by hunger, they cheerfully ate up. Some, we said, did not believe in the resurrection. Some did; and therefore they tied a camel to a man's sepulchre, without providing it with any food. If it ran away, that man was everlastingly damned—and, be it observed here, that the Jews alone among the Shemites protested against everlasting damnation; if not, its blackened bones would, on the day of judgment, form a handy and honorable conveyance to the abode of his bliss. The Phantoms of the Desert, the Fata Morgana, Angels and Demons, and the rest of embodied ideas or ideals, formed other objects of pious consideration, but only as intermediators with the great Allah. Long before Mohammed, the people were wont, in their distress, to pray at their pilgrimages to him alone, in this wise: "At thy service, O Allah! There is no Being like unto thee, and if there be one, it is thou and not it that reigneth;" and when asked what was the office of their idols, they would answer that they were intermediators —much as Roman Catholics in the lower strata revere Saints and their emblems. Let it not be forgotten also that the perpetuation of this pre-Islamic idolatry, if so we call it, was due to a great extent to political reasons.

The manifold sanctuaries and their incomes belonged to certain noble families and clans.

So much for Heathenism. We have now to consider the two other popularly assumed agents in that religious phase to which Mohammed has given its name, and which has changed the face of the world—Christianity and Judaism.

It has long been the fashion to ascribe whatever was "good" in Mohammedanism to Christianity. We fear this theory is not compatible with the results of honest investigation. For of Arabian Christianity, at the time of Mohammed, the less said perhaps the better. By the side of it, as seen in the Koran — and this book alone shows it to us authentically as Mohammed saw it—even modern Amharic Christianity, of which we possess such astounding accounts, appears pure and exalted. And as, moreover, the monk Behira-Sergius-Georgius-Nestor, who is said to have instructed Mohammed, is a very intangible person indeed, if he be not, as there is reason to believe, actually a Jew; and as the several Syrian travels during which Mohammed is supposed to have been further inured into Christianity have to be taken *cum grano*, nothing remains but his contact with a few freed Greek and Abyssinian slaves, who, having lived all their life among Arabians, could hardly boast of a very profound knowledge of the tenets and history of Christianity. We shall, therefore, not be surprised to see the Koran polemizing against some such extraordinary notions as that of

Mary-Maryam, "the daughter of Imran, the sister of Harun," being not only the mother of God, but forming a person in the Trinity; or, on the other hand, to meet with the extraordinary legends from the apocryphal Gospel of the Infancy, and from the "Assumption" of Mary, ascribed to John the Apostle himself. Or, again, to see it adopt the heretical view of certain early Christian sects that it was not Christ, but Judas, who was executed, and that Christ had to allow the "hallucination" as a punishment for having suffered people to call him God. But that fundamental tenet of Christianity, viz., the Sonship, Mohammed fought against with unswerving consistency; and never grew tired of repeating, in the most emphatic terms which he, the master of speech, could find, his abhorrence against that notion, at which "the Heavens might tear open, and the earth cleave asunder." There is a brief chapter in the Koran, the "Confession of God's Unity," which is considered tantamount to the third part of the whole Koran, though it only consists of these words —"Say, God is one: the Everlasting God. *He begetteth not, and he is not begotten*, and there is none like unto him." Still more distinctly is this notion expressed in another place: "The Christians say Christ is the Son of God. May God resist them ... how are they infatuated!" And again: "They are certainly infidels who say God is One of Three." ... "Believe in God and his Apostle, but speak not of a Trinity. There is but One God. Far be it from him that he should have a son." ...

"Christ the Son of Mary is no more than an Apostle." ... "It is not fit for Allah that he should have a Son. Praise to him!" (*i. e.*, far be it from him!).

Jesus, according to Mohammed, is only one of the six apostles who are specially chosen out of three hundred and thirteen to proclaim new dispensations, in confirmation of previous ones. These are Adam, Noah, Abraham, Moses, Jesus, and Mohammed. But this point must come under further consideration under the tenets of Islam.

We now turn to Judaism, which, as we have hinted before, forms *the* kernel of Mohammedanism, both general and special. Here merely the preliminary observation that when we spoke of the Talmud as a source of Islam we did not imply that Mohammed knew it, or, for the matter of that, had ever heard its very name; but it seems as if he had breathed from his childhood almost the air of contemporary Judaism, such Judaism as is found by us crystallized in the Talmud, the Targum, the Midrash.

Indeed, the geographical and ethnographical notices of Arabia in Scripture are to so astounding a degree in accordance with the very latest researches, that we can not but assume the connection between Palestine and Arabia to have been close from the earliest periods. The Ishmaelites of the Arabian midland are, in the earliest documents, carefully distinguished from the Yoctanites and Kushites of Marah in the south, not to speak of the minute information revealed by the later documents. At what time Jews first went to Arabia is a problem which we shall not endeavor to settle. Of Abraham and Ishmael, and the halo of legends that surrounds these national heroes, hereafter. But even rejecting, as we must do, the hallucinations of two most eminent scholars regarding the immigration of an entire Simeonitic regiment in the time of Saul, who having fought a battle near Mecca —hence called Makkah Rabbah (Great Defeat)—settled as Gorhoms or Gerim (Strangers), and so forth, we can not shut our eyes to the fact that Jews, "worshipers of the invisible God of Abraham," existed, though in small numbers, in Arabia, at a very primitive period indeed. Bokht-Nasar, as Nebuchadnezzar is called in early Arabic documents, caused many others to seek refuge in Arabia. The Hasmoneans forced a whole tribe of Northern Arabia to adopt Judaism; a Jewish king of Arabs fights against Pompey. The Talmud shows a rather unexpected familiarity with Arab manners and customs, and—to indicate one curious point—the prophet Elijah, who appears there as a kind of immortal tutelary genius—goes about in the guise of an Arab (the Khidhr of Mohammedan legend). The angels that appear to Abraham "look like Arabs" —not to speak of Job and his three friends, the Queen of Sheba, and other like Arab reminiscences. Centuries before Mohammed, Kheibar, five days from Medina, and Yemen, in South Arabia, were in the hands of the Jews. Dhu Nowas, the last Jewish king of Yemen, falls by the hands of the Abyssinian Negus. The question for us remains, what phase of faith these Jews represented.

It has been supposed that, though combined among themselves for purposes of war, they held little intercommunication with their brethren either in Palestine or even in Arabia, and therefore were ignorant of the development of "The Law" that went rolling on in Judæa and Babylonia. The chief proof for this was found in the absence of Judæo-Arabic literature before Mohammed. To us, this circumstance affords absolutely no proof. None, at least, that would not perhaps rather confirm our view to the exact contrary. We know how literatures may be and have been stamped out; or had the Phœnicians, the Chaldæans, the Etruscans, never any literature? We happen to know the contrary, though nothing, not to say worse than nothing, because more or less corrupt reminiscences, has remained of it all. And, further, we have distinct proof in the very Koran that not only did they keep *au courant* with regard to Haggadah — witness all the legends of Islam—but even to Halachah. Mohammed literally quotes a passage from the Mishnah,* and, further, gives special injunctions taken from the Gemara, such as the purification with sand in default of water, the shortening of the prayer in the moment of danger, etc.† There

---

* Notably the judge's admonition to the witnesses, that he who wantonly destroys one single human life will be considered as guilty as if he had destroyed a whole world.

† "Thy will be done in Heaven; grant peace to them that fear thee on Earth; and whatever pleaseth thee, do. Blessed art thou, O Lord,

is an academy, or Bethhamidrash, at Medina; and Akiba, when on his revolutionary mission, is consulted by the Arab Jews about one of the most minute and intricate points of the Oral Law.

In truth, these Jews stood not merely on the heights of contemporary culture, but far above their Arab brethren. They represented, in fact, the Culture of Arabia. They could all read and write, while the Arabs had occasionally to capture some foreign scholars and promise them their liberty on condition that they should teach their boys the elements of reading and writing. The Jews—nay, the Jewesses, as Mohammed had to learn to his grief—were specially gifted with the poetic vein, as we shall see farther on; and poetry in Arabia was at the time of Mohammed the one great accomplishment. There was a certain fair held annually, where, as at the Olympic Games, the productions of the last twelve months were read and received prizes. The beautiful tale of the hanging up of the prize poems in the Kaaba, whence they were called Moallakat, is unfortunately a myth, since Moallakat does not betoken suspended ones, but (pearls) loosely strung together. But, undoubtedly, to have made the best poem of the season was a great distinction, not merely for the individual poet, but for his entire clan.

These Jewish tribes, some of whom derived their genealogy from priestly families (Al-Kahinani), lived scattered

---

who hearest prayer"—is the formula suggested by the Talmud for the hours of mental distraction or peril.

all over Arabia, but chiefly in the south, in Yeman (Himyar), "the dust of which was like unto gold, and where men never died." They lived, as did other Arabs, either the life of roving Bedouins, or cultivated the land, or inhabited cities, such as Yathrib, the later Medina or City, by way of eminence—of the Prophet, to wit. Outwardly they had completely merged in the great Arabic family. Conversions of entire clans to Judaism, intermarriages, and the immense family likeness, so to speak, of the two descendants of Abraham—for the derivation of the Arabs from Ishmael, whatever may be alleged to the contrary, seems unquestionably an ante-Mohammedan notion—facilitated the leveling work of Jewish cosmopolitanism. Acquainted, as we said, with both Halachah and Haggadah, they seemed, under the peculiar story-loving influence of their countrymen, to have cultivated more particularly the latter with all its gorgeous hues and colors. Valiant with the sword, which they not rarely turned against their own kinsmen, they never omitted the fulfillment of their greatest religious duty—the release of their captives, though these might be their adversaries; and further, like their fathers, from of old, they kept the Sabbath holy even in war, though the prohibition had been repealed. They waited for the Messiah, and they turned their faces toward Jerusalem.* They fasted, they prayed,

---

* The synagogues were generally built in the form of a theatre, the portal due west, so that the worshiper's face was turned to the east, even to the Holy of Holies of the Temple of Jerusalem, in pious allusion to the words

and they scattered around them the seeds of such high culture as was contained in their literature. And Arabia called them the People of the "Book;" even as Hegel has called them the People of the "Geist." These seeds, though some fell on stones, and some on the desert sand, had borne fruit a thousand-fold. Of generally practical, nay vital, institutions which they had introduced, long before Mohammed, into the land of their adoption, may be mentioned the Calendar; and the intercalary month was by the Arabs called, in grateful acknowledgment, *Nassi* (Prince), the title of the Babylonian head of the Jewish Diaspora. The Kaaba and the Pilgrimage, Yoctan and Ishmael, Zemzem and Hagar, received their coloring from Jewish Arabs. They were altogether looked up to with much reverence, and their superiority would also politically have stood them in very good stead, when Mohammed subsequently turned against them, had they known what united action meant.

When we said that there were distinguished poets among them, we meant poets not Jewish, but purely Arabic. Their poems are all of intensely national Arabic type. Among others we have fragments by Assamael

---

(1 Kings viii., 29), "That their eyes may be open toward this house night and day . . . that thou mayest hearken to the prayers which thy servant shall make *toward this place.*" Daniel prayed toward Jerusalem and "the tower of David, builded for an armory" of the Song of Songs, is taken allegorically as an allusion to that enduring and mighty holiness that ever belonged to the spot, once hallowed by the presence of the Shechinah. And the early Church followed also in this respect.

(Samuel), "the faithful," a great chief, who dwelt in a strong castle, and who, rather than betray his friend's confidence, saw his boy cut in twain before his eyes. What has survived of his songs breathes noble pride and loftiness of soul, tempered at times by a strange sadness: joy of life and love of conviviality; as indeed one of his poems opens with the mournful question whether the women would lament him after his death, and how? Both his son Garid and his grandson Suba were poets; so were Arrabi, whose sons fought against Mohammed; and Aus, by whom we have a kind of characteristic, yet mild, protest against his wife's change of creed. "We live," he sings, "according to the Law (Thora) and Faith of Moses, but Mohammed's Faith is also good. Each of us thinks himself in the right path." Then there is Suraih, who " would drink from the cup of those that are of noble heart, even if there be twofold poison therein;" and about four or five more, who sing of love and wine, the sword and faithfulness, hospitality and the horse. There were also Jewish poetesses, whose poems, as we have already mentioned, were "bitterer to Mohammed than arrows," and who did not escape his vengeance.

We had to tarry somewhat on this out-of-the-way field of the circumstances and position of Arabian Jews—not a little of which would, but for Islam, never have been known. Of their tenets and ceremonies, their legends and dogmas, as transferred to Islam, we have to treat separately. And such was Arabia as to difference of creeds when Mohammed arose. We left him at the moment when he began to become aware of his "Mission." But he was not without special predecessors. These were the *Hanifs*, literally in Talmudical parlance—"hypocrites." "Four shall not see God," says the Talmud—"the scoffers, the *Hanifs*" ("who are to be exposed at all hazards," while generally it is considered better "to be thrown into a fiery furnace than bring any one to public shame"), "the liars, the slanderers." These Hanifs form a very curious and most important phase of Arabian faith before Mohammed—a phase of Jewish Christianity or Christian Judaism. They loved to style themselves also "Abrahamitic Sabians," and Mohammed, at the outset, called himself one of them. They were, to all intents and purposes, "heretics." They believed in One God. They had the Law and the Gospel, and, further, certain "Rolls of Abraham and Moses," called *Ashmaat*, to which Mohammed at first appeals. This word *Ashmaat*, or *Shamaata*, has likewise given rise to most hazardous conjectures. To us it appears very simply the Talmudical *Shemaata*, which is identical with Halachah or legal tradition. In Arabia it seems to have assumed the signification of Midrash in general, chiefly as regards its Haggadistic or legendary part. These mysterious Rolls, about which endless discussions have arisen, thus seem, to our mind, to have been neither more nor less than certain collections of Midrash, beginning, as is its wont, with stern Halachah, ending, as is still more its wont, with gorgeous dreams of fancy, woven around the sainted heads of the Patriarchs, with transcendental allegories—"tales of angels, fairy legends, festal songs, and words of wisdom." Nor does it much matter what were the original names of these rolls or collections in question (there must have been scores upon scores of them), since there is, as far as we can gather their probable contents, but little in them which has not survived in one form or other in our extant Midrash-books.

There were some very prominent men among this sect, if sect it may be called. Foremost among them stands one Omayya, a highly gifted and most versatile poet, who never would acknowledge Mohammed, and ceased not to write satires upon him; more especially as it had been his intention to proclaim himself prophet. Besides him there are recorded four special men (all relations of the Prophet, Waraka among them), who, disgusted with the fetichism into which their countrymen had sunk, once met at the Kaaba, during the annual feast, and thus expressed their secret opinion to each other. "Shall we encompass a stone which neither heareth nor seeth, neither helpeth nor hurteth? Let us seek a better faith," they said. And they went abroad to seek and to find the Hanifite creed—the "religion of Abraham."

This Religion of Abraham Mohammed came to re-establish, Mohammed the Hanifite, who succeeded where the others failed. He used the arguments, the doctrine, occasionally the very words of these his predecessors—

though we have here to be doubly on our guard against the possible coloring of later Mohammedan tradition—chiefly of Zaid, who refrained from eating blood and that which had been killed for idolatry—two things pointing emphatically to Jewish teaching.* Zaid, it is reported, also abhorred the barbarous burying alive of children, then customary among the Arabian savages, and "worshiped the God of Abraham." Also, did he say, "O Lord, if I knew what form of worship thou desirest, I would adopt it. But I know it not." And when his nephew after his death asked the Prophet to pray for him, Mohammed said, "Verily I will: he will form a Church of his own on the Day of Judgment." Nay, more, Zaid had actually taught at Mecca, and Mohammed openly declared himself his pupil.

We shall return to this "Religion of Abraham," which is the clew to Islam—and the mystery of which the Midrash alone solves satisfactorily. At this stage it behooves us to follow out the vicissitudes of Mohammed's career as briefly as we may; for without these we could never fully comprehend that religion, whereof he is the corner-stone and the pinnacle.

And first as to his early miracles, which nearly proved his ruin. The Jews required a sign, says the New Testament. The desire to see the Prophet, the chosen and gifted person, perform things apparently contrary to what is

---

* Foremost among the seven fundamental "Laws of the Sons of Noah."

called Nature—sights and sounds to wonder at, things by which to prove his intimate communication with and the command over the more or less personified powers of the Cosmos, of which ancient and mediæval times had so vague a notion—is very easily understood; and both the Old and New Testament are replete with extraordinary manifestations. The Talmud, while representing, to a certain extent, what is called the "advanced" opinion of the time, certainly contains views somewhat different from the popular one. "Esther's Miracle," it says, "was the last—*the end of all miracles.*" And she is called, in allusion to the well-known Psalm-heading, "Hind of the Dawn"—"*because with her it first became Light.*" And since there is nothing in the whole story of Esther which resembles in the faintest degree a "supernatural" act; and since, moreover, the name of God does not even appear in the book from beginning to end, this Talmudic parlance of "miracles" is very like the modern use of the word "prophet," of which it was remarked the other day that "many living writers, having first stripped the word of its ancient meaning, bestow it freely upon any body." Furthermore, the Mishnah had distinctly declared that miracles were "created" from the very beginning, in the gloaming of the sixth day. "God," says the Talmud, still more explicitly, "made it a condition upon the sea, when he created it, to open itself before the Israelites; the fire to leave the three martyrs unscathed; the heavens to open to the voice of Hezekiah," etc. No less clearly is the meaning of the

Masters further expressed in such sentences as these: "The healing of a sick person is often a greater miracle than that which happened to the men in the pit. Those who have been saved from flagrant sin may consider that a miracle has happened to them. Do not reckon upon a miracle—they do not happen every day. Those to whom a miracle happens often know it not themselves," etc., etc. But the old craving for wonders was either still strong among them, or they wished to vex Mohammed's soul—as they did in a thousand bitter little ways—when they found themselves disappointed in him, and so incited people to ask him for some miraculous performance. He is asked, he complains, to call wells and rivers to gush forth, to bring down the heaven in pieces, to remove mountains, to have a house of gold, to ascend to heaven by a ladder, to cause the dead to speak, and to make Allah and his angels testify to him — and he indignantly bursts out, "My Lord be praised! Am I more than a man sent as an apostle? . . . Angels do not commonly walk the earth, or God would have dispatched an angel to preach his truth to you;" and, he says, when they do see a sign—even the moon splitting—these unbelievers but turn aside, saying, "This is a well-devised trick, a sleight of hand."

How well he had entered into the meaning of those Talmudical notions on miracles—"Esther's being the last"—and how positively he spoke upon that point, though in vain, is best shown by his protest that "the miracles of all prophets were confined to their own times. My mira-

cle is *the Koran* which shall remain forever, and I am
hopeful of having more followers than any of the other
prophets." "Former prophets," he also used to say (and
this is one of the most momentous dicta) "were sent to
their own sects. I was sent to all. I have been sent for
one thing only: to make straight the crooked paths, *to
unite the strayed tribes*, and to teach that 'There is no
god but God by whom the eyes of the blind and the ears
of the deaf shall be opened, and the hearts of those who
know nothing.'" And over and over again he points to
those much greater signs "in Heaven and on Earth" than
any wondrous manifestation that had ever been wrought
by prophets—the sun, and the moon, and the stars, the
day and the night, the structure of men's bodies, the
mountains which steady the earth, the water that comes
from on high to slake the thirst of man and cattle, and
plant and tree: even the olive-tree, and the palm-tree,
and the vine—and he speaks to these desert folk of the
sea upon which walk the great ships. Are not all these
things made for man's use and service, even while they
serve Allah?... "I never said that Allah's treasures are
in my hands, that I knew the hidden things, or that I was
an Angel.... I, who can not even help or trust myself,
unless Allah willeth. Will ye not reflect a little?"...
Did they perceive the flashes of lightning and the thunderous rolls? Allah would show them his miracles in
good time—even the yawning mouth of Hell. Then they
would indeed believe, even as those people of the Cities

P

of the Plain had believed, when it was too late. Had their caravans passed the Dead Sea — even Sodom and Gomorrha? Did they know how Thamud and Ad were destroyed by a terrible cry from Heaven, or what had become of Pharaoh? "These are the signs of Allah. . . . He giveth Life, and he giveth Death, and unto him ye must return." . . . And to leave no doubt as to what his own signs and wonders really consist of, the single verses of the Koran are called *Ayat*=Heb. *Ot: letter, sign, wonder.*

But all these protests availed naught. Miracles there must be, and miracles there were. Three—and that is all —are *hinted* at in the Koran. First, Mohammed's seeing Gabriel "in the open horizon," when despair drove him to attempt self-destruction: "One mighty in power, endued with understanding," revealed himself to him, then "on the highest part of the horizon, at two bows' length." And again he appears to him under a certain tree, "the Tree of the Limit"—a lotos-tree, covered with myriads of angels, near the Garden of Repose. This second vision, however, it probably connected with the *Miraj*, or Mohammed's Night-journey. The Jews had told the Arabians that no prophet ever arose out of the Holy Land, and that Moses had gone up to Heaven. What they did not tell them probably was that other significant saying, that, since the destruction of Jerusalem, the gift of prophecy had fallen to fools and babes—a dictum we have often enough felt inclined to quote of our own days. And, further, that the Talmud states, as expressly as can be, that

"Moses never went up to Heaven"—even as it is written, "The Heavens are Jehovah's, and the Earth hath he given to the children of man."

It was therefore absolutely necessary that the Prophet should have been in the Holy Land—nay, in Jerusalem. And the *Miraj* happened, the transfiguration, the ascension, the real consummation of Mohammed's mission, and the centre of Islamic transcendental legend and creed. A whole volume of traditions exists on this one single point.

"'Praise be unto him,' says the Koran, 'who transported his servant by night from the temple Al Harâm (Mecca) to the remotest temple (of Jerusalem), the circuit of which we have blessed, that we might show him some of our signs. Verily he that heareth, that seeth . . .'"

And in verse sixty-two of that same chapter, this journey is emphatically declared to be a "Vision"—"a dream"—"a trial for men."

And these are its brief outlines, though Mohammed's own account was probably still more briefly and soberly conceived as compared with the worlds of golden dreams in which the later legend revels.*

In the middle of the night Gabriel appeared to Mohammed, and told him that the Lord had intended to bestow honor upon him such as he had not bestowed upon any

---

* We may have occasion to trace some of the gorgeous features of this Vision in the latter Haggadah, when we speak of Mohammed's Heaven and Hell. Exceedingly characteristic are the differences on some points: among other things, the entire omission in the Mohammedan legend of that Fifth Heaven of the Midrash, "Gan Eden," which is reserved for the souls of noble women—Pharaoh's daughter, who so tenderly took pity on the child Moses, occupying the first place in the first circle.

born being yet, such as had never come into any man's heart. He arose, and they went to the Kaaba, which they encompassed seven times. Gabriel then took out Mohammed's heart, washed it in the well Zemzem, filled it with faith and knowledge, and put it back in its place. He was then clothed in a robe of light, and was covered with a turban of light, in which in thousand-fold rays of light gleamed the words, "Mohammed is God's Prophet; Mohammed is God's Friend." Then, surrounded by myriads of angels, he bestrode the *Borak*—which only means Lightning—who had the face of a man; his red chest was as a ruby, and his back like a white pearl. His wings reached from the eastern point of the horizon to the western, and at every step he went as far as eye could see. Thrice Mohammed prayed while he flew—at Medina, at Madyan, at Bethlehem. Sweet voices were calling—to the left, to the right, before him, behind him; beautiful women flitted around: he heeded naught. And the angel told him that had he listened to the first voice, his followers would have become Jews; to the second, Christians; to the third, they would have given up Paradise for the pleasures of this world. At Jerusalem he entered, greeted by new hosts of angels, the Temple (and the ring by which the Borak was fastened has no doubt been seen by many of our readers near the "Dome of the Rock"); and here all the prophets, Christ among them, were assembled; and very striking are the likenesses given of them. Abraham resembled Mohammed most of all.

Prayers were said, and Mohammed acted as Priest Precentor. Most of the prophets then held a brief discourse in praise of God, and descriptive of their own individual mission on earth. Mohammed, having spoken last, ascended Jacob's ladder, standing upon *the* Rock, the same which forms, according to the Midrash, the foundation stone of the earth. And a very strange-looking rock it is, rising a few feet above the marble around, scarcely touched with the chisel; and at its southwestern corner there is seen the "footprint of the Prophet," and next to it the "handprint of Gabriel," who held down the rock as it tried to rise heavenward with God's Messenger. The ladder on which Mohammed mounted into the regions of light is the same which Jacob saw in his dream: it reaches from heaven to earth, and on it the souls of the departed return to God. It is made of ruby and emerald, of gold and silver, and of precious stones.

Having passed the angel who held the seven earths and the seven heavenly spheres, and the blue abyss in which float all ideal prototypes of things sublunary, he and Gabriel arrived at the Gates of the first Heaven of the World, where myriads of new angels held watch. Both he and Gabriel entered, and found other myriads praising God in the postures of Moslem prayer. On a magnificent throne sat Adam, dressed in light, the human souls arrayed by his sides—to his right the good souls, to his left the wicked ones. Farther on were Paradise and Hell. Punishments were wrought here according to earthly deeds.

The miserly souls were naked and hungry and thirsty; thieves and swindlers sat at tables filled with gorgeous things, of which they were not allowed to participate; and scoffers and slanderers carried heavy spiked logs of wood that tore their flesh, even as they had wounded the hearts of their fellow-men. Thus they passed heaven after heaven. In the second they found Christ and John the Baptist; in the third, Joseph and David; in the fourth, Enoch; in the fifth, Aaron; in the sixth, Moses, who wept because Mohammed was to be more exalted than he had been. In the highest heaven they found Abraham. Above the seventh heaven they came to a tree of vast leaves and fruits. In it is Gabriel's dwelling-place, on one branch of untold expanse; in another, myriads of angels are reading the Pentateuch; in another, other myriads of angels read the Gospel; yet in another they sing the Psalms; and in another they chant the Koran, from eternity to eternity. Four rivers flow forth from this region, one of which is the *River of Mercy*. There is also a House of Prayer there, right above the Kaaba.* Near it a tank of light, from which, when Gabriel's light approaches it, seventy thousand angels spring into existence—which will remind our readers of the river of fire that rolls its flames under the divine throne, and out of which rise ever new myriads of angels, who praise God and sink back into naught. They approach the temple, singing praises unto God; and

---

* In accordance with the Haggadistic notion of the "Jerusalem above," and the "heavenly Jerusalem" of the New Testament.

each time when their voices resound a new angel is born. "Not a drop of water is in the sea, not a leaf on a tree, not a span of space in the heavens that is not guarded by an angel." And to this day all these gorgeous transcendentalisms and day-dreams survive bodily in certain Jewish mystic liturgical poems (Piut), into which the golden rivers of the Haggadah have been turned by Poets or "Paitanas" at an early period.*

A space farther, a little space, after the Tree of the Limit, Mohammed found himself of a sudden alone. Neither Gabriel nor Borak dared go beyond it; and he heard a voice calling "Approach." And he passed on, and curtain after curtain, and veil after veil was drawn up before him and fell behind him. When the last curtain rose, he stood within two bow-shots from the Throne; and here—says the Koran—"he saw the greatest of the signs of his Lord." No pen dared to say more. "There was a great stillness, and nothing was heard except the silent sound of the reed, wherewith the decrees of God are inscribed upon the tablets of Fate." . . .

It would indeed be a labor of love, and not without its reward, to follow this Miraj-Saga through all its stages, down to the Persian and Turkish cycles. But it is not our task. All we have to add here is that Mohammed is not to be made responsible for some of his enthusiastic admirers when they transformed this Vision—a vision as

---

* In Western Europe this part of the Jewish Liturgy, as too mystical for the weaker brethren, has now mostly been abrogated.

grand as any in the whole Divine Comedy (which indeed has unconsciously borrowed some of its richest plumage from it), but which Mohammed, until he was sick of it, insisted on calling a *Dream* — into insipidity and drivel.

One feature more deserves mention. When Zaid asked the Prophet after his little daughter who had died, he answered that she was in Paradise and happy. And Zaid wept bitterly.

Remains, as of traditional miracles, the last one of the two angels who took out Mohammed's heart when he was a boy, purified it in snow, then weighed it, and found it weightier than all the thousands they put into the other scale — a parable equally transparent, and hardly a "miracle" in the conventional sense of the word.

Only one command was given to Mohammed on that occasion of the Ascension: that his faithful should pray fifty times daily. And when he returned to where Moses waited for him, and told him this, Moses made him return to pray God to reduce the number. And it was made forty. "This is still too much," Moses said; "I know that the faithful will not be able to do even thus much." And again and again was the number reduced till it came to five, and Mohammed no longer dared return to God, though Moses urged him to do so.

Very strikingly indeed does the Haggadah manifest her constant presence, not merely throughout this whole Vision, but even in such minute features, as this last, of God's instructing Mohammed about prayer.* For when the Pentateuch records that extraordinary manifestation of God to Moses on the rock, where the glory of the Lord passeth by and proclaims: " Jehovah, Jehovah, God, merciful and gracious, long-suffering, and abundant of goodness and truth, and keeping mercy for thousands, forgiving iniquity, and transgression and sin,"... the Talmud first of all introduces this passage, as is its wont in the like anthropomorphistic passages, with the awe-stricken, half-trembling words that, If Holy Writ had not said this, no man would dare to speak of a like manifestation; and, next, proceeds to explain that "*God showed Moses how that men should pray.*" "Let them invoke my Mercy and my Long-suffering. I will forgive them. Jehovah—twice repeated—means, It is Jehovah, even I, before man sinneth, and I, the self-same Jehovah, after he has sinned and repented."

It is time that we should now return, after these many indispensable little monographs, to the founder of Islam himself, as an historical personage. Ere we proceed to his book and faith, we must sum up the events that led first to his Flight, that event with which not only he, but Arabia, enters history, an event fraught with intense importance for all mankind.

When Mohammed had become clear as to his mission, he sought converts. And his first convert was his faith-

---

* For the shortening of it, see above, p. 327, note.

ful, motherly Chadija; his second, the freed slave Zaid, probably a Christian, whom he adopted; and his third, his small cousin Ali, ten years of age. Chadija, his good angel, Tradition reports,

> "believed in Mohammed and believed in the truth of the Revelation, and fortified him in his aims. She was the first who believed in God, in his messenger, and in the Revelation. Thereby God had sent him comfort, for as often as he heard aught disagreeable, contradictory, or how he was shown to be a liar, she was sad about it. God comforted him through her when he returned to her, in rousing him up again and making his burden more light to him, assuring him of her own faith in him, and representing to him the futility of men's babble."

And, in truth, when she died, not merely he but Islam lost much of their fervor, much of their purity. He would not be comforted, though he married many wives after her; and the handsomest and youngest of his wives would never cease being jealous of that "dead, toothless old woman." Abu Bakr, a wealthy merchant—energetic, prudent, and honest—joined at once. He had probably been a fellow-disciple of Mohammed at the feet of Zaid the Skeptic, and was his confidant and bosom friend throughout his life—the only one who unhesitatingly joined; "who tarried not, neither was he perplexed," Mohammed said of him. It was he who stood at the head of the twelve chosen Apostles who subsequently rallied around the Prophet, among whom we find Hamza, the Lion of God, Othman, Omar, and the rest, men of energy, talent, and wealth, and long before adverse to Paganism. Those twelve were his principal advisers while he lived, and after his death they founded an empire greater than that of Alexander or Rome. As to Abu Bakr, he was but two years younger than the Prophet, not a man of genius, but of calm, clear, impartial judgment, and yet of so tender and sympathetic a heart that he used to be called "the Sighing." He was not only one of the most popular men, but also rich and generous, and thus his influence can not well be overrated. It is his adherence to Mohammed throughout which, even by those who most depreciate the Prophet, is taken as one of the highest guarantees of the latter's sincerity. Nay, he is said to have done more for Islam than Mohammed himself—not to mention that, with his extensive knowledge of genealogy, one of the most important sciences of the period, he was able at the Prophet's desire to supply Hassan, the poet of the Faith, with matter for satires against the inimical Koreish.

Most of Mohammed's relations seemed to have treated his teachings with scorn. "There he goes," they used to say; "he is going to speak to the world about the heavens now." Abu Lahab, in open family council, called him a fool, instantly upon which followed that characteristic Surah, "Perish shall the hands of Abu Lahab. May he perish. . . . And his wife shall carry fuel for his hell-fire." The other Meccans treated the whole story of his mission, his revelations, and dreams with something like pitying contempt, as long as he kept to generalities, though the number of uninfluential adherents grew apace. But when he spoke of their gods—which they naively enough would call Thagût (Error), the technical Jewish word for Idols*—*as* Idols, they waxed wroth, and combined against him, until the stir both he and they made spread more and more rapidly and dangerously, and with it rose his own courage. He felt committed. All hesitations and doubts and fears and reconciliations he cast behind him now. He openly set the proud Meccans at defiance. He cursed those who reviled him with burning curses. He cursed their fathers in their graves; nay, his own father would undergo eternal punishment in hell, for that he had been an idolater. "There is no God but Allah!" He cried it aloud, day and night, and the echoes became more and more frequent.

His life was in jeopardy now, and his uncle, Abu Talib, under whose protection he had fallen when a youth, stood forth against the whole clan. He would protect him if they all combined against him. Did he believe in his mission? Not in the least. He remained steadfast in his own creed or skepticism to the day of his death. But he was an Arab, a Shemite. He had adopted him, and promised to protect him; and nothing, absolutely nothing, could cause him to break that holiest of engagements. He received the deputations of his kinsfolk, listened to their speeches, "how that Mohammed blasphemed their gods, called the living fools and the dead denizens of hell-

---

* See *Targums*, p. 319, *post.*

fire; that he was mad, brought disgrace upon their family and the whole clan; that he ought to be extinguished somehow—anyhow;" and he shook his head, saying nothing, or next to nothing. Again they returned and again, and at last demanded that the Possessed Man should be given up to them to be dealt with according to their judgment. If not—"We are determined no longer to bear his blasphemy toward our gods, nor his insults toward ourselves. If thou givest him protection, we will fight both him and thee, until one of us shall have been extinguished."

Abu Talib sent for Mohammed and told him what had happened, representing to him the position of affairs, and spoke to him about the danger he had brought upon their good old tribe. And very characteristic, not merely for the *dramatis personæ*, but for Arab feeling, is the further story of the interview. Mohammed, though fully believing now that even his uncle was about to abandon him to the mercies of his kinsfolk, replied—" By Allah, uncle, if they put the sun to my right hand, and the moon to my left, I will not give up the course which I am pursuing until Allah gives me success or I perish." And the tears starting to his eyes, he turned to depart. Then Abu Talib cried out aloud, "Son of my brother, come back!" And he returned. And Abu Talib said: "Depart in peace, O my nephew! Say whatever thou desirest, for, by Allah, I will in nowise abandon thee forever."

Fanaticism, here baffled, sought an outlet elsewhere.

As usual, the weak and the unprotected became the first victims and martyrs to their faith, while others apostatized, until Mohammed himself advised his converts to go to Abyssinia, where there ruled a pious and just king, and where they would find protection. Here also, when Meccan embassadors pursued them, and tried to obtain their extradition, they declared their creed to the Negus in these words:

"We lived in ignorance, in idolatry, and unchastity; the strong oppressed the weak; we spoke untruth; we violated the duties of hospitality. Then a prophet arose, one whom we knew from our youth, with whose descent, and conduct, and good faith, and morality we are well acquainted. He told us to worship one God, to speak the truth, to keep good faith, to assist our relations, to fulfill the rights of hospitality, to abstain from all things impure, ungodly, unrighteous. And he ordered us to say prayers, give alms, and to fast. We believed in him, we followed him. But our countrymen persecuted us, tortured us, and tried to cause us to forsake our religion, and now we throw ourselves upon your protection with confidence."

They then read him the nineteenth chapter of the Koran, which speaks of Christ and John the Baptist, and they all wept, and the king dismissed the Meccan messengers, refusing to give up the refugees. As to the nature of Christ they gave him a somewhat vague account, with which the king, however, agreed—to his later discomfiture.

This nineteenth chapter, which so moved them all, contains the story both of the Annunciation of John's birth to Zacharias and that of Christ's birth to the Virgin. It is here where Maryam=Mary, "the daughter of Amrán, the sister of Harún," is described, as in the Gospel of the

Infancy, as leaning on a barren trunk of a palm-tree when the throes come upon her, and she cries, "Would to God that I had been dead and forgotten before this." ... And a voice came from within, "Grieve not." And a rivulet gushed forth at her feet, and the erst withered palm glistened with luscious dates. Then, taunted by the people for having borne a child—"her father not being a bad man, nor her mother disreputable"—the child itself, even Christ, to whom she mutely points, answers to every body's wonderment, out of his cradle, in this wise: "I am a servant of Allah. He has given me the Book, and he has appointed me as a Prophet." And a few verses further on, a new rhyme indicates the commencement of a new episode, which reads as follows: "This is Jesus, the son of Maryam, according to the true doctrine" (not "the words of truth," as often translated), "which they doubt. It is not fit for God that he should have a son. Praise to him!" (*i. e.*, far be it from him). And finally, at the end of this same chapter—

"They say God has begotten a son. In this ye utter a blasphemy; and but little is wanting but the heavens should tear open, and the earth cleave asunder, and the mountains fall down, for that they attribute children to the Merciful, whereas it is not meet for God to have children. No one in Heaven and on earth shall approach the Merciful otherwise than as his servant."* ...

This is the first *Hejrah*, the first triumph of the Faith. But meanwhile Mohammed himself had recanted, aposta-

---

* Compare above, p. 324.

tized—twice. While the small band were proclaiming the purity of his Revelation before the Negus of Abyssinia, Mohammed had gone to the Kaaba, and in his sorely embittered state of mind, finding himself alienated from every body, in the midst of an absolutely hopeless, almost single-handed struggle, invoked, before the assembled Koreish, their three popular idols—"the sublime swans," whose intercession might be sought. The Assembly were delighted, and, though they despised his feebleness, they yet wished to put an end to the unseemly strife, and forthwith declared their readiness to believe in his doctrine, since it embraced the worship of their ancient gods. But on the day following Mohammed publicly rescinded that declaration. "The devil had prompted him," he declared boldly, and bitterer waxed the feud than before. But his mind was, as we said, in a sorely vexed state at that time. He was low-spirited, nervous, full of fear, and he was still ready to make concessions. To escape abuse he at about the same period declared that he had been commanded to permit the continuation of sacrifices to the idols; and then he repented again, and verses expressive of his contrition at his momentary weakness came and comforted him in the midst of the new troubles caused by his recantation. At that time it was also that great comfort came to him in the conversion of those two: Hamza, called the Lion of God, and Omar, the Paul of Islam, whilom Mohammed's bitterest adversary, who had entered the house of Mohammed girded with his sword, resolved on slaying him, and who returned a Moslem—the most zealous apostle of the faith, its most valiant defender and mainstay. Among the twelve of whom we spoke, Abu Bakr and Hamza became the principal heads and mainsprings of young Islam.

And now the breach in the clan was completed. The whole family of Mohammed, the Hashimites, were excommunicated. Great hardships ensued for both sides for the space of three years, until when both were anxious to remove the excommunication, the document itself was found to have been destroyed by worms — all but the name of God with which it commenced. While thus, on the one hand, Mohammed's star seemed in the ascendant, he having forced, if not recognition, at any rate toleration, a bitter grief befell him. Chadija, sixty-five years of age, died; shortly after, his protector, Abu Talib; and, as if to fill the cup of his misery, he now became aware also that he was a beggar. As long as Chadija lived she provided for him, leaving him to believe in his prosperity. For he was chiefly occupied with his Revelations, and with going about preaching to the caravans, the pilgrims, the people, at the fairs. And behind him went his other uncle, like a grim shadow; and when he exhorted the people to repeat after him, "There is no God but Allah," and promised that they would all be kings if they did— as indeed they became—Abu Lahab, "the squinter," with his two black side-curls, would mock at him, call him a liar and a Sabian. And the people mocked after him, and drove him away, and said, "Surely your own kinsfolk must know best what sort of a prophet you be." This Abu Lahab now had to stand forward, and as kinsman to take upon himself the galling charge of protecting Mohammed, whom he loathed. Abu Talib had resisted on his death-bed the entreaties both of Mohammed and of the Koreish —the one trying to induce him to embrace Islam, the others to give up his nephew. He did neither, and thus left the matter where it was. But Mohammed felt the awkwardness and danger of his position as the protected of his great foe very keenly, and he resolved to turn away from the place of his birth, even as Abraham had done, and Moses, and other prophets, and try to gain a hearing elsewhere. He accordingly went to Tayif, within three days' journey of Mecca; but he was unsuccessful. They hinted that his life would not be safe among them. The rabble hooted and pelted him with stones. He returned with a sad heart. On his road he stopped, and preached. And as whilom the stones had said Amen to the blind Saint's sermon, so now, legend says, the Jin listened to his words, as men would not hear him. And when Zaid, who went with him, asked him how he dared to return to the Koreish, he replied, "God will find means to protect his religion and his prophet."

And in the midst of these vicissitudes the event happened without which Mohammedanism would never have been heard of, save as one of the thousand outbreaks of sectarianism.

Medina, then Yathrib, was inhabited by a great number of Jews. They had, as mentioned before, an academy, where both Halachah and Haggadah were expounded, though very unostentatiously. They lived in peace and friendship with their neighbors, but had often religious conversations with them, in which the idolaters fared badly enough. With keenness of intellect, with sudden sparks of *esprit*, with all the arts of casuistry, they showed them the inanity of their form of belief. They further, as the keepers of holy books, told them such legends and tales about their common ancestor Abraham, their common kinsman Ishmael, and all that befell those before and those after them, that their imagination was kindled, their heart moved, their intellect fired, and that secretly they could not but agree to the mental and religious superiority of these their neighbors. But their Arab pride would not yield; and when they openly denied this superiority of Faith, the Jews would tell them that their Messiah would come and punish them for their unbelief, even as the unbelief of the legendary aborigines who had lived there before them had been punished.

When the few pilgrims who had patiently listened to Mohammed, at his many preachings, brought back the strange tidings to Medina that a certain man of good family had publicly renounced the old gods, and had spoken of the God of Abraham, and of his mission to convert his brethren to him—not a Jew, not preaching Judaism, but an Arab, a Gentile like themselves, a man of their own kith and kin, a man who had gradually acquired a certain position and following in spite of all attacks and hinderances—it struck some of the advanced and far-seeing men of that city that this was an opportunity not to be lost. If their people, "in whom more dissension was to be found than in any other on the face of the earth," could be united by one pure faith, which was emphatically their own, and which, though acknowledging some of the fundamental truths of Judaism, did not acknowledge Judaism itself, it would be a vast achievement; and if, further, they would acknowledge the coming man, the Messiah, with whom they had been threatened by the Jews, before even these knew of him, they would gain a doubly brilliant victory. And they went to Mohammed secretly as a deputation, and told him that if he were capable of creating that union, religious and political, which was needed, they would acknowledge him to be the foretold prophet, and "the greatest man that ever lived."

Mohammed then recited to them a brief summary of the commandments—to worship but One God, not to steal, not to commit adultery, not to kill their children, not to slander, and to obey his authority in things "right and just," which they repeated after him. This is called the women's vow, because the same points were afterward repeated for the benefit of the women in the Koran, and because there was no mention of fighting for the faith in this formula.

Shortly after this a solemn and secret compact was entered into between another influential deputation from Medina and himself: in the stillness of night, "so that the sleeper should not be awakened, and the absent not be waited for." Here he more fully declared his faith. There are, he told them, many forms of Islam or Monotheism; and each takes a different kind of worship or outer garment. The real points consist of the belief in the Resurrection, in the Day of Judgment, and, above all, unconditional faith in one only God, Allah, unto whom utter submission is due, and who alone is to be feared and worshiped. Other essential points are consistency in misfortune, prayer, and charity.

Whereupon they swore allegiance into his hands. This over, he selected twelve men among them—Jesus had chosen twelve Apostles, and Moses his elders of the tribes of Israel, he said—and exhorted those who had not been chosen not to be angry in their hearts, inasmuch as not he but Gabriel had determined the choice. These were the twelve "Bishops" (Nakib), while the other men of Medina are called "Aids" (Ansár).

Secretly as these things had been done, they soon became known in Mecca, and now not a moment was to be lost. The Koreish could no longer brook this; Mohammed's folly had become dangerous. And about one hundred families of influence in Mecca, who believed in the Prophet, silently disappeared, by twos and threes and fours, and went to Medina, where they were received with enthusiasm. Entire quarters of the city thus became deserted, and Otba, at the sight of these vacant abodes, once teeming with life, "sighed heavily," and recited the old verse: "Every dwelling-place, even if it have been blessed ever so long, at last will become a prey to wind and woe." . . . "And," he bitterly added, "all this is the work of our noble nephew, who hath scattered our assemblies, ruined our affairs, and created dissension among us." The position now grew day by day more embarrassing. A blow had to be struck. Still Mohammed was in Mecca—he, Ali, and Abu Bakr. An assembly of the Koreish met in all dispatch at the town-hall, and some chiefs of other clans were invited to attend. The matter had become a question for the commonwealth, not for a tribe.—And the Devil also came, according to the legend, in the guise of a venerable sheikh. Stormy was the meeting, for the men began to be afraid. Imprisonment for life, perpetual exile, and finally death, were proposed. It is for this that Satan is wanted by the legend. No Arab would have counseled death for Mohammed. The last proposal was accepted; its execution deferred to the first dark night. A number of noble youths were to do the bloody deed. Meanwhile they watched his house to prevent his escape.

But meanwhile, also, "the angel Gabriel" had told Mohammed what his enemies had planned against him. And he put his own green garment upon Ali, bade him lie on his own bed, and escaped, as David had escaped, through the window. A price was set upon his head. Abu Bakr, the "sole companion," was with him. They hid in a cave in the direction opposite from that leading to Medina, on Mount Thaur. A spider wove his web over the mouth of the cave, relate the traditions. Be it observed, by the way, that even this spider and web belong to the Haggadah,. and are found in the Targum to the ninety-fifth Psalm, where David is, by these means, hidden from his enemies. Two wild pigeons laid their eggs at the entrance of the cave, so that the pursuers were convinced that none could have entered it for many a long day; and the pigeons were blessed ever after, and made sacred within the Holy Territory. Once or twice danger was nigh, and Abu Bakr began to fear. "They were but two," he said. "Nay," Mohammed said, "we are three; God is with us." And he was with them. It was a hot day in September, 622, when Mohammed entered Yathrib, from that time forth honored by the name of *Medinat An-Nabi*, the City of the Prophet, at noon—ten, thirteen, or fifteen years (the traditions vary) after his assumption of the sacred office. This is the *Hejrah*, or the Mohammedan Era, which dates from the first month of the first lunar year after the Prophet's entry into the city. A Jew watching on a tower espied him first, in order that there might be fulfilled the words of the Koran, "The Jews know him better than they know their own children." Before entering the gate he alighted from his camel and prayed.

From that time forth Mohammed's life, hitherto obscure and dark, stands out in its minutest details. He now is judge, lawgiver, king; even to the day of his death. We shall leave our readers to follow out the minutiæ of his life in any of the biographies at their hand, which, from this period forth, no longer differ in any essential point.

But here we turn at once to that period of his open dissensions with the Jews, who, as we have said, formed a very influential section at Medina. He had by degrees come to sanction and adopt as much of their dogmas, their legends, their ceremonies, as ever was compatible with his mission as a Prophet of the Arabs, and one who, barring the fundamental dogma of the Sonship, wished to conciliate also the Christians. He constantly refers to the testimony of the Jews, calls them the first receivers of the Law, and not merely in such matters as turning in prayer toward Jerusalem, instead of the national sanctuary, the Kaaba, he had followed them—nay, at Medina he even adopted the Day of Atonement, date, name, and all. All he wanted in return was that they should acknowledge him as *the* Prophet of the Gentiles (*Ummi*), and testify to his mission. But the veil had been suddenly torn from the eyes of these Jews. If they had thought him a meet instrument to convert all Arabia to Judaism, and had eagerly fostered and encouraged him, had instructed him in law and legend, and had caused him to believe in himself and his mission, they of a sudden became aware that their supposed tool had become a thing of evergrowing power; and they had recourse to the most dangerous arms imaginable for laying that ghost which they had helped to raise. They laughed at him publicly. They told stories of how he came by his "Revelations." They who had been so anxious to inure him into the Midrash, challenged him by silly questions on Haggadistic lore—to which he was imprudent enough to give serious replies — to prove his Messiahship, with which they unceasingly taunted him. They produced the Bible, and showed how different the tales he told of the patriarchs and others were from those contained in that book: they who had begotten this Haggadistic guise themselves. Of course the stories did not agree, and even Christians (Omayyah and others) testified to that fact. What remained for Mohammed but to declare that in those instances both Jews and Christians had falsified their books? or that they did not understand them—applying to them the rabbinical designation of certain scholars: that though they had the books, they were but "as asses laden with them," and comprehended not their contents; or that they gave out foolish stories to be *the* Book itself. He now declared that, "of all men, Jews and Idolaters hate the Moslems most." And, in truth, when asked whether they preferred Mohammed's teaching or idolatry, they would reply—as their ancestors had done centuries before — "Idolatry, since idolaters did not know any better, while there were those who knowingly perverted the pure doctrine, and sowed strife and dissension between Israel and their Father which is in Heaven." Some Jewish fanatics even attempted his life—one, innocently enough, by witchcraft; another by the more earnest missile of a stone. They wrote satires and squibs upon him, men and women. There was no end to their provocations. They mispronounced his Koranic words —"twisting their tongues"—so as to give them an offensive meaning. Their "look down upon us" sounded like "Oh, our wicked one." For "forgiveness" they said "sin;" for "peace upon thee," "contempt upon thee," and the like. They mocked at his expression of "giving God a good loan"—"we being rich and he poor!" they said—evidently forgetting the similar expressions of the Mishnah itself, which speaks of certain good deeds* as bringing interest in this world, while the capital is reserved for the next. And the inevitable happened. The breach came to pass, and there was hatred even unto death on both sides. It was too late to substitute another faith, other doctrines, other legends, even had they been at hand. But as much as could be done without endangering the whole structure, to show the irreconcilable breach, was done now. The faithful were no longer to turn their faces toward Jerusalem, but toward Mecca. Friday was made the day of rest, and the

---

* Such as reverence for father and mother, charity, early application to study, hospitality, doing the last honors to the dead, promoting peace between man and his neighbor.

call to prayer was introduced as a supposed protest against the trumpet of the synagogue, though the trumpet was scarcely ever used for the purpose of the call to prayer. The Jews were not to be saluted in the streets; the Faithful were to abstain from eating with them; they are declared beyond the pale—and bitterly had they to rue their lost game.

In the first year of the *Hejrah* Mohammed proclaimed war against the enemies of the faith. At Badr the Moslems first stood face to face with the Meccans, and routed them, though but 316 against 600. The Koreish and certain Jewish tribes were the next object of warfare. Six years after the Flight he proclaimed a general pilgrimage to Mecca. Its inhabitants, though prohibiting this, concluded a peace with him, whereby he was recognized as a belligerent, and the pilgrimage was carried out the very next year. Next other Jewish tribes had to feel his iron rod, while he nearly lost his life at the hands of a Jewess, another Judith, who tried to poison him; and when charged with the crime, said that she had only wished to see whether Mohammed really was a prophet, and now she was convinced of it. She thus saved her own life; but the poison worked on, and in his dying hour Mohammed spoke of that poison "cutting his heartstrings." His missionaries now sought a larger sphere than Arabia. Letters were sent by him to Heraclius, to the Governor of Egypt, to Abyssinia, to Chosroës II., to Amra the Ghassanide. The latter resented this as an insult, executed the messenger, and the first war between Islam and Christianity broke out. Islam was beaten. Mecca at this news rose anew, threw off the mask of friendship, and broke the alliance. Whereupon Mohammed marched of a sudden 10,000 men strong upon them before they had time for any preparation, took Mecca by storm, and was publicly acknowledged chief and prophet. More strife and more, chiefly minor, contests followed, in which he was more or less victorious. In the year ten of the *Hejrah* he undertook his last solemn pilgrimage to Mecca with at least 40,000 Moslems, and there on Mount Arafat blessed them, like Moses, and repeated his last exhortations; chiefly telling them to protect the weak, the poor, and the women, and to abstain from usury.

Once again he thought of war. He planned a huge expedition against the Greeks; but he felt death approaching. One night, at midnight, he went to the cemetery of Medina, and prayed and wept upon the tombs, and asked God's blessing for his "companions resting in peace." Next day he went to the mosque as usual, ascended the pulpit, and commenced his exhortation with these words: "There was once a servant unto whom God had given the option of whatever worldly goods he would desire, or the rewards that are near God; and he chose those which are near God." And Abu Bakr, hearing these words, wept and said, "May our fathers and mothers, our lives and our goods, be a sacrifice for you, O messenger of God." And the people marveled at these words.

They wist not that the Prophet spoke of his near death, but Abu Bakr knew. For a few more days Mohammed went about as usual; but terrible headaches, accompanied by feverish symptoms, soon forced him to seek rest. He chose Ayisha's house, close to the mosque, and there took part as long as he could in public prayers. For the last time he addressed the Faithful, asking them, like Moses, whether he had wronged any one, or whether he owed aught to any one. To round the story off right realistically, there was an imbecile present who claimed certain unpaid pennies; which were immediately refunded to him, though not without a bitter word. He then read passages from the Koran preparing them for his death, and exhorted them to keep peace among themselves. Never after that hour did he ascend the pulpit, says the tradition, "till the day of the Resurrection." Whether he intended to appoint a successor—Mosaylima, perhaps, the pseudo-prophet, as Sprenger suggests—or not, must always remain a mystery. It is well known that the writing-materials for which he had asked were not given to him. Perhaps they did think him delirious, as they said. Some medicine was given to him, accompanied by certain superstitious rites and formulas. He protested with horror when he became aware of this. He wandered; somewhat of heaven and angels were his last words—"Denizens of Heaven ... Sons of Abraham ... prophets ... they fall down, weeping, glorifying His Majesty ..." Ayisha, in whose lap his head rested, felt it growing heavy and heavier; she looked into his face, saw his eyes gazing upward, and heard him murmuring: " No, the companions above . . . in Paradise." She then took his hand in hers, praying. When she let it sink, it was cold and dead. This happened about noon of Monday (12th or 11th) of the third month in the 11th year of the *Hejrah* (8th June, 632). Terrible was the distress which the news of his death caused. Many of the faithful refused to believe in it, and Omar confirmed them in their doubt. But Abu Bakr sprang forth, saying, " Whosoever among you has believed in Mohammed, let him know that Mohammed is dead; but he who has believed in Mohammed's God, let him continue to serve him, for he is still alive and never dies." . . .

We have in this succinct review of the stages through which Mohammed went carefully abstained from pronouncing upon him *ex cathedrâ*, from accusing or defending him. All this has been done, and public opinion is at rest on the point, for instance, of his marrying many wives, or committing wholesale slaughter when an example had to be made. Also with regard to his " cunning" and " craftiness," and the rest of it. There is, Mohammedans tell us now, polygamy and massacre enough and to spare in the Bible, and its heroes are in nowise exempt from human frailties. Moreover, " far-sighted prudence and energetic action "—provided always that they belong to the victorious camp—are not considered very grave faults. But we have also abstained from adducing many Koranic passages, however tempting it was to substitute for our own sober account the glowing words of "inspiration"—the cry out of the depths of an intensely human heart in its sore agony—the wail over the peace that is lost—the exultant bugle-call that proclaims the God-given triumph—the yell of revenge or the silent anguish, and the unheard, the unseen tear of a man. These things do indeed write a more faithful biography than the acutest historian will ever compile out of the infinite and infinitesimal mosaics at his disposal.

Mohammed has had many biographers, from the Byzantines, who could not satisfy their souls with heaping up mountains of silly abuse, from Maracci and Prideaux—the former of whom has, not without some show of reason, been accused of being a secret believer, while the latter wishes to stop by his biography "the great prevailing infidelity in the present age," more especially as he has reason to fear that "wrath hath sometime gone forth from the Lord," and that the "Wicked One may, by some other such instrument, overwhelm us with foulest delusions"—to those great authorities, Sprenger, Muir, Nöldeke, Weil, Amari. The work of the first of these we have placed at the head of our paper, because it is the most comprehensive, the most exhaustive, the most learned of all; because, more than any of the others, it does, by bringing all the material bodily before the reader, enable him to form his own judgment. Next to him in fullness and genuineness of matter, though not in genius, perhaps, stands, to our thinking, Muir; only that a certain preconceived notion anent Satan seems to have taken somewhat too firm a hold upon his mind. Both Muir and Sprenger have drunk out of the fullness of the East in the East, spending part of their lives in research on Indian and Mohammedan soil. Weil, Amari, Nöldeke have earned the first places among Koranic investigators in Europe; while Lane, that most illustrious master of Arab lexicography, has, both in his classical Notes on the "Arabian Nights" and in his "Modern Egyptians," thrown out most precious hints on the subject. And those that have written his life have all written it out of his book, the Koran, and its complement the Sunnah, and each has written it differently.

The Koran is a wonderful book in many respects, but chiefly in this, that it has no real beginning, middle, or end. Mohammed's mind is best portrayed here. It was not a well-regulated mind. Weil, in touching terms, almost appeals to the shadow of Mohammed to come and enlighten him as to what he said, when he said it, how he said it. He can not forgive him, he states at the commencement of his "Introduction," that he did not put every thing clearly and properly in order before his death —even as a man sends his "copy" to the printers. From date-leaves and tablets of white stone, from shoulder-bones and bits of parchment, thrown promiscuously into a box, and from "the breasts of men," was the first edition of the Koran prepared one year after the prophet's death, and the single chapters were arranged *according to their respective lengths:* organ-pipe fashion—and not even that accurately. And Mohammed's book is not even as the Pentateuch, according to the Documentary Theory. There are not several accounts of the same or different events vaguely put together. Nor is it even like the Talmud, which, though apparently leading us by the Ariadne-thread of the Mishnah through its labyrinths, yet every now and then plunges us into pathless wildernesses of cave and vault; through which ever and anon streams in the golden light of day, showing the wise aim and plan of their tortuous windings. But in the Koranic structure there is no cunning, no special purpose; and, indeed, you may begin at every page and end at every page, unless one should prefer to read it from beginning to end—and we warrant that, as it now stands, no one will easily perform that feat, unless he be a pious Moslem, or, perchance, makes it his Arabic text-book. Hence also not one of these *savans* agrees about the succession of the chapters. There is certainly a vast amount of truth or probability on the side of some suggestions; and Sprenger has, to our mind, come nearest, because he was the least fettered by conventionalities of view, but, son of the Alps and of the Desert, he set authority at defiance and sought out his path for himself. Yet with him, too, it is difficult to agree at times, according to the greater or less sympathy one feels with his stand-point, and the view he takes of the Prophet himself.

Broadly speaking, three principal divisions may, with psychological truth, be established; the first, corresponding to the period of early struggles, being marked by the higher poetical flight, by the deeper appreciation of the beauties of nature, in sudden, most passionate, lava-like outbursts, which seem scarcely to articulate themselves into words. The more prosaic and didactic tone warns us of the approach of manhood, while the dogmatizing, the sermonizing, the reiteration, and the abandoning of all Scriptural and Haggadistic helpmates point to the secure possession of power, to the consummation and completion of the mission. But these divisions must not be relied upon too securely. There rings through what may fairly be considered some of the very last Revelations ever and anon the old wild cry of doubt and despair; the sermon turns abruptly into a glowing vision; a sudden rhapsody inappropriately follows a small dogmatic disquisition, or a curse, fiery and yelling as any of the hottest days, is hurled upon some unbeliever's doomed head; while the very first utterances at times exhibit the theorizing, reflecting, arguing tendencies of ripe old age.

And it is exactly in these transitions, quick and sudden as lightning, that one of the great charms of the book, as it now stands, consists: well might Goethe say that "as often as we approach it, it always proves repulsive anew; gradually, however, it attracts, it astonishes, and, in the end, forces into admiration." The Koran, moreover, suffers more than any other book we could think of by a translation, however masterly. If any where, it is here that the *summum jus summa injuria* holds good. What makes the Talmud so particularly delightful is this peculiar fact, that whenever jurisprudence, with its thousand technicalities and uncouth terms, is out of the question, it becomes easy, translucent, and clear to the merest beginner. The pathetic *naïveté* of its diction, and the evident pains it takes to make all its sayings household words, is something for which we can not be too grateful. Hence also the fact that these words in their wisdom and grace must needs find an echo in every true heart, if told exactly as they stand, without attempt to color them. The grandeur of the Koran, on the other hand, consists, its contents apart, in its diction. We can not explain the peculiarly dignified, impressive, sonorous nature of Semitic sound and parlance; its *sesquipedalia verba*, with their crowd of prefixes and affixes, each of them affirming its own position, while consciously bearing upon and influencing the central root—which they envelop like a garment of many folds, or as chosen courtiers move around the anointed person of the king.

May be some stray reader remembers a certain thrill on waking suddenly in the middle of his first night on Eastern soil—waking, as it were, from dream into dream. For there came a voice, solitary, sweet, sonorous, floating from on high through the moonlight stillness—the voice of the blind Mueddin singing the Ulah, or first Call to Prayer. At the sound whereof many a white figure would move silently on the low roofs, and not merely, like the palms and cypresses around, bow his head, but prostrate and bend his knees. And the sounds went and came—" Allahu Akbar... Prayer is better than sleep... There is no god but He... He giveth life, and He dieth not... Oh! thou Bountiful... Thy mercy ceaseth not... My sins are great, greater is Thy mercy... I extol His perfection... Allahu Akbar!"—and this reader may have a vague notion of Arabic and Koranic sound, one which he will never forget.

But the Koran is *sui generis*, though its contents be often but the old wine in new bottles, and its form strikingly resembling that of pre-Islamic poetry, which it condemns. It is rhythmical, rhymed, condescends to word-plays, and indulges—and in one place to an appalling degree—in refrains. As usual, the rhyme — the swaddling clothes of unborn thought — here too seems to run away at times, if not with the sense, at all events with the numbers. Yet not far; only that for the sake of the soft dual termination certain gardens and fountains and fruits are doubled; while on the other hand a lofty contempt for this thraldom is shown by m being made to answer to n, l to r, and so forth. Yet here, as in all these critical exoteric questions, we are treading on very dangerous ground, and we shall content ourselves with mentioning that there are at least three principal schools at variance on the very question whether the Koran *is* rhymed throughout: one affirming it, the other denying it, and the third taking a middle course.

We reserve all that we have to say on the outer or critical aspect of the Koran for the present; the scientific terms on this field — rules, divisions, and subdivisions — most minute and manifold, and the entire Masoretic apparatus, with all the striking analogies with the corresponding Jewish labors that reveal themselves at every step.

We turn, in preference, at once to the intrinsic portion of this strange book — a book by the aid of which the Arabs conquered a world greater than that of Alexander the Great, greater than that of Rome, and in as many tens of years as the latter had wanted hundreds to accomplish her conquests; by the aid of which they, alone of all the Shemites, came to Europe as kings, whither the Phœnicians had come as tradesmen, and the Jews as fugitives or captives; came to Europe to hold up, together with these fugitives, the light to Humanity—they alone, while darkness lay around; to raise up the wisdom and knowledge of Hellas from the dead, to teach philosophy, medicine, astronomy, and the golden art of song to the West as well as to the East, to stand at the cradle of modern science, and to cause us late Epigoni forever to weep over the day when Granada fell.

We said that there is a great likeness between pre-Islamic poetry (even that of those inane "priests") and the Koran. If Mohammed wished to go straight to the heart of his people, it could only be through the hallowed means of poetry—the sole vehicle of all their "science," all tradition, all religion, all love, and all hatred. And, indeed, what has remained of fragments of that period of pre-Islamic poetry which immediately preceded Mohammed—broken, defaced, dimmed, as it is, by fanaticism and pedantic ignorance—prove it sufficiently to have been of all the brilliant periods of Arabic literature the most brilliant. There arises out of the Hamasa, the Moallakat, the Kitab, Al-Aghani, nay, out of the very chips that lie embedded in later works, such a freshness and glory and bloom of desert-song—even as out of Homer's epics rise the glowing spring-times of humanity and the deep blue heavens of Hellas—as has never again been the portion of Arab poetry. Wild and vast and monotonous as the yellow seas of its desert solitudes, it is withal tender, true, pathetic, soul-subduing; much more so than when in beauteous Andalus the great-grandchildren of these wild rovers sang of nightly boatings by torchlight, of the moon's rays trembling on the waves, of sweet meetings in the depths of rose-gardens, of Spain's golden cities and gleaming mosques, and the far-away burning desert whence their fathers came. Those grand accents of joy and sorrow, of love and valor and passion, of which but faint echoes strike on our ears now, were full-toned at the time of Mohammed; and he had not merely to rival the illustrious of the illustrious, but to excel them; to appeal to the superiority of what he said and sang as a very sign and proof of his mission. And there were, at first, many and sinister tokens of rivalry and professional hatred visible, to which religious fanaticism carried fuel. Those that had fallen fighting against him were lamented over in the most heartrending and popular dirges. Poets of his time said, even as Jehuda Al-Hassan-Halevi, that great Hebræo-Arabic minstrel, did hundreds of years after them, that they failed to see any thing extraordinary in his verses. Nay, they called him names —a fool, a madman, a ridiculous pretender and impostor; they laughed at the people of Medina for listening to "such a one." And these rival poets formed a formidable power. Their squibs told, while the counter-satires he caused to be written fell flat. Not even "sudden visitations," by which some of the worst offenders were found struck to death, stopped the "press." Until there came a revelation — "Shall I declare unto you," he asks in the Sura called "the Poets," "on whom the devils descend? They descend upon every lying and wicked person... most of them are liars. And those who err follow the steps of the poets. Seest thou not how they rove as bereft of their senses through every valley?"... Which reminds us strikingly of Kutayir, a pre-Islamic poet, and the answer he gave to people asking him "How he managed when poetry became difficult to him?" and he said, "I walk through the deserted habitations and through the blooming greenswards; then the most perfect songs become easy, and the most beautiful ones flow naturally"—"roving bereft of his senses through every valley!"...

Mohammed is said to have convinced a rival, Lebid, a poet-laureate of the period, of his mission by reciting to him a portion of the now second Sura. Unquestionably it is one of the very grandest specimens of Koranic or Arabic diction, describing how hypocrites "are like unto those who kindle a fire without, and think themselves safe from darkness. But while it is at its biggest blaze, God sends a wind; the flame is extinguished, and they are shrouded in dense night. They are deaf and dumb and blind. . . . Or when in darkness, and, amid thunder and lightning, rain-filled clouds pour from heaven, they in terror of the crash thrust their fingers into their ears. . . . But God compasseth the infidels around. . . . The flash of the lightning blindeth their eyes—while it lights up all things, they walk in its light—then darkness closes in upon them, and they stand rooted to the ground."

But even descriptions of this kind, grand as they be in their own tongue, are not sufficient to kindle and preserve the enthusiasm and the faith and the hope of a nation like the Arabs, not for one generation, but for a thousand. Not the most passionate grandeur, not the most striking similes, not the legends, not the parables, not the sweet spell of rhyme-fall and the weaving of rhythmic melodies, and all the poet's cunning craft—but the kernel of it all, the doctrine, the positive, clear, distinct doctrine. And this doctrine Mohammed brought before them in a thousand, so to say, symphonic variations, modulated through the whole scale of human feeling. From prayer to curse, from despair to exultant joy, from argument, often casuistic, largely spun-out argument, to vision, either in swift and sudden and terrible transition, or in repetitions and reiterations—monotonous and dreary and insufferably tedious to the outsider, but to him alone.

The poets before him had sung of love. One of the principal forms of pre-Islamic poetry was, indeed, the Kasida, which almost invariably commenced with a sorrowful remembrance of her who had gone none knew whither, and the very traces of whose tent, but yesterday gleaming afar in the midst of the wide solitudes, had disappeared overnight. Antara, himself the hero of the most famous novel, sings of the ruins, around which ever hover lovers' thoughts, of the dwelling of Abla, who is gone, and her dwelling-place knows her not; it is now desolate and silent. Amr Al-Kais, "the standard-bearer of poets, but on the way to hell," as Mohammed called him, of all things praises his fortune with women, chiefly Oneisa, and in brilliant, often Heinesque, verse sings of the good things of this world; until his father banishes him on account of an adventure wherein he, as usual, had been too happy. And of a sudden, in the midst of a wild revel, he hears that his father has been slain, and not a word said he. But higher and louder waxed the revel, and he drank deep, and gamed till the gray dawn; when he arose of a sudden, and swore a holy oath that neither wine nor woman should soothe his senses until he had taken bloody vengeance for his father; and when, consulting the oracle, he drew an arrow with the inscription "Defense," he threw it into the idol's face, saying, "Wretch, if thy father had been killed, thou wouldst have counseled Vengeance, not Defense."

They sang of valor and generosity, of love and strife and revenge, of their noble tribe and ancestors, of beautiful women, "often even of those who did not exist, so that woman's noble fame should be spread abroad among kings and princes," as the unavoidable scholiast informs us; of the valiant sword, and the swift camel, and the darling horse, fleeter than the whirlwind's rush. Or of early graves, upon which weeps the morning's cloud, and the fleeting nature of life, which comes and goes as the waves of the desert sand, and as the tents of a caravan, as a flower that shoots up and dies away—while the white stars will rise and set everlastingly, and the mountains will rear their heads heavenward, and never grow old. Or they shoot their bitter arrows of satire right into the enemy's own soul.

Mohammed sang none of these. No love-minstrelsy his, not the joys of this world, nor sword nor camel, nor jealousy or human vengeance, not the glories of tribe or ancestor, nor the unmeaning, swiftly, and forever extinguished existence of man, were his themes. He preached *Islam*.

And he preached it by rending the skies above and tearing open the ground below, by adjuring heaven and hell, the living and the dead. The Arabs have ever been proficient in the art of swearing, but such swearing had never been heard in and out of Arabia. By the foaming waters and by the grim darkness, by the flaming sun and the setting stars, by Mount Sinai and by Him who spanned the firmament, by the human soul and the small voice, by the Kaaba and by the Book, by the Moon and the dawn and the angels, by the ten nights of dread mystery and by the day of judgment. That day of judgment, at the approach whereof the earth shaketh, and the mountains are scattered into dust, and the seas blaze up in fire, and the children's hair grows white with anguish, and like locust-swarms the souls arise out of their graves, and Allah cries to Hell, Art thou filled full? and Hell cries to Allah, More, give me more; ... while Paradise opens its blissful gates to the righteous, and glory ineffable awaits them—both men and women.

The kernel and doctrine of Islam Goethe has found in the second Sura, which begins as follows:

"This is the Book. There is no doubt in the same. A *Guidance* to the righteous. Who believe in the *Unseen*, who observe the *Prayer*, and who give *Alms* of that which we have vouchsafed unto them. And who believe in that which has been sent down unto thee—(the *Revelation*)—which had been sent down to those before thee, and who believe in the *Life to come*. They walk in the guidance of their Lord, and they are the blessed. As to them who believe not—it is indifferent to them whether thou exhortest them or not exhortest them. They will not believe. Sealed hath Allah their hearts and their ears, and over their eyes is darkness, and theirs will be a great punishment.—'And in this wise,' Goethe continues, 'we have Sura after Sura. Belief and unbelief are divided into upper and lower. Heaven and hell await the believers or deniers. Detailed injunctions of things allowed and forbidden, legendary stories of Jewish and Christian religion, amplifications of all kinds, boundless tautologies and repetitions, form the body of this sacred volume, which to us, as often as we approach it, is repellent anew, next attracts us ever anew, and fills us with admiration, and finally forces us into veneration.'"

Thus Goethe. And no doubt the passage adduced is as good a summary as any other. Perhaps, if he had gone a little further in this same chapter, he might have found one still more explicit. When Mohammed at Medina told his adherents no longer to turn in prayer toward Jerusalem, but toward the Kaaba at Mecca, to which their fathers had turned, and he was blamed for this innovation, he replied:

"That is not righteousness: whether ye turn your faces toward East or West, God's is the East as well as the West. But verily righteousness is his who believes in God, in the day of judgment, in the angels, in the Book and the prophets; who bestows his wealth, for God's sake, upon kindred, and orphans, and the poor, and the homeless, and all those who ask; and also upon delivering the captives; he who is steadfast in prayer, giveth alms, who stands firmly by his covenants when he has once entered into them; and who is patient in adversity, in hardship, and in times of trial. These are the righteous, and these are the God-fearing."

Yet these and similar passages, characteristic as they be, do not suffice. It behooves us to look somewhat deeper.

First of all, What is the literal meaning of Islam, the religion of a Moslem? We find that name Moslem already applied to those *Hanifs*, of whom we have spoken above, who had renounced, though secretly, idolatry before Mohammed, and had gone out to seek the "religion of Abraham," which Mohammed finally undertook to re-establish. The Semitic root of the word Moslem yields a variety of meanings, and accordingly Moslem has had many interpretations. But in all these cases—even as is now becoming so universally clear in the terms of the New Testament—it is as useless to go back to the original root for the elucidation of some special or technical, dogmatic, scientific, or other term of a certain period, as it is to ask those for an explanation who lived to use that same term long after it had assumed an utterly new, often the very opposite, meaning. *Salm*, the root of *Islam*, means, in the first instance, to be tranquil, at rest, to have done one's duty, to have paid up, to be at perfect peace, and, finally, to hand one's self over to Him with whom peace is made. The noun derived from it means peace, greeting, safety, salvation. And the Talmud contains both the term and the explanation of the term Moslem, which in its Chaldee meaning had become naturalized in Arabia. It indicates a "Righteous Man." In a paraphrase of Proverbs xxiv., 16, where the original has *Zadik* (*Ziddik* in Koran), which is rightly translated by the Authorized Version, "Just Man," the Talmud has this very word. "Seven pits are laid for the 'Moslem'" (*Shalmana*—Syr., *Msalmono*), it says, and "one for the wicked, but the wicked falls into his one, while the other escapes all seven."* The word thus implies absolute submission to God's will—as generally assumed—neither in the first instance, nor exclusively, but means, on the contrary, one who strives after righteousness with his own strength. Closely connected

---

* There is also the story in the Talmud of the Master whose name was *Shalman* (Solomon); and they said to him, "'Thou art full of peace, and thy teaching is peace [perfect], and thou hast made peace between the disciples."

with the misapprehension of this part of Mohammed's original doctrine is also the popular notion on that supposed bane of Islam, Fatalism; but we must content ourselves here with the observation that, as far as Mohammed and the Koran are concerned, Fatalism is an utter and absolute invention. Not once, but repeatedly, and as if to guard against such an assumption, Mohammed denies it as distinctly as he can, and gives injunctions which show as indisputably as can be that nothing was further from his mind than that pious state of idle and hopeless inanity and stagnation. But to return to Islam. The real sum and substance of it is contained in Mohammed's words: "We have spoken unto thee by revelation: *Follow the religion of Abraham.*" . . .

What did Mohammed and his contemporaries understand by this religion of Abraham? "Abraham," says the Koran, pointedly and pregnantly, "was neither a Jew nor a Christian, but he was pious and righteous, and no idolater." Have we not here the briefest and the most rationalistic doctrine ever preached? Curious and characteristic is the proof which the Koran finds it necessary to allege (partly found, by the way, in the Midrash) for this: There *was* no Law (or Gospel) revealed then—there were, in fact, no divisions of Semitic creed, no special and distinctive dogmas in Abraham's time yet. The Haggadah, it is true, points out that, when Scripture says "he heard my voice," it meant that to him were given, by anticipation, all that the Law and the Prophets contain.

And in order rightly to understand the drift of Mohammed's words, we must endeavor to gather the little mosaics as they lie scattered about in all directions in the Talmud and Midrash. Perchance a picture, anent Abraham's faith and works, may arise under our hands—a not unworthy ideal of Judaism, which formed it, and Mohammedanism, which adopted it; of Abraham, the righteous, the first and the greatest Moslem. It may also further elucidate, by the way, the words of the Mishnah, "Be ye of the Disciples of Abraham." "The divine light lay hidden," says the Midrash, "until Abraham came and discovered it."

Again we have to turn—driven by absolute necessity—to one of those indigestible morsels, one of the many *cruces* of the exegetes of Orient and Occident. The word used in the Koran for the "Religion of Abraham" is generally *Milla*. Sprenger, after ridiculing the indeed absurd attempts made to derive it from an Arabic root, concludes that it must be a foreign word, introduced by the teachers of the "Milla of Abraham" into the Hejaz. He is perfectly right. Milla=Memra=Logos, are identical: being the Hebrew, Chaldee (Targum, Peshito in slightly varied spelling), and Greek terms respectively for "*Word*"—that surrogate for the divine Name used by the Targum, by Philo, by St. John. This Milla, or "Word," which Abraham proclaimed—he " who was not an astrologer, but a prophet"—teaches, according to the Haggadah, first of all, the existence of One God, the Creator of the

Universe, who rules this universe with mercy and loving-kindness.* He alone also, neither angel nor planet, guides the destinies of man. Idolatry, even when combined with the belief in him, is utterly to be abhorred; he alone is to be worshiped; in him alone trust is to be placed in adversity. He frees the persecuted and the oppressed. You must pray to him and serve him in love, and not murmur when he asks for your lives, or even for lives still dearer to you than your own. As to duties toward man, it teaches—"Loving-kindness and mercy are the tokens of the faith of Abraham." "He who is not merciful is not of the children of Abraham." "What is the distinguishing quality of Abraham's descendants? Their compassion and their mercy." (Be it observed, by the way, that in all these Talmudical passages the word *Rachman* is used, which term for "Merciful" forms an emphatic mark in the Koran.) "Abraham not merely forgave Abimelech, but

---

* "God," says the Talmud, in boldest transcendental flight, "*prays*." And what is that prayer? "Be it my will that my mercy overpower my justice." The Koran says: "God has laid down for himself the Law of Mercy."

God's Mercy, says the Midrash, was the only link that held the universe together before the "Law" came to be revealed to man. And very beautifully does the Haggadistic version of the manner in which the universe, which, spite of all, would not rest firmly, but kept swaying to and fro in space, "even as a great palace built of mortal man, the foundations whereof are not firmly laid," contrast from all those well-known wild heapings-up of monsters begotten for steadying purposes. "The earth shook and trembled, and would not find rest until God created Repentance: then it stood."

he prayed for him;" and this mercy, charity, and loving-kindness is to be extended to every being, without reference to "garment," birth, rank, creed, or nationality. Disinterestedness and unselfishness are self-understood duties. Though the whole land had been promised to Abraham by God, he *bought* the ground for Sarah's tomb. After the victorious campaign he took nothing, no, not even "from a thread to a shoe-latchet," from the enemy. Modesty and humility are other qualities enjoined by him. Rule yourself, he said, before you rule others. Eschew pride, which shortens life—modesty prolongs it. It purifies from all sins, and is the best weapon for conquest. His humility was shown even by the way in which he exercised his hospitality. He himself waited on his guests; and when they tried to thank him, he said, "Thank Him, the One who nourisheth all, who ruleth in heaven and earth, who killeth and giveth life, who causeth the plants to grow, and who createth man according to his wisdom." He inaugurated the Morning Prayer—even as did Isaac that of the Evening, and Jacob that of the Night. He went, even in his old age, ever restless in doing good, to succor the oppressed, to teach and preach to all men. He "wore a jewel around his neck, the light of which raised up the bowed-down and healed the sick, and which, after his death, was placed among the stars. And see how he was chosen to be tempted with the bitterest trial, in order that mankind might see how steadfast he remained—"even as the potter proves the strength of his

R

ware, not by that which is brittle, but by that which is strong." And when he died, he left to his children four guardian angels — "Justice and Mercy, Love and Charity."

Such are the floating outlines of the faith of Abraham to be gathered from the Haggadah; and these traits form the fundamental bases of Mohammed's doctrine—often in the very words, always in the sense, of these Jewish traditions. The most emphatic moment, however, we find laid upon the Unity of God, the absence of Intermediators, and the repudiation of any special, exclusive, "privileged" creed. This is a point on which the Talmud is very strong—not merely declaring its aversion to proselytism, but actually calling every righteous man, so that he be no idolater, a "Jew" to all intents and purposes. The tracing of the minutiæ of general human ethics is, comparatively speaking, of less import, considering that these, in their outlines, are wonderfully alike, in Hellas and India, and Rome and Persia and Japan; so that it would indeed be difficult to say who first invented the great law of good-will toward fellow-creatures. But the manner and the words in which these things are inculcated mark their birthplace and the stages of their journey clearly enough in the Semitic creeds.

And with the doctrines—if so we may call them—of Abraham, as we gathered them from the Jewish writings, Mohammed also introduced the whole legendary cycle that surrounds Abraham's head, like a halo, in these same writings. We have in the Koran, first of all, that wondrous Haggadistic explanation how Abraham first came to worship, in the midst of idolaters, the one invisible God — how he first lifted up his eyes heavenward and saw a brilliant star, and said, This is God. But when the star paled before the brightness of the moon, he said, This is God. And then the sun rose, and Abraham saw God in the golden glory of the sun. But the sun, too, set, and Abraham said, "Then none of you is God; but there is one above you who created both you and me. Him alone will I worship, the Maker of heaven and earth!" How he then took an axe and destroyed all the idols, and placed the axe in the hands of the biggest, accusing him of the deed; how he is thrown into the fiery furnace, and God said to the fire, "Be thou cold;" how he entertained the angels, and how he brought his beloved son to the altar, and an "excellent victim" (a ram from Paradise) was sacrificed in his stead; and so on. All this, though only sketched in its outlines in the Koran, is absolute Haggadah, with scarcely as much of alteration as would naturally be expected in the like fantastic matter, even as is the rest of that "entire world of pious Biblical legend which Islam has said and sung in its many tongues, to the delight of the wise and simple, for twelve centuries now, to be found either in embryo or fully developed in Haggadah."

But here, in the midst of our discourse, we are compelled to break off, reserving its continuation: notably with regard to the theoretical and practical bearing of the religion of Mohammed, and the relation of its religious terms* and individual tenets to those of Judaism; also its progress and the changes wrought within the community by many and most daring sects; and the present aspect of the Faith and its general influence. And this our Exordium we will sum up with the beginning of the Sura, called the Assembly, revealed at Medina:

"In the name of God, the Merciful, the Compassionate. Whatsoever is in heaven and on earth praises God the King, the Holy One, the Almighty, the All-wise. It is he who out of the midst of the illiterate Arabs has raised an Apostle to show unto them his signs, and to sanctify them, and to teach them the Scripture and the Wisdom, them who before had been in great darkness. . . . This is God's free Grace, which he giveth unto whomsoever he wills. God is of great Mercy!".

---

* *E. g.*, Koran, Forkan (= Pirke, exposition of Halachah), Torah (Law), Shechinah (presence of God), Gan Eden (Paradise), Gehinnom (Hell), Haber (Master), Darash (search the Scriptures), Rabbi (teacher), Sabbath (day of rest), Mishnah (Oral Law), etc., all of which are bodily found in the Koran, as well as even such words as the Hebrew *Yam* (for Red Sea), etc.

THE END.

VALUABLE & INTERESTING WORKS

FOR PUBLIC AND PRIVATE LIBRARIES,

Published by HARPER & BROTHERS, New York.

☞ *For a full List of Books suitable for Libraries, see* HARPER & BROTHERS' TRADE-LIST *and* CATALOGUE, *which may be had gratuitously on application to the Publishers personally, or by letter enclosing Ten Cents.*

☞ HARPER & BROTHERS *will send any of the following works by mail, postage prepaid, to any part of the United States, on receipt of the price.*

SCHWEINFURTH'S HEART OF AFRICA. The Heart of Africa: or, Three Years' Travels and Adventures in the Unexplored Regions of the Centre of Africa. From 1868 to 1871. By Dr. GEORG SCHWEINFURTH. Translated by ELLEN E. FREWER. With an Introduction by WINWOOD READE. Illustrated by about 130 Woodcuts from Drawings made by the Author, and with Two Maps. 2 vols., 8vo, Cloth, $8 00.

FLAMMARION'S ATMOSPHERE. The Atmosphere. Translated from the French of CAMILLE FLAMMARION. Edited by JAMES GLAISHER, F.R.S., Superintendent of the Magnetical and Meteorological Department of the Royal Observatory at Greenwich. With 10 Chromo-Lithographs and 86 Woodcuts. 8vo, Cloth, $6 00.

HUDSON'S HISTORY OF JOURNALISM. Journalism in the United States, from 1690 to 1872. By FREDERICK HUDSON. Crown 8vo, Cloth, $5 00.

DR. LIVINGSTONE'S LAST JOURNALS. The Last Journals of David Livingstone, in Central Africa, from 1865 to his Death. Continued by a Narrative of his Last Moments and Sufferings, obtained from his faithful Servants Chuma and Susi. By HORACE WALLER, F.R.G.S., Rector of Twywell, Northampton. With Maps and Illustrations. 8vo, Cloth, $5 00.

SIR SAMUEL BAKER'S ISMAILÏA. Ismailïa: A Narrative of the Expedition to Central Africa for the Suppression of the Slave Trade. Organized by ISMAIL, Khedive of Egypt. By Sir SAMUEL W. BAKER, PASHA, F.R.S., F.R.G.S. With Maps, Portraits, and upward of Fifty full-page Illustrations by ZWECKER and DURAND. 8vo, Cloth, $5 00.

MYERS'S REMAINS OF LOST EMPIRES. Remains of Lost Empires. Sketches of the Ruins of Palmyra, Nineveh, Babylon, and Persepolis, with some Notes on India and the Cashmerian Himalayas. By P. V. N. MYERS, A.M. Illustrations. Crown 8vo, Cloth, $3 50.

EVANGELICAL ALLIANCE CONFERENCE, 1873. History, Essays, Orations, and Other Documents of the Sixth General Conference of the Evangelical Alliance, held in New York, Oct. 2-12, 1873. Edited by Rev. PHILIP SCHAFF, D.D., and Rev. S. IRENÆUS PRIME, D.D. With Portraits of Rev. Messrs. Pronier, Carrasco, and Cook, recently deceased. 8vo, Cloth, nearly 800 pages, $6 00.

VINCENT'S LAND OF THE WHITE ELEPHANT. The Land of the White Elephant: Sights and Scenes in Southeastern Asia. A Personal Narrative of Travel and Adventure in Farther India, embracing the Countries of Burma, Siam, Cambodia, and Cochin-China (1871-2). By FRANK VINCENT, Jr. Magnificently illustrated with Map, Plans, and numerous Woodcuts. Crown 8vo, Cloth, $3 50.

TRISTRAM'S THE LAND OF MOAB. The Result of Travels and Discoveries on the East Side of the Dead Sea and the Jordan. By H. B. TRISTRAM, M.A., LL.D., F.R.S., Master of the Greatham Hospital, and Hon. Canon of Durham. With a Chapter on the Persian Palace of Mashita, by JAS. FERGUSON, F.R.S. With Map and Illustrations. Crown 8vo, Cloth, $2 50.

SANTO DOMINGO, Past and Present; with a Glance at Hayti. By SAMUEL HAZARD. Maps and Illustrations. Crown 8vo, Cloth, $3 50.

SMILES'S HUGUENOTS AFTER THE REVOCATION. The Huguenots in France after the Revocation of the Edict of Nantes: with a Visit to the Country of the Vaudois. By SAMUEL SMILES. Crown 8vo, Cloth, $2 00.

POETS OF THE NINETEENTH CENTURY. The Poets of the Nineteenth Century. Selected and Edited by the Rev. ROBERT ARIS WILLMOTT. With English and American Additions, arranged by EVERT A. DUYCKINCK, Editor of "Cyclopædia of American Literature." Comprising Selections from the Greatest Authors of the Age. Superbly Illustrated with 141 Engravings from Designs by the most Eminent Artists. In elegant small 4to form, printed on Superfine Tinted Paper, richly bound in extra Cloth, Beveled, Gilt Edges, $5 00; Half Calf, $5 50; Full Turkey Morocco, $9 00.

THE REVISION OF THE ENGLISH VERSION OF THE NEW TESTAMENT. With an Introduction by the Rev. P. SCHAFF, D.D. 618 pp., Crown 8vo, Cloth, $3 00.
This work embraces in one volume:
  I. ON A FRESH REVISION OF THE ENGLISH NEW TESTAMENT. By J. B. LIGHTFOOT, D.D., Canon of St. Paul's, and Hulsean Professor of Divinity, Cambridge. Second Edition, Revised. 196 pp.
  II. ON THE AUTHORIZED VERSION OF THE NEW TESTAMENT in Connection with some Recent Proposals for its Revision. By RICHARD CHENEVIX TRENCH, D.D., Archbishop of Dublin. 194 pp.
  III. CONSIDERATIONS ON THE REVISION OF THE ENGLISH VERSION OF THE NEW TESTAMENT. By J. C. ELLICOTT, D.D., Bishop of Gloucester and Bristol. 178 pp.

NORDHOFF'S CALIFORNIA. California: For Health, Pleasure, and Residence. A Book for Travelers and Settlers. Illustrated. 8vo, Paper, $2 00; Cloth, $2 50.

MOTLEY'S DUTCH REPUBLIC. The Rise of the Dutch Republic. By JOHN LOTHROP MOTLEY, LL.D., D.C.L. With a Portrait of William of Orange. 3 vols., 8vo, Cloth, $10 50.

MOTLEY'S UNITED NETHERLAND'S. History of the United Netherlands: from the Death of William the Silent to the Twelve Years' Truce—1609. With a full View of the English-Dutch Struggle against Spain, and of the Origin and Destruction of the Spanish Armada. By JOHN LOTHROP MOTLEY, LL.D., D.C.L. Portraits. 4 vols., 8vo, Cloth, $14 00.

MOTLEY'S LIFE AND DEATH OF JOHN OF BARNEVELD. Life and Death of John of Barneveld, Advocate of Holland. With a View of the Primary Causes and Movements of "The Thirty Years' War." By JOHN LOTHROP MOTLEY, D.C.L. With Illustrations. In Two Volumes. 8vo, Cloth, $7 00.

HAYDN'S DICTIONARY OF DATES, relating to all Ages and Nations. For Universal Reference. Edited by BENJAMIN VINCENT, Assistant Secretary and Keeper of the Library of the Royal Institution of Great Britain; and Revised for the Use of American Readers. 8vo, Cloth, $5 00; Sheep, $6 00.

MACGREGOR'S ROB ROY ON THE JORDAN. The Rob Roy on the Jordan, Nile, Red Sea, and Gennesareth, &c. A Canoe Cruise in Palestine and Egypt, and the Waters of Damascus. By J. MACGREGOR, M.A. With Maps and Illustrations. Crown 8vo, Cloth, $2 50.

WALLACE'S MALAY ARCHIPELAGO. The Malay Archipelago: the Land of the Orang-Utan and the Bird of Paradise. A Narrative of Travel, 1854–1862. With Studies of Man and Nature. By ALFRED RUSSEL WALLACE. With Ten Maps and Fifty-one Elegant Illustrations. Crown 8vo, Cloth, $2 50.

WHYMPER'S ALASKA. Travel and Adventure in the Territory of Alaska, formerly Russian America—now Ceded to the United States—and in various other parts of the North Pacific. By FREDERICK WHYMPER. With Map and Illustrations. Crown 8vo, Cloth, $2 50.

ORTON'S ANDES AND THE AMAZON. The Andes and the Amazon; or, Across the Continent of South America. By JAMES ORTON, M.A., Professor of Natural History in Vassar College, Poughkeepsie, N. Y., and Corresponding Member of the Academy of Natural Sciences, Philadelphia. With a New Map of Equatorial America and numerous Illustrations. Crown 8vo, Cloth, $2 00.

WINCHELL'S SKETCHES OF CREATION. Sketches of Creation: a Popular View of some of the Grand Conclusions of the Sciences in reference to the History of Matter and of Life. Together with a Statement of the Intimations of Science respecting the Primordial Condition and the Ultimate Destiny of the Earth and the Solar System. By ALEXANDER WINCHELL, LL.D., Professor of Geology, Zoology, and Botany in the University of Michigan, and Director of the State Geological Survey. With Illustrations. 12mo, Cloth, $2 00.

WHITE'S MASSACRE OF ST. BARTHOLOMEW. The Massacre of St. Bartholomew: Preceded by a History of the Religious Wars in the Reign of Charles IX. By HENRY WHITE, M.A. With Illustrations. 8vo, Cloth, $1 75.

Harper & Brothers' Valuable and Interesting Works. 3

LOSSING'S FIELD-BOOK OF THE REVOLUTION. Pictorial Field-Book of the Revolution; or, Illustrations, by Pen and Pencil, of the History, Biography, Scenery, Relics, and Traditions of the War for Independence. By BENSON J. LOSSING. 2 vols., 8vo, Cloth, $14 00; Sheep, $15 00; Half Calf, $18 00; Full Turkey Morocco, $22 00.

LOSSING'S FIELD-BOOK OF THE WAR OF 1812. Pictorial Field-Book of the War of 1812; or, Illustrations, by Pen and Pencil, of the History, Biography, Scenery, Relics, and Traditions of the Last War for American Independence. By BENSON J. LOSSING. With several hundred Engravings on Wood, by Lossing and Barritt, chiefly from Original Sketches by the Author. 1088 pages, 8vo, Cloth, $7 00; Sheep, $8 50; Half Calf, $10 00.

ALFORD'S GREEK TESTAMENT. The Greek Testament: with a critically revised Text; a Digest of Various Readings; Marginal References to Verbal and Idiomatic Usage; Prolegomena; and a Critical and Exegetical Commentary. For the Use of Theological Students and Ministers. By HENRY ALFORD, D.D., Dean of Canterbury. Vol. I., containing the Four Gospels. 944 pages, 8vo, Cloth, $6 00; Sheep, $6 50.

ABBOTT'S FREDERICK THE GREAT. The History of Frederick the Second, called Frederick the Great. By JOHN S. C. ABBOTT. Elegantly Illustrated. 8vo, Cloth, $5 00.

ABBOTT'S HISTORY OF THE FRENCH REVOLUTION. The French Revolution of 1789, as viewed in the Light of Republican Institutions. By JOHN S. C. ABBOTT. With 100 Engravings. 8vo, Cloth, $5 00.

ABBOTT'S NAPOLEON BONAPARTE. The History of Napoleon Bonaparte. By JOHN S. C. ABBOTT. With Maps, Woodcuts, and Portraits on Steel. 2 vols., 8vo, Cloth, $10 00.

ABBOTT'S NAPOLEON AT ST. HELENA; or, Interesting Anecdotes and Remarkable Conversations of the Emperor during the Five and a Half Years of his Captivity. Collected from the Memorials of Las Casas, O'Meara, Montholon, Antommarchi, and others. By JOHN S. C. ABBOTT. With Illustrations. 8vo, Cloth, $5 00,

ADDISON'S COMPLETE WORKS. The Works of Joseph Addison, embracing the whole of the "Spectator." Complete in 3 vols., 8vo, Cloth, $6 00.

ALCOCK'S JAPAN. The Capital of the Tycoon: a Narrative of a Three Years' Residence in Japan. By Sir RUTHERFORD ALCOCK, K.C.B., Her Majesty's Envoy Extraordinary and Minister Plenipotentiary in Japan. With Maps and Engravings. 2 vols., 12mo, Cloth, $3 50.

ALISON'S HISTORY OF EUROPE. FIRST SERIES: From the Commencement of the French Revolution, in 1789, to the Restoration of the Bourbons, in 1815. [In addition to the Notes on Chapter LXXVI., which correct the errors of the original work concerning the United States, a copious Analytical Index has been appended to this American edition.] SECOND SERIES: From the Fall of Napoleon, in 1815, to the Accession of Louis Napoleon, in 1852. 8 vols., 8vo, Cloth, $16 00.

BALDWIN'S PRE-HISTORIC NATIONS. Pre-Historic Nations; or, Inquiries concerning some of the Great Peoples and Civilizations of Antiquity, and their Probable Relation to a still Older Civilization of the Ethiopians or Cushites of Arabia. By JOHN D. BALDWIN, Member of the American Oriental Society. 12mo, Cloth, $1 75.

BARTH'S NORTH AND CENTRAL AFRICA. Travels and Discoveries in North and Central Africa: being a Journal of an Expedition undertaken under the Auspices of H. B. M.'s Government, in the Years 1849-1855. By HENRY BARTH, Ph.D., D.C.L. Illustrated. 3 vols., 8vo, Cloth, $12 00.

HENRY WARD BEECHER'S SERMONS. Sermons by HENRY WARD BEECHER, Plymouth Church, Brooklyn. Selected from Published and Unpublished Discourses, and Revised by their Author. With Steel Portrait. Complete in 2 vols., 8vo, Cloth, $5 00.

LYMAN BEECHER'S AUTOBIOGRAPHY, &c. Autobiography, Correspondence, &c., of Lyman Beecher, D.D. Edited by his Son, CHARLES BEECHER. With Three Steel Portraits, and Engravings on Wood. In 2 vols., 12mo, Cloth, $5 00.

BOSWELL'S JOHNSON. The Life of Samuel Johnson, LL.D. Including a Journey to the Hebrides. By JAMES BOSWELL, Esq. A New Edition, with numerous Additions and Notes. By JOHN WILSON CROKER, LL.D., F.R.S. Portrait of Boswell. 2 vols., 8vo, Cloth, $4 00.

DRAPER'S CIVIL WAR. History of the American Civil War. By JOHN W. DRAPER, M.D., LL.D., Professor of Chemistry and Physiology in the University of New York. In Three Vols. 8vo, Cloth, $3 50 per vol.

DRAPER'S INTELLECTUAL DEVELOPMENT OF EUROPE. A History of the Intellectual Development of Europe. By JOHN W. DRAPER, M.D., LL.D., Professor of Chemistry and Physiology in the University of New York. 8vo, Cloth, $5 00.

DRAPER'S AMERICAN CIVIL POLICY. Thoughts on the Future Civil Policy of America. By JOHN W. DRAPER, M.D., LL.D., Professor of Chemistry and Physiology in the University of New York. Crown 8vo, Cloth, $2 50.

DU CHAILLU'S AFRICA. Explorations and Adventures in Equatorial Africa with Accounts of the Manners and Customs of the People, and of the Chase of the Gorilla, the Crocodile, Leopard, Elephant, Hippopotamus, and other Animals. By PAUL B. DU CHAILLU. Numerous Illustrations. 8vo, Cloth, $5 00.

BELLOWS'S OLD WORLD. The Old World in its New Face: Impressions of Europe in 1867-1868. By HENRY W. BELLOWS. 2 vols., 12mo, Cloth, $3 50.

BRODHEAD'S HISTORY OF NEW YORK. History of the State of New York. By JOHN ROMEYN BRODHEAD. 1609-1691. 2 vols. 8vo, Cloth, $3 00 per vol.

BROUGHAM'S AUTOBIOGRAPHY. Life and Times of HENRY, LORD BROUGHAM. Written by Himself. In Three Volumes. 12mo, Cloth, $2 00 per vol.

BULWER'S PROSE WORKS. Miscellaneous Prose Works of Edward Bulwer, Lord Lytton. 2 vols., 12mo, Cloth, $3 50.

BULWER'S HORACE. The Odes and Epodes of Horace. A Metrical Translation into English. With Introduction and Commentaries. By LORD LYTTON. With Latin Text from the Editions of Orelli, Macleane, and Yonge. 12mo, Cloth, $1 75.

BULWER'S KING ARTHUR. A Poem. By EARL LYTTON. New Edition. 12mo, Cloth, $1 75.

BURNS'S LIFE AND WORKS. The Life and Works of Robert Burns. Edited by ROBERT CHAMBERS. 4 vols., 12mo, Cloth, $6 00.

REINDEER, DOGS, AND SNOW-SHOES. A Journal of Siberian Travel and Explorations made in the Years 1865-'67. By RICHARD J. BUSH, late of the Russo-American Telegraph Expedition. Illustrated. Crown 8vo, Cloth, $3 00.

CARLYLE'S FREDERICK THE GREAT. History of Friedrich II., called Frederick the Great. By THOMAS CARLYLE. Portraits, Maps, Plans, &c. 6 vols., 12mo, Cloth, $12 00.

CARLYLE'S FRENCH REVOLUTION. History of the French Revolution. Newly Revised by the Author, with Index, &c. 2 vols., 12mo, Cloth, $3 50.

CARLYLE'S OLIVER CROMWELL. Letters and Speeches of Oliver Cromwell. With Elucidations and Connecting Narrative. 2 vols., 12mo, Cloth, $3 50.

CHALMERS'S POSTHUMOUS WORKS. The Posthumous Works of Dr. Chalmers. Edited by his Son-in-Law, Rev. WILLIAM HANNA, LL.D. Complete in 9 vols., 12mo, Cloth, $13 50.

COLERIDGE'S COMPLETE WORKS. The Complete Works of Samuel Taylor Coleridge. With an Introductory Essay upon his Philosophical and Theological Opinions. Edited by Professor SHEDD. Complete in Seven Vols. With a fine Portrait. Small 8vo, Cloth, $10 50.

DOOLITTLE'S CHINA. Social Life of the Chinese: with some Account of their Religious, Governmental, Educational, and Business Customs and Opinions. With special but not exclusive Reference to Fuhchau. By Rev. JUSTUS DOOLITTLE, Fourteen Years Member of the Fuhchau Mission of the American Board. Illustrated with more than 150 characteristic Engravings on Wood. 2 vols., 12mo, Cloth, $5 00.

GIBBON'S ROME. History of the Decline and Fall of the Roman Empire. By EDWARD GIBBON. With Notes by Rev. H. H. MILMAN and M. GUIZOT. A new cheap Edition. To which is added a complete Index of the whole Work, and a Portrait of the Author. 6 vols., 12mo, Cloth, $9 00.

HAZEN'S SCHOOL AND ARMY IN GERMANY AND FRANCE. The School and the Army in Germany and France, with a Diary of Siege Life at Versailles. By Brevet Major-General W. B. HAZEN, U.S.A., Colonel Sixth Infantry. Crown 8vo, Cloth, $2 50.

HARPER'S NEW CLASSICAL LIBRARY. Literal Translations. The following Volumes are now ready. Portraits. 12mo, Cloth, $1 50 each. CÆSAR.—VIRGIL.—SALLUST.—HORACE.—CICERO'S ORATIONS.—CICERO'S OFFICES, &C.—CICERO ON ORATORY AND ORATORS.—TACITUS (2 vols.).—TERENCE.—SOPHOCLES.—JUVENAL.—XENOPHON.—HOMER'S ILIAD.—HOMER'S ODYSSEY.—HERODOTUS.—DEMOSTHENES.—THUCYDIDES.—ÆSCHYLUS.—EURIPIDES (2 vols.).—LIVY (2 vols.).

DAVIS'S CARTHAGE. Carthage and her Remains: being an Account of the Excavations and Researches on the Site of the Phœnician Metropolis in Africa and other adjacent Places. Conducted under the Auspices of Her Majesty's Government. By Dr. DAVIS, F.R.G.S. Profusely Illustrated with Maps, Woodcuts, Chromo-Lithographs, &c. 8vo, Cloth, $4 00.

EDGEWORTH'S (Miss) NOVELS. With Engravings. 10 vols., 12mo, Cloth, $15 00.

GROTE'S HISTORY OF GREECE. 12 vols., 12mo, Cloth, $18 00.

HELPS'S SPANISH CONQUEST. The Spanish Conquest in America, and its Relation to the History of Slavery and to the Government of Colonies. By ARTHUR HELPS. 4 vols., 12mo, Cloth, $6 00.

HALE'S (MRS.) WOMAN'S RECORD. Woman's Record; or, Biographical Sketches of all Distinguished Women, from the Creation to the Present Time. Arranged in Four Eras, with Selections from Female Writers of each Era. By Mrs. SARAH JOSEPHA HALE. Illustrated with more than 200 Portraits. 8vo, Cloth, $5 00.

HALL'S ARCTIC RESEARCHES. Arctic Researches and Life among the Esquimaux: being the Narrative of an Expedition in Search of Sir John Franklin, in the Years 1860, 1861, and 1862. By CHARLES FRANCIS HALL. With Maps and 100 Illustrations. The Illustrations are from Original Drawings by Charles Parsons, Henry L. Stephens, Solomon Eytinge, W. S. L. Jewett, and Granville Perkins, after Sketches by Captain Hall. 8vo, Cloth, $5 00.

HALLAM'S CONSTITUTIONAL HISTORY OF ENGLAND, from the Accession of Henry VII. to the Death of George II. 8vo, Cloth, $2 00.

HALLAM'S LITERATURE. Introduction to the Literature of Europe during the Fifteenth, Sixteenth, and Seventeenth Centuries. By HENRY HALLAM. 2 vols., 8vo, Cloth, $4 00.

HALLAM'S MIDDLE AGES. State of Europe during the Middle Ages. By HENRY HALLAM. 8vo, Cloth, $2 00.

HILDRETH'S HISTORY OF THE UNITED STATES. FIRST SERIES: From the First Settlement of the Country to the Adoption of the Federal Constitution. SECOND SERIES: From the Adoption of the Federal Constitution to the End of the Sixteenth Congress. 6 vols., 8vo, Cloth, $18 00.

HUME'S HISTORY OF ENGLAND. History of England, from the Invasion of Julius Cæsar to the Abdication of James II., 1688. By DAVID HUME. A new Edition, with the Author's last Corrections and Improvements. To which is Prefixed a short Account of his Life, written by Himself. With a Portrait of the Author. 6 vols., 12mo, Cloth, $9 00.

JAY'S WORKS. Complete Works of Rev. William Jay: comprising his Sermons, Family Discourses, Morning and Evening Exercises for every Day in the Year, Family Prayers, &c. Author's enlarged Edition, revised. 3 vols., 8vo, Cloth, $6 00.

JEFFERSON'S DOMESTIC LIFE. The Domestic Life of Thomas Jefferson: compiled from Family Letters and Reminiscences by his Great-Granddaughter, SARAH N. RANDOLPH. With Illustrations. Crown 8vo, Illuminated Cloth, Beveled Edges, $2 50.

JOHNSON'S COMPLETE WORKS. The Works of Samuel Johnson, LL.D. With an Essay on his Life and Genius, by ARTHUR MURPHY, Esq. Portrait of Johnson. 2 vols., 8vo, Cloth, $4 00.

KINGLAKE'S CRIMEAN WAR. The Invasion of the Crimea, and an Account of its Progress down to the Death of Lord Raglan. By ALEXANDER WILLIAM KINGLAKE. With Maps and Plans. Two Vols. ready. 12mo, Cloth, $2 00 per vol.

KINGSLEY'S WEST INDIES. At Last: A Christmas in the West Indies. By CHARLES KINGSLEY. Illustrated. 12mo, Cloth, $1 50.

KRUMMACHER'S DAVID, KING OF ISRAEL. David, the King of Israel: a Portrait drawn from Bible History and the Book of Psalms. By FREDERICK WILLIAM KRUMMACHER, D.D., Author of "Elijah the Tishbite," &c. Translated under the express Sanction of the Author by the Rev. M. G. EASTON, M.A. With a Letter from Dr. Krummacher to his American Readers, and a Portrait. 12mo, Cloth, $1 75.

LAMB'S COMPLETE WORKS. The Works of Charles Lamb. Comprising his Letters, Poems, Essays of Elia, Essays upon Shakspeare, Hogarth, &c., and a Sketch of his Life, with the Final Memorials, by T. NOON TALFOURD. Portrait. 2 vols., 12mo, Cloth, $3 00.

LIVINGSTONE'S SOUTH AFRICA. Missionary Travels and Researches in South Africa; including a Sketch of Sixteen Years' Residence in the Interior of Africa, and a Journey from the Cape of Good Hope to Loando on the West Coast; thence across the Continent, down the River Zambesi, to the Eastern Ocean. By DAVID LIVINGSTONE, LL.D., D.C.L. With Portrait, Maps by Arrowsmith, and numerous Illustrations. 8vo, Cloth, $4 50.

LIVINGSTONES' ZAMBESI. Narrative of an Expedition to the Zambesi and its Tributaries, and of the Discovery of the Lakes Shirwa and Nyassa. 1858-1864. By DAVID and CHARLES LIVINGSTONE. With Map and Illustrations. 8vo, Cloth, $5 00.

M'CLINTOCK & STRONG'S CYCLOPÆDIA. Cyclopædia of Biblical, Theological, and Ecclesiastical Literature. Prepared by the Rev. JOHN M'CLINTOCK, D.D., and JAMES STRONG, S.T.D. 5 vols. now ready. Royal 8vo. Price per vol., Cloth, $5 00; Sheep, $6 00; Half Morocco, $8 00.

MARCY'S ARMY LIFE ON THE BORDER. Thirty Years of Army Life on the Border. Comprising Descriptions of the Indian Nomads of the Plains; Explorations of New Territory; a Trip across the Rocky Mountains in the Winter; Descriptions of the Habits of Different Animals found in the West, and the Methods of Hunting them; with Incidents in the Life of Different Frontier Men, &c., &c. By Brevet Brigadier-General R. B. MARCY, U.S.A., Author of "The Prairie Traveller." With numerous Illustrations. 8vo, Cloth, Beveled Edges, $3 00.

MACAULAY'S HISTORY OF ENGLAND. The History of England from the Accession of James II. By THOMAS BABINGTON MACAULAY. With an Original Portrait of the Author. 5 vols., 8vo, Cloth, $10 00; 12mo, Cloth, $7 50.

MOSHEIM'S ECCLESIASTICAL HISTORY, Ancient and Modern; in which the Rise, Progress, and Variation of Church Power are considered in their Connection with the State of Learning and Philosophy, and the Political History of Europe during that Period. Translated, with Notes, &c., by A. MACLAINE, D.D. A new Edition, continued to 1826, by C. COOTE, LL.D. 2 vols., 8vo, Cloth, $4 00.

NEVIUS'S CHINA. China and the Chinese: a General Description of the Country and its Inhabitants; its Civilization and Form of Government; its Religious and Social Institutions; its Intercourse with other Nations; and its Present Condition and Prospects. By the Rev. JOHN L. NEVIUS, Ten Years a Missionary in China. With a Map and Illustrations. 12mo, Cloth, $1 75.

THE DESERT OF THE EXODUS. Journeys on Foot in the Wilderness of the Forty Years' Wanderings; undertaken in connection with the Ordnance Survey of Sinai and the Palestine Exploration Fund. By E. H. PALMER, M.A., Lord Almoner's Professor of Arabic, and Fellow of St. John's College, Cambridge. With Maps and numerous Illustrations from Photographs and Drawings taken on the spot by the Sinai Survey Expedition and C. F. Tyrwhitt Drake. Crown 8vo, Cloth, $3 00.

OLIPHANT'S CHINA AND JAPAN. Narrative of the Earl of Elgin's Mission to China and Japan, in the Years 1857, '58, '59. By LAURENCE OLIPHANT, Private Secretary to Lord Elgin. Illustrations. 8vo, Cloth, $3 50.

OLIPHANT'S (MRS.) LIFE OF EDWARD IRVING. The Life of Edward Irving, Minister of the National Scotch Church, London. Illustrated by his Journals and Correspondence. By Mrs. OLIPHANT. Portrait. 8vo, Cloth, $3 50.

RAWLINSON'S MANUAL OF ANCIENT HISTORY. A Manual of Ancient History, from the Earliest Times to the Fall of the Western Empire. Comprising the History of Chaldæa, Assyria, Media, Babylonia, Lydia, Phœnicia, Syria, Judæa, Egypt, Carthage, Persia, Greece, Macedonia, Parthia, and Rome. By GEORGE RAWLINSON, M.A., Camden Professor of Ancient History in the University of Oxford. 12mo, Cloth, $2 50.

Harper & Brothers' Valuable and Interesting Works. 7

RECLUS'S THE EARTH. The Earth: a Descriptive History of the Phenomena and Life of the Globe. By ÉLISÉE RECLUS. Translated by the late B. B. Woodward, and Edited by Henry Woodward. With 234 Maps and Illustrations, and 23 Page Maps printed in Colors. 8vo, Cloth, $5 00.

RECLUS'S OCEAN. The Ocean, Atmosphere, and Life. Being the Second Series of a Descriptive History of the Life of the Globe. By ÉLISÉE RECLUS. Profusely Illustrated with 250 Maps or Figures, and 27 Maps printed in Colors. 8vo, Cloth, $6 00.

SHAKSPEARE. The Dramatic Works of William Shakspeare, with the Corrections and Illustrations of Dr. JOHNSON G. STEEVENS, and others. Revised by ISAAC REED. Engravings. 6 vols., Royal 12mo, Cloth, $9 00.

SMILES'S LIFE OF THE STEPHENSONS. The Life of George Stephenson, and of his Son, Robert Stephenson; comprising, also, a History of the Invention and Introduction of the Railway Locomotive. By SAMUEL SMILES. With Steel Portraits and numerous Illustrations. 8vo, Cloth, $3 00.

SMILES'S HISTORY OF THE HUGUENOTS. The Huguenots: their Settlements, Churches, and Industries in England and Ireland. By SAMUEL SMILES. With an Appendix relating to the Huguenots in America. Crown 8vo, Cloth, $2 00.

SPEKE'S AFRICA. Journal of the Discovery of the Source of the Nile. By Captain JOHN HANNING SPEKE. With Maps and Portraits and numerous Illustrations, chiefly from Drawings by Captain GRANT. 8vo, Cloth, uniform with Livingstone, Barth, Burton, &c., $4 00.

STRICKLAND'S (MISS) QUEENS OF SCOTLAND. Lives of the Queens of Scotland and English Princesses connected with the Regal Succession of Great Britain. By AGNES STRICKLAND. 8 vols., 12mo, Cloth, $12 00.

THE STUDENT'S SERIES.
France. Engravings. 12mo, Cloth, $2 00.
Gibbon. Engravings. 12mo, Cloth, $2 00.
Greece. Engravings. 12mo, Cloth, $2 00.
Hume. Engravings. 12mo, Cloth, $2 00.
Rome. By Liddell. Engravings. 12mo, Cloth, $2 00.
Old Testament History. Engravings. 12mo, Cloth, $2 00.
New Testament History. Engravings. 12mo, Cloth, $2 00.
Strickland's Queens of England. Abridged. Engravings. 12mo, Cloth, $2 00.
Ancient History of the East. 12mo, Cloth, $2 00.
Hallam's Middle Ages. 12mo, Cloth, $2 00.
Hallam's Constitutional History of England. 12mo, Cloth, $2 00.
Lyell's Elements of Geology. 12mo, Cloth, $2 00.

TENNYSON'S COMPLETE POEMS. The Complete Poems of Alfred Tennyson, Poet Laureate. With numerous Illustrations by Eminent Artists, and Three Characteristic Portraits. 8vo, Paper, 75 cents; Cloth, $1 25.

THOMSON'S LAND AND THE BOOK. The Land and the Book; or, Biblical Illustrations drawn from the Manners and Customs, the Scenes and the Scenery of the Holy Land. By W. M. THOMSON, D.D., Twenty-five Years a Missionary of the A. B. C. F. M. in Syria and Palestine. With two elaborate Maps of Palestine, an accurate Plan of Jerusalem, and several hundred Engravings, representing the Scenery, Topography, and Productions of the Holy Land, and the Costumes, Manners, and Habits of the People. 2 large 12mo vols., Cloth, $5 00.

TYERMAN'S WESLEY. The Life and Times of the Rev. John Wesley, M.A., Founder of the Methodists. By the Rev. LUKE TYERMAN. Portraits. 3 vols., Crown 8vo, Cloth, $7 50.

TYERMAN'S OXFORD METHODISTS. The Oxford Methodists: Memoirs of the Rev. Messrs. Clayton, Ingham, Gambold, Hervey, and Broughton, with Biographical Notices of others. By the Rev. L. TYERMAN. Crown 8vo, Cloth, $2 50.

VÁMBÉRY'S CENTRAL ASIA. Travels in Central Asia. Being the Account of a Journey from Teheran across the Turkoman Desert, on the Eastern Shore of the Caspian, to Khiva, Bokhara, and Samarcand, performed in the Year 1863. By ARMINIUS VÁMBÉRY, Member of the Hungarian Academy of Pesth, by whom he was sent on this Scientific Mission. With Map and Woodcuts. 8vo, Cloth, $4 50.

WOOD'S HOMES WITHOUT HANDS. Homes Without Hands: being a Description of the Habitations of Animals, classed according to their Principle of Construction. By J. G. WOOD, M.A., F.L.S. With about 140 Illustrations. 8vo, Cloth, Beveled Edges, $4 50.

Harper's Catalogue.

The attention of gentlemen, in town or country, designing to form Libraries or enrich their Literary Collections, is respectfully invited to Harper's Catalogue, which will be found to comprise a large proportion of the standard and most esteemed works in English and Classical Literature—COMPREHENDING OVER THREE THOUSAND VOLUMES—which are offered, in most instances, at less than one-half the cost of similar productions in England.

To Librarians and others connected with Colleges, Schools, &c., who may not have access to a trustworthy guide in forming the true estimate of literary productions, it is believed this Catalogue will prove especially valuable for reference.

To prevent disappointment, it is suggested that, whenever books can not be obtained through any bookseller or local agent, applications with remittance should be addressed direct to Harper & Brothers, which will receive prompt attention.

Sent by mail on receipt of Ten Cents.

Address   HARPER & BROTHERS,
FRANKLIN SQUARE, NEW YORK.

www.ingramcontent.com/pod-product-compliance
Lightning Source LLC
Chambersburg PA
CBHW032010220426
43664CB00006B/196